MY WIFE MY BABY…AND HIM

D1362116

[Scan barcode w/mobile device for more information]

SEP – – 2014

NorthStar Books
An Imprint of Bonita And Hodge Publishing
Published by Bonita And Hodge Publishing Group LLC

My Wife My Baby...And Him Copyright © 2014 Shelia E. Lipsey
All rights reserved.

No part of this book may be reproduced or transmitted in any form or by any means, electronic or mechanical, including photocopying, recording or by any information storage and retrieval system without written permission from the author, except for the inclusion of brief quotations in a review.

ISBN-10:0983893551
ISBN-13: 978-0-9838935-5-4

Library of Congress Control Number: 2013913769
Printed in the United States of America

This is a work of fiction. Names, characters, places, and incidents either are products of the author's imagination or are used fictitiously. Any resemblance to actual events or locales or persons, living or dead, is entirely coincidental.

WWW.BONITAANDHODGEPUBLISHING.COM

MY WIFE MY BABY...AND HIM

SHELIA E. LIPSEY

NorthStar
BONITA AND HODGE PUBLISHING GROUP, LLC

COVER BY MARION DESIGNS

CENTRAL ARKANSAS LIBRARY SYSTEM
SUE COWAN   WILLIAMS BRANCH
LITTLE ROCK, ARKANSAS

Other Books by Shelia E. Lipsey

Beautiful Ugly Series
True Beauty (Book 2)
Beautiful Ugly (Book 1)

My Son's Wife Series
My Sister My Momma My Wife (Book 4)
My Son's Next Wife (Book 3)
My Son's Ex-Wife: The Aftermath (Book 2)
My Son's Wife (Book 1)

Stand Alone Books
What's Blood Got To Do With It?
House of Cars (YA)
Sinsatiable
Into Each Life
Always, Now and Forever Love Hurts
Show A Little Love

Anthologies
Bended Knees – *Against the Grain*
Weary And Will – *A Purpose Realized*

Non-fiction
A Christian's Perspective – Journey through Grief

Acknowledgements

It goes without fail, but I will say it anyway: Thanks to ALL of the loyal, dedicated, and committed supporters along my literary journey. Thanks to every book club, every reader, and every person who has shared in my literary dreams. Thanks to every library, every bookstore, and any and every one who believes in me enough to showcase my work.

I want to thank Lacricia Wilson of His Pen Publishing. Thank you for your professionalism, and for being real with me when it comes to editorial decisions and changes.

Of course, I want to thank Bonita And Hodge Publishing Group for being a company where my literary dreams can be fully expressed.

Thanks to Keith Saunders of Marion Designs for making the world's best book covers!

Thanks to my sons, Kevin and Jay, who support me, believe in me, encourage me, pray for me, and love me unconditionally. I will forever sing your praises.

Thanks always to my mother and my sisters.

Thank you to my precious grandchildren and my first great granddaughter, Harlynn Monroe. I write because of you. I write to leave a legacy for you to know that if you can Dream It, You Can Do It!

A special thanks to Regina "aka Robinette" Dobbins for your support in so many ways.

This literary journey has been more than I can ever think, hope, and imagine, and I give my awesome God the glory! I have not come this far without Him being my guide, my director, my forgiver, and my redeemer. He is truly blessing me each and every day with the desires of my heart.

I want to encourage anyone reading this book, who is not living their dreams now, to start today, *right now.* Do not waste another second, moment or minute. You can achieve what you believe. It is already embedded in you, perfectly designed by God, the Father for you to accomplish your dreams and fulfill your passions.

Shelia E. - 'God's Amazing Girl'

Dedication

To All Who Have Done Something In Your Life
That You Are Not Proud Of

"There is no sense in punishing your future for the mistakes of your past. Forgive yourself, grow from it and then let it go."
Melanie Koulouris

Do not judge someone
just because they SIN
differently than you. *Unknown*

1

"Falling in love is like jumping off a really tall building. Your brain tells you it is not a good idea, but your heart tells you, you can fly."
Unknown

Stiles scanned the perimeter of the private dining room at Bonefish Grill. He watched the interaction of the deacons gathered around the long table for their monthly Pastor and Deacons outing. Stiles enjoyed getting the men together outside of Holy Rock from time to time where they could do more than discuss the business of the church. They could enjoy one another's company as men.

Looking at the deacons reminded him of Jesus and the twelve disciples because he had exactly twelve men on his deacon board.

"So the consensus is that the position of associate pastor be offered to Reverend Hezekiah McCoy?" Stiles asked.

"Yes, Pastor Graham. The final vote is unanimous in favor of Reverend Hezekiah McCoy," announced Leo Jones, chairman of the deacon board and one of Stiles' friends since back during their high school days. "Reverend McCoy has been faithful in his ministry at Holy Rock since he and his wife joined the church two years ago. I believe he loves the Lord, and he knows the Bible too."

Several of the deacons nodded in agreement.

"Okay, then. It's a go. I'll meet with him later this evening and tell him our decision. We'll announce it to the congregation this Sunday. Okay, is that all? Anything else on the agenda?"

"No, that was the final item of discussion," Leo told him.

Stiles picked up his cloth napkin, wiped his mouth, laid it back on the table and stood up. "Great meeting. Since I'm at the mall, I think I'll run over to Macy's and get the first lady a little something. You know we have to keep our women happy, guys. You know what they say: happy wife, happy life."

Skip Madison laughed and added, "What if you're a confirmed bachelor like me?"

Stiles shook his head and laughed. "Man, there's no hope for you. I wouldn't dare send you out to get a thing. You have too many women to buy for."

"Ooooo," several of the deacons said and laughed.

"Pastor Graham, we need to help Skip get a wife," one of the deacons said, hitting Skip on the back.

"I couldn't agree with you more." Stiles chuckled, turned, and looked at Leo. "You ready?"

"Yes, sir."

The two men left the restaurant, got in Pastor's Audi A6, and drove to the west entrance of the mall, close to Macy's.

Stiles walked through the Women's Department of Macy's in search of the perfect gift for Detria. It had been a while since he'd actually bought her a 'just because' gift.

"I think I'm going to try to find her this purse I heard her and Brooke talking about."

"What kind of purse?"

"Uh, I think it's called Coors, something like that."

They walked to the handbag section and Stiles saw the actual name was Michael Kors. He looked at the different styles. To keep from picking out something Detria might not like, he asked the sales clerk for help.

Less than an hour after walking into Macy's, he walked out with an iris colored Michael Kors Grab Bag. The sales clerk assured Stiles that Detria would love the purse.

"Man, you just dropped three hundred bucks on a purse?"

"Look, I told you I'm trying to keep the lady of the house happy. You know what I mean?" Stiles laughed and Leo did too.

"I hear you but I hope Cynthia doesn't see it, because next thing I know, she'll be asking me to buy her one. And unless it's Christmas or her birthday, I'm sorry, but the only surprise gift she'll get from me will be a bouquet of flowers or maybe a bottle of perfume."

"Man, you better learn how to treat your wife good."

"I treat her good but my dollars are limited, you know."

"Yeah, I hear you," said Stiles.

They made small talk as they walked through Macy's and out into the mall.

Without reason, Stiles looked to his right over at Zales Jewelers and suddenly stopped walking. "Hold up, that looks like Detria."

"Where?" asked Leo.

"Over there...at Zales." Stiles pointed.

"Aww, looks like she's not the only one who's going to get surprised."

Stiles smiled. He felt good inside with the thought that Detria might actually be thinking of him. The past year of their marriage had been a difficult one, and he was praying that their marriage would solidify and become even stronger since they recommitted themselves to one another. He walked toward the store.

"You going over there?" Leo asked.

"Yeah, but I'm not going to say anything. I just want to see what she's up to."

Stiles ventured toward where Detria was standing. He had a clear view of her and his daughter. Audrey was asleep in her stroller.

It made his heart swell with joy every time he witnessed how rapidly Audrey was growing. And Detria, well if Stiles had anything to say about Detria, she had made vast improvements in the motherhood department. Maybe it was because Audrey was growing up, walking, and even talking. She was a spunky, fun, and bright little two-year old girl and Stiles adored her.

"May I see that one right there?" Stiles heard Detria ask as she pointed to something behind the glass enclosure.

The sales clerk reached inside the jewelry case and pulled out a black men's bracelet. "Oh, this is a very good choice."

"What is it made out of?" Detria asked.

Stiles nudged Leo and smiled. Both men maintained a proper distance so they would not be detected but were still close enough to hear the conversation.

"This is a half carat, diamond, black titanium, and sterling silver bracelet. The retail price is eight hundred dollars, but it's marked down to six fifty. You can get an extra fifteen percent off if you use your Zales card. Would you like me to box it for you?"

"Umm, I don't know."

"Is it for a special occasion? For your husband or significant other?" the sales associate asked while Detria looked at other pieces of jewelry inside the case.

"May I have a closer look at it?" Detria asked, ignoring the sales clerk's question.

"Certainly." The sales associate gave Detria the bracelet. She toyed with it, and examined it carefully.

Stiles looked at Leo again and stepped back when he thought Detria was about to turn around. She didn't.

"You're going to ruin her surprise," Leo whispered.

"No, I'm not."

"You know what; I think I *will* get it," Stiles heard Detria say.

"Great. I think you made a good choice. Would you like me to put it on your Zales card?"

"No." Detria went in her purse and pulled out her cranberry clutch, opened it and retrieved a credit card. "Put it on this." She gave the sales clerk a MasterCard.

Stiles turned and walked in the other direction after he saw Detria pay for the item. He felt good, real good. Detria was thinking about him just as much as he was thinking about her.

As soon as he saw her leave, he turned back around, went into the store, and approached the sales clerk. Leo followed, shaking his head.

"If you don't mind, I'd like to see whatever that woman just purchased. I'm looking for a bracelet too, and I heard you telling her she made a good choice."

"I don't have another one exactly like the one she purchased, but I can show you one that's similar." The sales clerk unlocked the glass case and removed a bracelet. "This is almost identical to the one she purchased, except it's one tenth of a carat total weight. The one she bought was half a carat. This one is also two hundred dollars cheaper."

The sales clerk passed Stiles the bracelet, allowing him to get a good feel for it, hoping that she would make another easy sale.

Stiles looked at the bracelet, and his chest puffed out at the thought of Detria buying him such a nice gift.

"Would you like to purchase this one today? You can get fifteen percent off the price if you use your Zales card."

Stiles studied the bracelet again. "Ummm. You know what? I think I'll wait. Thanks anyway." He passed the bracelet back to the sales clerk who looked disappointed that she didn't make the sale.

Stiles turned to leave. "Have a blessed day."

"You too, and thank you for shopping at Zales."

"You're welcome," Stiles replied.

"What was that all about?' Leo asked as they left out the store. "Why did you want to see what she bought? It's bad enough you spied on her."

"I was not spying. I didn't know she was going shopping today, and to think my lady is shopping for *me*. Man, I feel real good right about now." Stiles tapped Leo on the arm.

"Hi," Detria said, talking into the hands-free phone inside her car. She glanced in the rear view mirror and saw Audrey playing with her toy cell phone. "I guess you're still in your meeting. Call me. No, on second thought, I'll try calling you back. I'm out running some errands, so I'll try to get with you a little later. Bye," Detria pushed the button on her steering wheel, ending the call.

Ever since returning from what she called their 'patch up' trip to Myrtle Beach almost a year ago, Detria had been trying to make things work in her strained marriage. Sure, she had been guilty of committing adultery, but Stiles had no idea about it. As for Skip, she didn't know what it was about that man, other than she was crazy about him, and she believed he was crazy about her. She promised herself, and God, that she wouldn't sleep with him again. That promise was short-lived, because a week after returning from Myrtle Beach, she succumbed to Skip's demands.

She couldn't deny that Skip Madison mesmerized her. She couldn't explain it, but there was just something about him. Seeing him, being around him, and talking to him made her weak for the man. He was tall, dark, handsome, and sexy with depthless grayish eyes. He had the ability to make her feel like she was the only girl in the world whenever she was with him, unlike Stiles who was the exact replica of how Pastor used to be - all about Holy Rock.

Stiles had resigned as adjunct professor of Theology at the University of Memphis so he could spend more time with her and Audrey, but that wasn't working out because now he was spending more time at Holy Rock. She was still stuck 24/7 on motherhood duty. Now that Audrey was two years old, walking and talking, Detria was beginning to enjoy being a mother a little more than she had in the past, but she still believed that Stiles could pay both her and Audrey more attention.

Ring, ring.

She looked at the console. It was Skip's number.

She pushed the button. "Hi, there."

"Hey, gorgeous. What's up?"

"Oh, just out and about. I left you a message."

"Yeah, I know. I'm just leaving Bonefish Grill."

"Bonefish Grill?"

"Yeah, we had the deacon's meeting there today. Remember?"

"Oh, yeah. At which one?"

"The one at Carriage Crossing Mall."

"I just left that mall. So you're still out this way?"

"Actually, I just got on the interstate. But hey, turning around is just a word."

"I have Audrey with me, but I still want to see you."

"Tell you what. I'll turn around, and let's see, I can meet you at—"

"No, hold up. Never mind. We'll just talk later."

"Why?"

"I better not take the chance. Stiles or some of the other deacons could still be around."

"Okay, but when am I going to see you? It's been two weeks since I've held you next to me. I miss you, girl."

"I don't know, Skip. I keep telling myself that I have to stop seeing you, but it's like you've cast a spell on me, and I can't break free."

Skip laughed aloud over the phone. Detria smiled, checked her rearview mirror, and maneuvered over into the right hand lane, turned on to Forest Hill Irene and continued driving.

"What's so funny?"

"You. I think you're the one who cast a spell on me."

This time Detria laughed. "I know I'm laughing, but really, you know what we're doing is not a laughing matter." She grew serious. "I have to do something about this before stuff hits the fan. You know I don't want to hurt Stiles or jeopardize my marriage."

"Tell you what. You finish running your errands, and don't worry your pretty little head about me and you."

"But, Skip, I can't help it. I feel bad about going behind Stiles' back."

"Didn't I say stop worrying, Detria? We'll talk tonight at church. I'll meet you in your office, say around seven thirty. How does that sound?"

Detria sighed. "Okay. Bye."

"Bye, babe."

Detria made two more stops before heading home. The phone rang again as she was turning on to her street.

"Hello."

"Mrs. Graham?"

"Yes, this is Mrs. Graham."

"This is Riley Hollingsworth."

"Hello, Riley. How are you?"

"I'm good. Thanks for asking."

"Do you have news about the house?"

"I'm pleased to tell you that I do. Your offer was accepted. After we schedule the home inspection and get a thumbs up from them, then closing on your new home should take place in a few weeks."

"Thank you soooo much, Riley. I can't wait to tell Pastor Graham. God bless you, and have a good day."

"You're welcome, First Lady. I'll be in touch. In the meantime, if you or Pastor Graham have any questions, just give me a call."

"Okay, Riley. Goodbye."

"Goodbye, First Lady."

Riley Hollingsworth was one of the daughters of Michael Hollingsworth, owner of Hollingsworth Realtors. She was Stiles and Detria's real estate agent. Riley and her family were also longtime members of Holy Rock.

Detria and Stiles had been house hunting for the past several months. She felt like they had outgrown their present home and to be honest, the neighborhood too. She wanted a home that they could grow into, especially since Stiles wanted more children. Detria still wasn't too keen on having more children, but if that's what she had to do to make Stiles happy, she told Stiles she would do it, but under one condition, and that was he would have to move her into a new house. At first, Stiles was reluctant, because Detria wanted to move out in the suburbs. He, on the other hand, didn't want to be too far away from Holy Rock. Finally, he gave in to his wife's desires and the house hunting started.

Riley had shown them at least twenty or thirty houses. Stiles was ready to call it quits until last week when Detria found what she called her dream house. It was in the suburbs, of course. It was farther away from Holy Rock than Stiles wanted, but he gave in to Detria, and they put an offer in on the $475,000 southern colonial style home that boasted five bedrooms, four and a half baths, a bonus room, formal dining room, family room, separate living room, an all-season room, and a dedicated office for Stiles, plus a swimming pool. The swimming pool was already gated for protection, which made Stiles feel better, considering his daughter's safety.

Detria turned into the driveway of her home while at the same time pushing the overhead remote in her car. The left side of their three-car garage opened and she drové inside.

"Mommy," Audrey said.

Detria turned around. "Audrey, did you hear that? Mommy got her dream house." Detria was elated.

As usual, when the garage door opened, Stiles' side of the garage was empty. Detria gathered her packages, ran inside, and put them on the kitchen island. She came back out to the car and unbuckled Audrey from her car seat. As soon as the buckles came loose Audrey slid out of her car seat and jumped out of the car.

"You are such a big girl." Detria told her as she reached on the middle console and grabbed the two fruit smoothies she had stopped and bought for her and Audrey on the way home.

"Gimme...joosh," Audrey said and reached up toward Detria.

"Okay, when we get in the house mommy will give it to you. Okay?"

Audrey wasn't having it. She started crying. "Joosh, joosh," she cried. "Joosh."

"Audrey, calm down. Go on in the house. I'll put you in your high chair and then I'll give it to you."

Audrey screamed louder.

Detria rolled her eyes up in her head, and pursed her lips. "Audrey, I am not in the mood. Now get in the house!"

Audrey continued crying. She wouldn't budge. Instead, she held her head down, put her hands to her face, and started screaming like she was being tortured.

Detria snatched her by the arm. "Shut up. I don't want to hear all that screaming. Now get your butt in this house!"

Audrey still didn't move. She screamed even louder and then started stomping her feet. "Joosh, joosh," she screamed repeatedly.

Detria leaned down, swatted Audrey on her bottom a couple of times, and then practically drug the girl inside the house.

"Just for that, you're not getting anything. Cry as long as you want to. That temper tantrum mess might work with your daddy, but all it's going to get you from me is a good spanking. That's why your little butt is going to start going to daycare. I don't have time for all of this hollering." Detria picked up her shopping bags and stormed out of the kitchen, leaving Audrey screaming in the middle of the kitchen.

She went upstairs and put everything away. Afterwards, she sat on the edge of her bed and removed the small box out of the Zales bag. She opened it, removed the bracelet, and smiled as she studied it. "This is sooo fiyah," she said, talking to herself. "You are going to be so surprised." She studied the bracelet for a few seconds longer, and then put it back inside the box and the Zales bag. Standing up, she placed one hand on her hip. "Umm, let's see. Where can I hide this so you won't find it?" She walked over to the walk-in closet, looked up and down the shelves, then turned and walked back out. "Nope, that won't do. Let's see." She stood in the middle of the bedroom, and then turned and paraded downstairs with the Zales bag in her hand.

Detria disregarded Audrey's screams. Sometimes that little girl could work her last nerves. She seemed to think that pitching tantrums would get her her way, but Detria could be just as stubborn as Audrey. Sometimes she would let her cry for what seemed like hours while she went about doing whatever she had to do or wanted to do around the house. Today was one of those days.

When she went back downstairs, Audrey was sitting on the kitchen floor, looking rather content. She had somehow managed to get both smoothies from off the kitchen island. Raspberry and pomegranate smoothie was smeared all over the kitchen floor, all over her face and all over her clothes.

"Aaaahh," Detria screamed. "You little monster." She stormed over to her daughter, placed the Zales bag on the island counter, snatched Audrey up off the floor by her arm, and proceeded popping the child on her legs and bottom. Audrey screamed so loud and cried so hard until she started jerking.

"I told you not to mess with me, little girl!" She picked her up and carried her upstairs to her bedroom, put her in her crib, and stormed back downstairs. Grabbing the Zales bag, she went outside to her car, opened the trunk, and placed the bag inside.

When she got back upstairs, she ran some bath water and in a flash, she undressed Audrey, bathed her, and took her back to her crib, closed the little girl's bedroom door and went back downstairs to clean up the mess Audrey had made.

"I know I said I'd give you another child, but we'll just have to see about that. We'll definitely have to see."

2

"Everyone deserves a chance to clean up their mistakes." Unknown

"Pastor Graham, God is good. Thank you so much for entrusting me to serve as your associate pastor. I will make you proud. That's a promise."

"You don't have to make me proud. Make God proud." Stiles patted Hezekiah on the back.

"You know, since me and Fancy have been members of Holy Rock, nothing but favor and blessings have been raining down on us. God has truly shown us that this is where He wants us. Who knew that moving to Memphis from Chicago, finding a church like Holy Rock, and getting to know you and First Lady Graham would turn out to be our biggest blessing. It's all a bit overwhelming."

"You know when God moves, He moves in a mighty way. Sometimes we think we're doing something for one reason, when God has another plan. I'm glad that the Lord led you and Fancy to us. You've done an outstanding job here; you've made a difference. You know the Word and the people of Holy Rock love you and Fancy."

"Thanks, Pastor Graham. I can't wait to tell Fancy the news. You know my wife is my rock. She supports me and prays with me and for me. The woman is remarkable. I'm telling you, Pastor, when she hears this, she's going to be up in Holy Rock dancing all over the place." Hezekiah McCoy smiled.

"Yeah, she knows she is not ashamed to celebrate the Lord in song and dance. She'll run around that sanctuary in a minute, won't she?" Stiles laughed.

"You got that right."

"What about your boys? Xavier, and uh…"

"Khalil," Hezekiah stated.

"Are you still planning on moving them here?"

"I'm not sure. They both love Chicago and they're really close to Fancy's parents. So, I guess for now everything is still up in the air."

"But I thought you wanted the youngest one to come here and attend school."

"You know how these young people are, Pastor Graham. He has friends; he loves his school."

"How old is he? Fifteen? Sixteen?"

"No, fourteen, going on fifteen. Khalil is the one that's sixteen. "Xavier is into his books. Khalil, well," Hezekiah shook his head. "Let's just say he's at the stage where you can't tell him a thing. Thinks he knows it all."

Hezekiah didn't tell Stiles that Khalil had been addicted to heroin since age fourteen. The boy was currently serving time in a youth detention center for troubled teens for breaking into the home of one of his grandparents' neighbors. He would be incarcerated until he turned eighteen.

"You know how kids are. I'm sure you were the same way when you were coming up. I know I was."

Hezekiah crooked his head to the side. Raising his eyebrows he said, "Maybe, but anyway, at the end of the day I'm proud of Xavier. He does well in school, but he already says that he doesn't want to go to college."

"Oh, and why is that?"

"He says he wants to go to a trade school to be an electrician. To tell you the truth, I wouldn't mind if he didn't go to college. If he can take up a good trade, he can start his own business, and that'll sure save a lot on my pockets. Don't get me wrong, I value a good education, but a good education doesn't always equate to having a four-year degree or a doctorate. As long as he can get out into this world, provide for himself, position himself to take care of a family somewhere down the line if he so chooses, and make an honest living, then I'm fine with that."

"You can only lead them and guide them. The final choice of what a child does with his life is on that child," Stiles responded. "I'll be in prayer for both of them to make wise decisions about their futures, but as for now, they're still young. And Xavier, he has a few years ahead of him. Between now and the time he graduates, he'll probably change his mind a thousand times about what he wants to do."

"Yeah, I'm sure you're right about that."

"I was thinking that I would make the official announcement Sunday at both services. Then after church service, I want you and Fancy to join me and Detria for a celebratory dinner. I'll probably invite the deacons too."

"Sounds good, and I'm sure Fancy would love it. She and First Lady seem to get along well."

"You and I both know that's a plus. Think of the alternative."

"I don't want to," answered Hezekiah and laughed.

"Neither do I," Stiles agreed.

Stiles decided to let Hezekiah lead midweek service. There were times like tonight, when he wanted his soul to be ministered to. Whenever he went on sabbatical, which was rare, he often visited the churches of some of his minister friends in order to be spiritually fed. Since Hezekiah McCoy's arrival, Stiles found him to be not only a confidante, but also an anointed speaker who could deliver a powerful, soul-stirring word.

Hezekiah, the total opposite of Stiles, was average height, thin as a wafer, with honey colored skin, a thin, carefully clipped mustache and a balding head.

"Holy Rock, first John chapter five, starting with verse four, states, 'For everyone who has been born of God overcomes the world. And this is the victory that has overcome the world—our faith.' Where is your faith? Where is your trust in God?" Hezekiah preached. "Holy Rock, keep your eyes on the prize. Speak good things over your own life. Release the negative, usher in the positive."

Fancy sat in the audience second row from the front. She raised both hands in the air, and stood to her feet. "Preach, Reverend. Say it."

Hezekiah was thirty-eight and Fancy was two years younger. They'd been a couple since their teens.

Fancy McCoy lived up to her name. She was a sharply dressed woman with a petite, size six or eight frame. One could probably count on one hand the times she wore any kind of shoe other than her signature stiletto heels. Fancy also had a melodious voice, and there were times when some of the senior members of Holy Rock requested she sing one of their favorite songs or hymns.

"Don't look back," Hezekiah preached. "Keep moving forward. Keep looking ahead at the author and finisher of your faith."

Where is that woman? Stiles asked himself. *Probably in the church nursery with Audrey or in her office.* He refocused himself on Hezekiah's preaching.

"Skip, no." Detria pushed him away using very little force. He didn't budge. "You know we can't do anything in my office," she moaned as Skip planted traces of kisses from her lips to her neckline all the way to her cleavage.

His hands caressed her curves, and he held her close to him. "You know you miss me. Tell me you miss me, Detria."

"I do, Skip, but, but..."

"But what?" he asked as he continued to kiss and fondle her.

She pushed him back gently and looked into his eyes. "Why do you do me like this?"

"Like what? Tell me what I'm doing that's so wrong?"

Detria laughed. "Are you serious? You and I both know everything about this is wrong."

"Okay." Skip stepped all the way back and showed his palms. "First, tell me that you honestly do not want me, that you don't want me to talk to you, to see you, to hold you, or make love to you," he began to whisper. "If you can look me in the eyes and tell me all those things, then I promise you, I will walk out of this office and never bother you again."

"Skip, please."

"Say it. Tell me you don't want me. Just say it, and I'll go. I swear I will." Skip's face was rigid. He stared at Detria, not flinching once.

"I...You...," she began to say then she rushed into his arms and planted her lips on top of his. "I will, but not now, not tonight."

Detria jumped, smoothed down her dress, and started wiping her sweaty face when she heard someone trying to open the door to her office. Thank God, it was locked.

"Detria? You in there?"

"Oh, my God. It's Stiles. What's he doing here? Bible study shouldn't be over this quick. What are we going to do?"

"Think. Be cool. He doesn't have a key, unless you gave him one."

"No, he doesn't have one." Detria watched the knob turn again. "Go to my bathroom; close the door. I'll get rid of him."

Skip dashed off to the bathroom.

Detria slowly walked to the door, taking one glance at herself in the wall mirror in her modern styled office. She patted her hair in place then opened the door.

"Hey," she said as soon as she opened the door and Stiles walked in. She kissed him on the cheek and walked toward her desk.

"What's with the locked door?" he asked, looking around like he expected someone else to be in the office with her.

"Because anybody can just up and walk in here. I know we're in church, but criminals come to church too, you know."

Stiles nodded. "Why aren't you in service?"

"I had some paperwork I wanted to finish." It appeared that he didn't notice the nervousness in her voice.

"Where's Audrey?"

"In the nursery." Detria sat down at her desk, and started pulling up files on her computer. She stole a look over her shoulder toward the bathroom. "Is church over?"

"Yeah, we got out early. I let Hezekiah preach tonight. You know he gets right to the point."

"Why did you let him preach? I mean, I have no problem with it. He's really a great speaker, but it's unusual for you to let someone else carry on the service unless you're away."

"I know, but since he's going to be the associate pastor, I thought I might as well get used to the idea of having him fill my shoes every now and then."

Detria looked up from her computer. "Associate Pastor? When did you make that decision?" Her furrowed brows revealed her concern.

"I've been thinking about it and praying on it for a while. I told you that."

"Thinking and praying is not the same as doing, Stiles, and you know it." She sounded agitated.

"I discussed it with the deacons and they supported my decision. The main thing is I believe that God directed me to do it. You know we have some fantastic ministers at Holy Rock, but we've never offered a full-time paid position to any of them."

"Exactly. Which is why I can't understand why you would make him the associate pastor when you have other ministers who have been here far longer than him."

"Look." Stiles rubbed his head back and forth with his hand. "I don't want to get into this right now. It's been a long day. I'm ready to go home."

"See, that's what I'm talking about. When it comes to sharing what's going on at this church, you never want to talk. You could have told me. That's all I'm saying. Why do you have to make stuff so difficult?" She stared at him with contempt, jumped up from her chair, shuffled some papers around, and walked from behind the desk.

"So, now you got an attitude?"

She rolled her eyes. "Should I have one? You know what? Do what you want to do. I'm through with it."

Stiles turned and walked toward the door. "I'll go get Audrey. I'll see you at the house."

Detria flipped him off. "Whatever."

As soon as Stiles left out of her office, she closed the door and locked it again, then ran back to the bathroom. "Okay, you can come out."

Skip came out with a big smile on his face.

"What are you smiling about?"

"You and preacher boy always into it about something. But I have to admit, you know how to handle dude."

"You know how Stiles is. He can be an arrogant jerk." Detria smirked. "Look, you better leave. I'm getting ready to get out of here myself. I've had enough of Holy Rock for one night."

Skip grabbed her, pulled her into the bathroom, pushed her against the cold tile wall, and resumed doing what they were doing before Stiles interrupted.

Detria didn't resist. What was it about Skip Madison that captivated her so? Why couldn't she just say, no? Detria's eyes connected with his, and the fat lady began to sing.

3

"Such is the way of an adulterous woman; she eateth, and wipeth her mouth, and saith, I have done no wickedness." Proverbs 30:20 KJV

Detria walked in the house and heard the sound of the blaring television. She walked into the family room; it was empty. She hated when Stiles left the television on. He had a bad habit of leaving it on for hours at a time. She turned it off and headed upstairs to the bedroom.

"Hey," she said when she walked in the bedroom and saw him and Audrey laying in the middle of the bed. Of course, the mounted flat screen was on. Detria looked at the television screen. "You left the television downstairs on, again."

"Sorry about that. You better?"

"Better? What are you talking about?"

Stiles looked at her questioningly. "Never mind."

Detria was so caught up in Skip back at the church that she had forgotten all about their little shouting match. "Since when did you start watching Love and Hip Hop?" she asked with a slight smile etched on her face.

"You'd be surprised at the great sermons I pull from watching shows like this. Nothing like real life drama and people scrambling to find the answers to their life's choices. Many of them don't understand that what's missing in their lives is a relationship with God."

Detria nodded. She didn't feel like listening to Stiles holier than thou reasoning, not tonight. She went into the bathroom, undressed, and prepared to take a shower.

"Any word about the house yet?" he asked.

Detria halted just before stepping into the shower. She grabbed her robe from off the back of the bathroom door and slipped it on. "I can't believe I forgot to tell you." She opened the door and stepped back out into the master bedroom.

"What did you forget?"

Detria threw her head back, clapped her hands, and jumped up and down with excitement. "We got the house. We got the house!" she repeated, while running over to the bed and plopping down next to Audrey.

Stiles sat upright. "We got the house? Are you serious?"

"Yes. Riley called earlier today. She said once they do the home inspection we should be able to close in a few weeks. Oh, Stiles, I'm so happy." She leaned over Audrey and kissed Stiles on the side of his face.

Stiles remained pensive.

"What's wrong?"

Audrey played with her toys like she had been the sweetest little girl all day instead of the temper tantrum tyrant Detria knew she could be.

"Uh, have you forgotten that we haven't sold this house yet?"

"I know, but we have people who've expressed an interest in it. Riley said she feels confident that one or two of them will put in an offer. Surely, one of them will go through. If not, then we'll just have to keep paying the mortgage until it sells."

"Humph. I guess. But you act like we have money flowing out the wazoo. I don't want to pay a note here and plus our new mortgage is twice the amount as this one. I don't want to be house poor."

"What?" Detria moved from off the bed ready to go at it again with Stiles. Sometimes he could be so cheap that it sickened her. "You know what; you always have to put a tear in every silver lining that comes our way."

"What are you talking about now?" Stiles frowned.

"House poor? Puhleeze. You are paid more than some of these top of the line corporate executives, not to mention the other perks we have. The church pays our car notes, our Y memberships, and they pay for two 30-day sabbaticals a year for you." Her voice rose as she counted each thing off on her fingers. "And, let's see, we don't have to pay for childcare, we practically eat free because the church keeps the fridge and pantry stockpiled with food. All we have to pay is a mortgage and property taxes and you're complaining? Give me a break."

"I don't want to take advantage of the church, sweetheart. That's all I'm saying. I know we can make the payments, but I still don't want to be paying two house notes. That's all."

"Hey, I have an idea," Detria said.

"What?"

"Hezekiah and Fancy."

"What about Hezekiah and Fancy?"

"They're still living in an apartment, right?"

A wrinkle appeared on Stiles forehead. Audrey reached for her daddy, and he picked her up in his arms, and kissed her on the forehead. He had her spoiled rotten.

"Yeah, but what's this got to do with them?"

"Maybe they would like to buy this house, or lease it. Better yet, you said you wanted Holy Rock to have a pastor's parsonage. This house can be it. It's close to the church and the mortgage isn't that much, so the church board shouldn't have a problem buying it from us and paying it off. Maybe you can just quit claim the house over to Holy Rock and make everything official. Riley can tell you how to go about it, I'm sure. If you do it like that then maybe Hezekiah and Fancy can move here."

Stiles stood up from the bed, still holding Audrey who seemed quite content in her daddy's arms.

"You know what, I hadn't thought about that. That's a great idea. As a matter of fact, I love it." He walked around to the other side of the bed and kissed Detria on the lips. "Thank you, baby."

Detria smiled, happy that Stiles liked her suggestion.

"I'll talk to the trustees tomorrow and of course to Hezekiah. He may not want to move here. You never know."

"Oh, please. He'll like it. Who wouldn't want to live somewhere rent-free? And it's not like this is a small house either. They'll have plenty of room for when their boys come to Memphis."

"That is, if either one of them comes."

"But Fancy told me they were coming soon, maybe this summer."

"I know, but Hezekiah said they're having second thoughts. You know how teenagers are."

"Anyway, talk to him, Stiles. Why don't you call him tonight?"

"Yeah, I guess I can do that."

"Good. See how everything worked out? I'm going to take my shower."

"You want some company?" Stiles asked with a twinkle in his eye and a naughty smile on his face.

Detria smiled and answered quickly, "Who would watch your sweet little baby girl?"

Stiles looked at Audrey and hugged her against his chest. "You're right. We can't leave daddy's girl out here all by her lonesome now, can we?" He kissed Audrey again. "Come on, let Mommy take her shower. Me and you are going to go downstairs and get us some animal crackers. How about that?"

"Crackus," Audrey repeated.

"Yep, let's go."

Detria entered the bathroom, closed the door behind her, and exhaled. She was glad she managed to dissuade Stiles from taking a shower with her. One thing would lead to another and she didn't want that, not tonight. That would be nasty, just plain nasty. A cheater she may be, but nasty with it, that wasn't her.

Detria stepped into the master bedroom fresh from a warm, relaxing shower. She saw a large Macy's bag on the bed. *What's that?* She was baffled as to what could be inside. She slowly walked over to the bed. Looking up again, as if she expected Stiles to walk in, she stood at the side of the bed, staring at the bag. "What *is* this?" She reached for the bag, opened it, and pulled out the purse.

"It's for you. The mother of my child. My wife. My lover," Stiles said as he appeared at their bedroom door.

"Stiles, I," Detria sounded shocked. "Oh, baby. I love it! But wh...why?" she turned toward him and asked.

"I told you. Because I love you. I know sometimes I'm not the easiest person to get along with. I know I can be stubborn, insensitive, and inconsiderate, but I love you, Detria. I really do love you, and I just wanted to do something to show you, to brighten your day."

Detria held the purse in her hands. She proceeded to go through its compartments. "Thank you." She placed the purse back down on the bed, ran over to him, and kissed him.

Stiles reciprocated with a deep kiss. He brought her into his arms and allowed his hands to travel to her most intimate places. His kiss grew more intense, and his body came alive for her.

Detria moved out of his arms. "Where's Audrey?"

"In her crib, down for the night. You should have seen her. She fell asleep while she was eating her animal crackers. It was the cutest thing.

"Good. That child has given me the blues today. Stiles, I can't wait to show off my purse," she said, hurriedly trying to change the atmosphere. "How did you know I wanted it?"

"How did I know? Because, I know you. I know how much you love designer purses. I heard you a couple of times telling Brooke about some Kors handbag you wanted. I didn't know what style; I just knew that I wanted to surprise you with something nice. Sooo, after the deacon's meeting, Leo and I went to Macy's and looked around. That's when I saw the handbags. I talked to the sales clerk and got some advice from her. So, I take it, you like it, huh?"

Detria walked back over to the bed and picked up the designer handbag again. "Like it? I love it!"

Stiles walked up behind her and nibbled on her neck. "I know a way you can thank me," he said in a husky voice.

Detria immediately tensed up.

"What is it?" Stiles asked, obviously detecting her apprehension.

"Nothing, I'm just tired. It's been a long day."

"I can help you relax," he crooned softly in her ear.

"But, I—"

"Shhh, relax." He turned her around to face him and again started kissing her while at the same time, gently pushing her back down onto the bed.

Detria had conflicting thoughts. Part of her wanted to satisfy her husband, but the other part of her wanted to do like that song Whitney used to sing, "Saving All My Love For You."

While Stiles made love to her, Detria's mind raced. She had to stop committing adultery, stop cheating on her husband. She was the first lady of Holy Rock Church. What kind of example was she setting? What if someone else, or Stiles, discovered that she was being unfaithful?

Get your act together. If you want your marriage to work, you have to cut it off with Skip. Thought after thought raced through her mind. With each stroke, with each groan of satisfaction coming from her husband, she retreated to a place where guilt did not exist. Only this moment, and right now, she had the responsibility and the duty to please her husband.

When their lovemaking session ended, Stiles insisted that they shower together. This time Detria didn't put up a fuss. The warm jets of water streaming down the contours of her body somehow gave her a sense that she was washing away her sinful acts of betrayal.

"Penny for your thoughts…."

"Huh?" Detria turned in the shower and faced Stiles.

"Wow, where is your mind? I only said it twice."

"Said *what* twice?"

"Penny for your thoughts."

"Oh."

"So, tell me. What's on your mind? You seem preoccupied." Stiles turned off the water and stepped out of the shower. Detria followed. He passed her a towel and she eagerly took hold of it and started drying off.

"I was thinking about how blessed I am."

"Is that right? Are you sure that's what you were thinking about?"

"What kind of question is that? Of course, I'm sure." Detria chuckled lightly.

"So I take it you really loved the purse." Stiles laughed.

"It's not just about the purse. I'm blessed to have a thoughtful, kind, considerate husband who also happens to be a great father. And who also has a birthday coming up in a couple of months. Maybe this is your way of making sure I get you something extra special." Detria laughed and continued drying off.

"That is *not* why I got it. I told you; I wanted to show you how much I love you. You're the mother of my child." Stiles dried off his lower legs and feet, walked out of the bathroom, and stood next to the chest of drawers. "Hey, maybe we made a baby tonight. You think so?"

"Uhhh, I don't know about that, but I was thinking that for your birthday me and you could go—"

"Daaada. Daaada," Audrey screamed, halting their conversation.

Stiles and Detria looked at each other.

"Umm, wonder what's she's doing awake? I'll go check on her," Stiles said.

"She should be sleep for the night," Detria retorted. "I don't understand that child. She's two years old and she *still* wakes up at night. For goodness sakes. Gimme a break!"

Audrey belted out her signature scream. Stiles hurried and finished drying off.

"Daddy's coming, sweetheart. Hold on, precious."

How can he be so patient with her when she behaves like a little tyrant? "You sure you don't want me to go check on her?" Detria asked, knowing full well that she did not intend to cater to her daughter tonight. She was exhausted, and the only call she was going to answer was the call of sleep.

4

"Everybody's got a past. The past does not equal the future
unless you live there." Tony Robbins

Hezekiah and Fancy McCoy were a private couple. When Stiles
asked if their sons were moving to Memphis, he had no idea how
much that inquiry pricked at Hezekiah's spirit. If he had his way, his
sons would most definitely come to Memphis once he and Fancy
were better established.

Unlike his younger brother, Khalil had always been somewhat of
a wayward child. Hezekiah and Fancy didn't want to think that they
could be at fault for the manner in which their sons were growing up.
They hadn't exactly been ideal parents or role models.

Hezekiah had served six and a half years in the Metropolitan
Correctional Center in Chicago and Fancy five. They committed fraud
and started embezzling small to larger sums of money from several
churches in the past, without being caught, but like many criminals,
they became comfortable in their crimes. Their luck ran out at the last
church where Hezekiah was financial administrator and Fancy was
his secretary. Auditors discovered the couple had embezzled tens of
thousands of dollars.

While incarcerated, Hezekiah started a preaching ministry. He
studied the Bible, having been brought up in the church since infancy
by his parents, as was Fancy. That's actually how the two of them
met. They attended the same church as youth and went to the same
school. He was weeks shy of turning seventeen, and she was fifteen
when they started dating.

Hezekiah always had the desire to make plenty of money. He
grew up in the worse housing project there was: Cabrini–Green
located on Chicago's North Side. It was where his father was gunned
down after getting off work one evening. Some thugs robbed and shot
him dead when Hezekiah was thirteen years old. Cabrini-Green had
since been demolished. After his father's murder, Cabrini-Green was
where Hezekiah learned the game of hustling, drug dealing, and

gangbanging. He was a great mathematician when he was in school and he had the gift of gab to add to those skills. He could convince anybody to do just about anything, even if it was wrong. By the time the person realized the error of their ways, Hezekiah had done his dirty deeds and gotten away with it.

When he and Fancy went to prison, they left behind their boys to be raised by Fancy's parents. Hezekiah's mother suffered from pancreatic cancer when he went to prison and later died from the painful disease while he was still incarcerated. He had a half-brother seven years his senior who lived in Buffalo, New York, but Hezekiah hadn't seen or heard from him in ages.

A minister, who came inside the prison and held a weekly church service, took a liking to Hezekiah. He recognized Hezekiah's determination to make a positive change in his life. Having come from Memphis, the minister suggested to Hezekiah to consider relocating there. He told Hezekiah that he believed he could make the perfect new start in Memphis once he and Fancy finished their sentence. The cost of living in Memphis was far below that of Chicago, according to the minister. So several months after the power couple was released from prison, they worked odd jobs until they had enough money saved, and then took a bus to Memphis where they rented a small one-bedroom apartment.

"What if Pastor Graham finds out we're convicted felons?" Fancy asked. "I'm worried, Hezekiah."

Hezekiah sat across from her in their modest living room. He looked away from the television and focused on his wife.

"You are still just as radiant and tempting as the first time we met." He smiled. "Remember, we were both teenagers, living a hard life on Chicago's North Side. But at least you didn't live in the projects."

"Yeah, I'm glad about that, but my family still struggled to make ends meet. It was hard back then. I'm glad they've finally torn those projects down. You had some near death encounters living in Cabrini-Green, but God brought you through it all."

True, so why are you worried about something we did in the past?"

"So far, since being here, we've been blessed that no one has found out about us, but you know that can all change with one good

Internet search by the church staff or anybody who, for whatever reason, decides they want to investigate our backgrounds. Suppose they ask you to turn in a résumé of your past church or ministerial affiliations, what then?"

"We aren't the same people anymore. We aren't going by our real names anyway, so how will anybody find out? And even if somehow they were able to find out who we really are and what we did, we have nothing to be ashamed of, Fancy. Nothing at all. It's all in the past."

"Nothing to be ashamed of? If that's the case then why didn't you tell Pastor Graham that we went to prison for stealing from Cradle of Love Church? A hundred and fifty thousand dollars to be exact. And why haven't you told him Khalil is locked up right today and that he's a heroin addict?"

Hezekiah's nose flared open, revealing his anger. "Do you think we're the only ones in the church who've messed up? Who've made mistakes? Do you think we're the only ones who have a wayward child?"

"No, I know better than that, but you know for yourself how Christian people can be. They're the main ones that are quick to judge. And I'm just saying, I don't want you to step into the position of associate pastor and then lose it all because of the mistakes of the past."

"So you want me to tell Pastor Graham about us and Khalil?"

Fancy got up and walked to where her husband was seated. She sat down beside him. "I don't want you to lose what you're trying to build; that's all. I mean, when you told me that Pastor Graham asked you to be the associate pastor, you know I was ecstatic. This will open up so many doors for you in your ministry. For that, I'm grateful. But, you know as well as I do, if he or anyone at Holy Rock for that matter finds out that we kept our past a secret, you can say buh-bye to the associate pastor role. And me, you know I've had hopes of one day being a first lady, and I don't want anything creeping up from my past to ruin that."

"I have the position, Fancy. There's no need to worry. We did the crime and we served our time. That's that on that. God has forgiven us, and we're trying to do what's right in His eyes now. As far as Khalil is concerned, where he is, is nobody's business. He's in a detention center where he can get some help. Hopefully, he will come out a better person. He's a bright young man and he can still make a wonderful future for himself. We just have to remain prayerful. I know he can kick the heroin habit, and once he does that, he won't be out there trying to rob people."

Fancy sighed heavily before laying her head on her husband's shoulder. "I hope you're right."

"I *am* right. You'll see. Listen, Fancy. What we did is done. There's nothing we can do about it. Our sons will be fine. I believe God for that."

"I know, Hezekiah, but I'm still worried."

"Anyway, like I said, it will be hard for Pastor Graham, or anyone, to find out about our past. We are no longer Horace and Felicia McKellar. Those names, those people, are dead and gone. We have new lives and new names. God is giving us a second chance to live a life holy and acceptable to Him."

The phone rang and interrupted their conversation.

"I'll get it." Fancy stood up and walked over to the table where the home phone rested on its base. "Hello. Ohhh, good evening, Pastor Graham. How are you?" Fancy nodded and smiled. "Yes, I'm blessed, blessed and highly favored. Here's Hezekiah."

Fancy carried the phone over to where Hezekiah was seated and gave it to him.

"Hello, Pastor Graham. How are you this evening?"

"Hello, Pastor McCoy. I hope I'm not interrupting your family time. I won't hold you but a minute."

"Oh, no problem. Me and Fancy were just relaxing, watching a little television. What's on your mind?"

Fancy stood in front of him, listening to his end of the conversation.

Hezekiah listened as Stiles told him about the offer to move into him and Detria's house. When they finished talking, Hezekiah popped off the sofa, grabbed Fancy in his arms, and started twirling her around.

"Baby, I told you God has forgiven us. He is opening doors, baby!" Hezekiah laughed and kissed her all over her face.

"What did he say?" she asked when Hezekiah finally released her.

"He wants us, you and me," Hezekiah pointed at Fancy then himself, "to move into their house. They're closing on their new home in a few weeks. Pastor Graham is going before the trustees tomorrow to discuss turning the house they live in now to a pastor's parsonage. We can live there rent-free, baby. Do you hear me, woman? Tell me that God ain't got our back?"

Fancy started dancing all around the room. "Thank you, Lord, thank you, thank you, thank you." Fancy stopped, grinned and looked at Hezekiah. "Pastor McCoy, I think we better start packing."

"Sister Fancy McCoy, I couldn't agree with you more."

5

"Advice is like castor oil, easy enough to give but dreadfully uneasy to take." Josh Billings

Brooke opened the door to her home and stepped aside to let Detria in. "Well, it's about time my favorite sister came to visit."

"I'm your only sister," Detria laughed as she held onto Audrey's chubby fingers.

"Hi, Audrey. How's Auntie Brooke's favorite niece in the entire world?" Brooke reached down to pick her up.

"Ahhhh," Audrey screamed and jerked out of Brooke's reach.

"Ughh, she makes me so mad when she acts like she's so untouchable," Detria complained and walked further into Brooke's house.

"Girl, don't worry about that. She's just being Audrey. She's still a baby and little girls can be over-the-top dramatic sometimes."

"I wish I had boys instead, if this is the kind of attitude I have to deal with the rest of my life."

"You'll be just fine, and so will Auntie Brooke's gorgeous little niece. Isn't that right, Audrey?"

Audrey clung to Detria's leg and didn't say a word.

"Where are John and the boys?"

"I told John that I didn't feel like cooking this evening, so they went to get pizza. They should be back anytime now. You and Audrey are just in time to join us. Come on, let's go in the family room where we can sit down, relax, and talk."

"Thanks." Detria sat in the chair and Audrey stood next to her, still clinging to her and acting like she didn't want her aunt to touch her or say anything to her. Detria ignored her.

"So, fill me in on what's been going on in the life of my sister, the first lady." Brooke sat down across from Detria on the wraparound sectional sofa. "I assume that all is going well at home?"

"Everything is cool, but why did you ask me that?"

"Because, I haven't talked to you that much lately, and I can count the times you've been over here in the past few months."

"Girl, please. That works both ways. You're the one that's always on the go."

"You got that right. Between the boys and John, and working a full time job, it seems like I rarely get a chance to sit back and chill."

"Yeah, tell me about it. I talked to Mom and Dad the other day. Momma said she was thinking about cooking a big dinner next weekend. She said she asked John if he would put some meat on the grill."

"I know, but I told her she doesn't need to be doing all that cooking. She's still not in the best of health."

"You know our mother. She wants to do the things she enjoys doing as often as she can and for as long as she can. Cooking just happens to be one of those things; you know that. So, like me and you agreed, we are not going to discourage her or slow her down."

"I know that, but still, she needs to be careful. If she stands up in that kitchen cooking, the days following she's going to be complaining about how much pain she's in. Her lupus can flare up at any time. You know that."

"Yeah, that's true."

Audrey tugged on Detria's arm until Detria picked her up and placed her on her lap. "If you get up here, you're going to have to sit still. You could be in the floor playing, but you have to act all babyfied with your Aunt Brooke. You ought to be ashamed of yourself."

"Leave that child alone. She'll warm up in a few minutes. You know how kids are. Anyway, let's hear it."

"Hear what?"

"Girl, you know I know you. Something's on your mind. You didn't just come over here for nothing. I can see it in your face and hear it in your voice. So tell me, what is it?"

Detria looked down at Audrey, picked her up, and stood her on the floor. Audrey poked out her lips, a warning to Detria that she was about to start her signature *give me what I want and give me what I want right now cry.* "Don't you even th—?"

"Hold up. That sounds like John and the boys. Don't forget what we were talking about. Audrey can hang with the boys and eat some pizza. You and me can eat outside on the porch."

"That sounds good, but it's nothing that serious that I have to keep it all hush-hush."

"Detria, hey. What's up sister-in-law?" John said as he walked into the open area family room. He walked over to where Detria sat, leaned over, and gave her an around the shoulder, one-armed hug. The side of her face rested almost squarely against the side of his waist. "Long time no see. Where have you been hiding?" John smiled, as he stood upright and stepped back so they could see each other face to face.

"I haven't been hiding. Just busy. I'm learning more each day that motherhood is not an easy thing, and then there's the church. It goes without saying, there's always something going on around there. Anyway, enough of that. How are you?"

"I'm good. Hi, Audrey," John said with a smile on his face and a slightly raised happy tone.

Detria was mortified when Audrey started wiggling and grinning at John like she'd just seen her daddy. "I can't believe this. Look at her, Brooke."

"She likes men. What can you say?" Brooke's head slightly bobbled as she laughed.

"Don't hate. It's obvious my little niece has good taste." John's laughter connected with Brooke's, while Detria looked at the both of them.

"Since she likes you so much, you can entertain her." Detria laughed this time.

"No problem. Hey, where's Stiles?"

"Where else? At church," replied Detria.

"I heard that. Well, me, the boys, and my sweet little niece here are going to go have a little fun." He swooped Audrey up in his arms and she yelped in joy. "Come on, let's go eat some pizza." He paused then stole a two-second glance at Brooke.

"Yeah, come on, Detria," Brooke said. "John, me and Detria are going to eat our pizza in the sunroom."

"I heard that," he replied and walked out of the family room, up the hall and into the kitchen with Detria and Brooke in tow.

"Jayce...Jayden," Brooke called for her seven and nine year old sons as she walked into the kitchen.

Jayden looked up first, followed by Jayce. They were already munching on cheese breadsticks.

"Hey, Mama," Jayden said as Brooke entered the kitchen.

"Hi, Mama," Jayce said next.

"Hi, boys," said Detria.

They both looked at Detria. "Hi," they practically said in unison, and not with much enthusiasm, but their faces lit up when they saw their little cousin, Audrey. John walked over to the kitchen table. He pulled out a chair and sat down, placing Audrey on his lap. Three large pizza boxes lined the oblong table that seated eight.

Brooke fixed John and Audrey's food and instructed the boys to start off with one slice of pizza each. "If you eat that, you can get some more." She went to the stainless steel refrigerator, opened it, and took out several bottles of water. "You want a bottled water, Detria?"

"Yeah, I'll have one. Thanks."

"Okay." Brooke brought six bottled waters to the table. "Now that that's done, let's eat. I'll let y'all have a few slices of the supreme pizza and take the rest of it for me and Detria."

John shrugged like he could care less. He broke off some pizza and gave it to Audrey. She quickly reached for it and stuffed it into her mouth.

"She acts like she's in heaven." Detria grinned.

"Yeah, so while she's enjoying herself, let's go do the same. Remember to get your water," Brooke said as she turned and walked out of the kitchen.

"So what's up with you and Stiles?" Brooke asked while they devoured their pizza.

"You know my problem with Stiles. I've told you a thousand and one times. He's just selfish, plain selfish."

"What didn't he tell you this time?" She stopped chewing for a second to look at her sister.

"See, you know how he is too. He acts like I don't need to know anything that happens at that church. Do you know as of a week ago, this past Sunday, we have an official associate pastor? He gets paid, Brooke. He's on staff. Can you believe it? But, do you think that husband of mine told me?"

"How did you find out?"

Detria took a swallow of water before she proceeded. "From him."

"But you said—"

"I know what I said, but what I meant to say is he was just talking and then he just up and casually mentions it." Detria slapped the table and both of their bottled waters shook. "I didn't go off like I should have, but you know I wanted to go back to Egypt on that man."

Brooke burst out laughing.

At first Detria looked at Brooke like she wanted to jump across the table, but in less than a second, she was laughing too.

"It's not funny, Brooke."

"I wasn't laughing at the way he told you, I was laughing at what you said about how you should have gone off on him. But you do have a point. As the first lady, you should know what's going on at the church, to some extent. But to defend Stiles, I have to say that he *did* tell you. And it's not like he waited forever to do it. If you want your marriage to work, and I mean really work, you have to stop sweating over little stuff that really doesn't matter."

"Brooke...I need someone to talk to." Detria looked at her sister then dropped her head.

"Talk to? About what?"

"Me."

Brooke returned Detria's stare with a serious glare of her own. "I'm your sister. You know you can tell me anything. What's going on?"

"I don't need you judging me."

"I said you can talk to me. Now what is it?"

"I'm having an affair." Detria suddenly looked away and then back over her shoulder like she wanted to make certain no one had come in and overheard what she was saying.

"What? Are you serious? With who?"

"I don't think that matters, plus I don't think you would know him anyway."

"Detria, tell me. Who is he? Are you in love with him?" Brooke got up, went over to where Detria sat, and took a seat next to her.

Detria sucked in her breath, then started talking again. "His name is Skip. He's the building engineer and a deacon at Holy Rock, and no, I'm not in love with him. At least I don't think I am."

"How long has this been going on?"

"You're not going to like the answer to that question."

"How long, Detria?" Brooke didn't relent.

"Over a year."

"What! Over a year? So is this why you and Stiles have been having problems?"

"No. Stiles has no idea that I'm involved with Skip. Anyway, I plan on breaking it off."

"You *plan* on it? When are you going to do it?"

Detria shrugged. "Soon."

"Look, I'm sorry, Sis. I love you, but I have to tell you what's right. And cheating on your husband is wrong. You're dead wrong. What if somebody finds out? For goodness sakes, Detria, you're the first lady. Why would you even do something like this?"

Detria stood up suddenly, folded her arms, and rolled her eyes. "You act like Stiles is Mr. Perfect. You have no idea how difficult that man can be. He's selfish, self-centered, and all he thinks about is that dang church and his precious little daughter."

"You sound like a fool, Detria. You act like you're jealous of your own child. As for the church, you knew he had a commitment to the church and to his ministry. If you thought you weren't going to be able to deal with that, then you shouldn't have married the man."

"So, it's okay for him to threaten me and to raise his hand at me?" Detria's voice escalated an octave. "What do you have to say about that?"

"You have never said a word about Stiles being violent toward you. Not ever. Has he hit you?"

"No, he hasn't hit me, but he's acted like he wanted to, and on more than one occasion too. Sometimes I get scared of him because I don't know what he'll do."

This time Brooke stood up. She paced for a few seconds around the sunroom then turned toward Detria. "You are not the kind of woman who will let a man push her around, so I'm not falling for that crap. I've never known you to be afraid of anybody."

"Look, I need to go. I have to get home. I see there's no use in talking to you. I should have known better. You're *Little Miss Perfect*. Perfect marriage. Perfect children. Perfect everything. You're so blinded by the fact that Stiles is a preacher that you don't want to hear anything else."

"You are really something else, Detria. You're sitting up here in my house telling me that you're sleeping with another man, and you want to call *me* names? Girl, please. Don't try to justify your actions. You better get it together, and you better do it real soon, before all of this hits the fan."

Detria huffed, got up, and then waltzed out of the sunroom. "John," she called and walked through the house to go get Audrey.

John came out of the kitchen holding Audrey by her hand. "You getting ready to leave already?"

"Yeah, I have a couple of more stops to make. Come on here, Audrey."

Audrey held on to John's leg when Detria reached for her.

"Nooo," she screamed.

Jayce appeared from the kitchen. "Can she spend the night with us?"

"Yeah, can she?" Jayden asked when he walked up.

"No, sweeties, not today. Maybe another time. Come on, Audrey. I'm not playing with you!" Detria reached out to her daughter again, and again Audrey pulled back and started screaming.

"Noooo!"

"Why don't you just let her stay," said Brooke, standing behind Detria. "I'll drop her off later this evening, or bring her home tomorrow."

"She doesn't have enough pull-ups."

"That's no problem. I'll run up the street and get a package. Does she have a change of clothes in her backpack?"

"Yeah."

"Then she'll be fine. You go on and handle your business," Brooke told her.

Detria looked at her daughter and then without another word, she turned and walked toward the front door.

Brooke followed. "You can have an attitude all you want, but right is right and wrong is wrong. And you are wrong, and you know it," she said softly so John wouldn't hear her. "You need to end it, and you need to do it today. You're going down a dangerous path, Sis. I don't want to see you get hurt, your family destroyed, and your marriage fail."

Detria stood silently at the door. Tears welled in her eyes. "I know. You're right; it's just that it's hard. I feel torn. I care about my husband; and I think I love him. But Skip, well he makes me feel special, like he cares about me and nobody else, just me."

"End it. Today," Brooke said adamantly. "He knows you're a married woman, so what does that say about him. Is he married too?"

"No."

"What does that tell you? Wake up, Detria. You're just a booty call to him."

"Let me go. I have to clear my head, do some thinking."

"Well, don't worry about Audrey; she'll be fine over here. You just pray, and ask God to give you the strength to do what's right. I love you, Sis."

Brooke hugged Detria. Detria returned the embrace.

"I'll call you later," Detria said, then opened the door and left.

Detria turned the corner and headed out of her sister's neighborhood. At the traffic light, she searched for her phone until she found it, pulling it out of her new handbag. She dialed a number. "I need to see you," she said to the person on the other end of the phone. "I need to see you now."

6

"Bad boys ain't no good. Good boys ain't no fun." Mary J Blige

Detria turned swiftly into Skip's driveway. They had long since stopped meeting at his house, but today was an exception. After talking to Brooke, she agreed, she had to call things off between them. If Stiles discovered her infidelity, her life would be in a shamble and like his ex; she would be hated by just about everyone at Holy Rock. One thing her mother-in-law had told her, God rest her soul, was to never let your right hand know what your left hand is doing, 'cause some things are better left untold.

Now that she'd confided in her sister, Detria felt like she had no choice but to face the fact that her life could turn pretty ugly, real fast unless she broke it off with Skip. She cared about him deeply, and she honestly believed he cared about her; but when Brooke asked if she was in love with Skip, Detria couldn't give her an honest answer. Maybe it was because she didn't know her own true feelings.

Detria was careful not to use the tip of her perfectly polished and manicured nail to push Skip's doorbell.

"Hey, come on in," Skip told her as soon as he opened the door. "What's going on? You sounded upset on the phone. What has preacher boy done now?"

Detria swiftly walked into the house. She was familiar with almost every inch of his modern style, tastefully furnished home. She strolled nervously into the open area living room that Skip had made into a man cave. "I can't see you anymore. It's over." She talked, fast, like she had to hurry up and get it out before she couldn't say what needed to be said. "I shouldn't have let this go on this long." She waved her hands flippantly through space. "I never should have let this happen in the first place."

Skip walked up on her, grabbed her in his arms, and hungrily covered her mouth with his. His sweet tasting kiss almost cut her breath off.

She nudged him away, but he didn't stop. "Uh, no, stop. I'm serious," she managed to say, nudging him harder in his lower rib cage.

Skip stepped off. "What's this all about?"

"I just told you, it's over. I can't do this anymore. Here I am, a married woman, a mother *and* a first lady and look at me." She looked herself up and down, turned up her nose and then looked at Skip with tears forming in the crest of her eyes. "Lord, what have I been doing?"

"Okay, if this is the way you want it, fine." Skip turned and started walking out of the room.

"Where are you going?"

"To fix myself a drink."

Detria followed. "You do understand, don't you?" She sounded pitiful. She didn't want to end things with him, but part of her knew that it was best that she did. She couldn't believe that no one had discovered that she was messing off on Stiles, but she was glad no one had. She had to make things right in her marriage and with God.

"No, to tell you the truth, I don't understand," Skip snapped. "I don't understand why you want to stay in a marriage that you don't want to be in. If you did, then you wouldn't be with me. I don't get it. First lady or no first lady, if you're unhappy, I say kick preacher boy to the curb and move on with your life."

Stiles opened a bottle of vodka that was sitting on the kitchen counter top with other bottles of liquor. He got a glass from out of the overhead cabinet, turned around, filled it with a couple of ice cubes from the refrigerator door, poured himself a shot, and immediately turned it up. He grimaced like he was in pain as the liquor went down his throat.

"Please, don't do this, Skip. Don't make it harder for me than it already is. I care about you a lot. You know that."

"Oh, really?" Skip said with sarcasm. "Are you sure I haven't been your little boy toy all this time? I mean, do you realize that I could be with whoever I want to be with, Detria? I'm a single guy, no obligations to any one, not even to you. I care about you, but I guess you're right, this has to end. I'm not going to let you keep on using me for your pleasure whenever your husband rubs you the wrong way."

Skip made himself another drink and swallowed it just as quickly as he did the first one.

Detria walked up to him, then stopped. "I'm sorry. I only hope God forgives me. And I hope you will find it in your heart to forgive me too."

Detria turned, walked off, and didn't stop until she was outside standing next to her car. She got ready to open the car door and then stopped suddenly. Wiping tears from her eyes, she pushed the button on her key set and the trunk popped open. "I'm sorry," she kept saying to herself as she retrieved the package and went back to Skip's door. It was still open and she walked back into his house, closing the door behind her.

Back in his kitchen, she said, "Here." She pushed the small bag toward him.

"What's this?"

"It's yours." She stood on her tiptoes and kissed him softly on his lips.

Skip looked at it then removed the box out of the bag and opened it. He studied the bracelet like he was contemplating whether he should keep it or give it back.

"Humph," he said. "So this is what it's come down to, huh?"

"What are you talking about?"

"Nothing, Detria. Go back to your husband and your daughter. Go back to pretending you're the perfect little wife."

Detria looked at him while tears streamed down her face.

Skip placed the bracelet on the kitchen counter. Walking up to her, he pulled her into his arms. His hands roamed her curves and the heat from his body set her on fire with desire. She melted under his touch. She heard her breath grow short and the sound of want eased from the depths of her soul as her body reacted to his touch.

"One more time," he said as he continued kissing her passionately. "That's all I ask, baby. One more time, and I'll leave you alone. I promise."

Detria didn't resist as he kissed her salty tears away.

Skip paused. Looking deep into her eyes, he took hold of her hand and led her to his bedroom.

Detria laid up with him for the remainder of the afternoon, savoring the last time they would be together intimately like this.

Skip reached over and nuzzled her on the neck. "I'm going to miss you. I'm going to miss holding you, kissing you, making love to you," he whispered in her ear.

Detria slowly turned and faced him. "I'm going to miss you too, but you know this is what we need to do, don't you?" She sat up in his bed, not bothering to shield her nakedness. She stared at him, silently tracing his cheek with the tip of her thumb. Her eyes landed on the bracelet. "When did you put it on?"

"While you were sleeping," he answered, smiling and studying the bracelet on his wrist. "This is nice. I like it."

"I'm glad." Slowly, she got up. "Every time you wear it, I want you to think of me." Climbing out of the bed, she ambled to the bathroom, closing the door behind her. This was hard to do, breaking it off with Skip, but what else was she supposed to do? She called herself a Christian woman and it was high time she started acting like it.

Skip sat on the side of his bed then got up and walked to the bathroom door. He was about to turn the knob but decided not to. If this is what Detria wanted, he was going to let her have her way. He went to his guest bathroom down the hall to clean himself up then went to his man cave to wait on Detria.

Minutes passed before Detria came out of the bathroom and into the man cave. Skip was sitting on the sofa in front of his TV playing a sports game on his Xbox One.

Standing in front of him, Detria said solemnly, "I'm leaving now." Her face was etched with hurt and she felt a tinge of uncertainty about her decision. Once she left Skip's house, there was going to be no turning back. The past would be just that, the past. It was time for her to move forward, see if she could truly be happy being Stiles' wife and the mother of his child.

Skip put the game on Pause and looked up at her. No words were exchanged between them.

Detria leaned over slightly and kissed him before she turned and walked away, refusing to look back.

7

"It's easier to be with someone you can't love, than to admit you love someone you can't have." J. Johnson

Detria surveyed their spacious 4,100 square foot home. The luxurious space was all she had dreamed of and more. They had been living at their new, gated address for six and a half weeks, and Detria absolutely loved it. She had spent the past month decorating it. The dark oak hardwoods, trey ceilings throughout, wainscoting, and open space layout, combined with her excellent taste in furnishings made the house look like something off HGTV.

Detria was equally excited that she had everything moved into the new house in time to host Stiles' birthday dinner. Today he was thirty-six years old, and Detria had planned a sit down dinner for fifty. A dozen or so women from Holy Rock's Women's and Kitchen Ministry were busy helping to prepare food and decorating the family room and the outside kitchen area. Initially, Detria planned to have the dinner catered by one of the upscale restaurants located downtown, until the Women's Ministry convinced her that they could prepare a menu of food that would rival the best of restaurants.

Stiles tried to convince Detria more than once not to go all out for his birthday. He would rather have spent an intimate evening with her and his daughter, but Detria, being the attention seeker she was, refused. More than celebrating his birthday, she wanted to show off their new address.

Detria hurried and finished getting dressed. She expected the guests to start arriving in less than an hour.

"Stiles, honey, are you ready?"

Stiles appeared in the doorway of the master bedroom. "What did you say?

"Are you ready?" She turned around and her mouth dropped open when she saw him inside the doorway. He looked so fine in his black suit and tie. She grew excited seeing him, something that surprised her. Since ending things with Skip recently, she found herself enjoying being around Stiles more. When she was at Holy

Rock during the week, the two of them often ate lunch together. Detria had even persuaded Stiles to make love to her a time or two in his church office, something Stiles would never agree to do in the past.

Stiles acted like he was enjoying the new and improved Detria. She had confided in Brooke that she'd taken her advice and broken it off with Skip, and since doing so she admitted that maybe she hadn't given Stiles or her marriage a real chance before. But, now, things were slowly turning around. Whenever she did see Skip at church, he spoke to her and kept on stepping. That was the down side, seeing him almost every day. She fought against the temptation to be with him by trying to channel her emotions toward Stiles.

The birthday dinner was a success. The deacons, trustees, the church secretary, and many of their closest friends and family attended.

Detria had asked Skip not to come but he told her that Stiles would be expecting him, and that she had to get used to them being in the same space at times. It turned out that everything was so busy that she actually didn't have much time to focus on Skip being there.

Hezekiah and Fancy came all decked out in their finest. Pastor and his wife, Josie, were there acting like two star struck teenagers. Everyone seemed to be having a good time.

Gathered around tables strategically placed outside in the open area, guests had a choice of premium cuts of steak, grilled salmon, and perfectly baked chicken breasts. There was a huge array of grilled and steamed seasoned veggies, various salads, breads, pastas, plus a cupcake station. Hired servers made sure everyone was properly served.

"Um, excuse me." Skip stood up and clinked his glass of sparkling juice. "I'd like to propose a toast."

Detria swallowed deeply and stared at him. Her heart beat rapidly.

Stiles was busy talking to Pastor and Hezekiah. He stopped talking, as did the other guests, when Skip proposed to make a toast.

"Pastor Graham, May this next year bring you the very best of happiness, the best of health, and may God's favor abound in your life. Happy birthday, friend."

"Whaaat?" Stiles whispered underneath his breath, then slowly looked from side to side until he saw his wife standing next to her parents and sister. He swallowed hard, frowned, but said nothing. He refocused his piercing gaze on Skip, only Stiles really didn't hear a word Skip was saying. He was too engrossed with the diamonds glistening from the bracelet on Skip's wrist as Skip held the raised glass in his hand. Stiles quickly did an instant mental replay to that day, over a month ago, when he and Leo saw Detria shopping at Zales.

Skip was wearing a bracelet identical to the one Stiles saw Detria purchase, the bracelet he thought she was buying for him. He shook his head and tried to tell himself that it was just a coincidence, but he felt differently.

For his birthday, she gave him a Parallel Study Bible with his initials engraved in gold and season tickets to the Grizzlies games, which paled in comparison to the bracelet Skip was wearing.

Stiles remained dumbfounded until Pastor poked him in the side. "Cheers, son."

Stiles shook his head slightly as if he was coming from under a spell. "Oh, yeah. Cheers," Stiles said under his breath, his eyes remaining glued on Skip. He took a sip of the sparkling juice, as he tried to contain his mounting anger.

The remainder of the dinner party went smoothly. Stiles and Skip talked and he was able to get a closer look at the bracelet. It was definitely the same bracelet. While Skip and some of the other deacons stood around in a circle talking to Stiles, Stiles' mind started racing. He thought back to that night, a little over a year ago, when he heard Detria on the phone with who he suspected was another man. He thought about the times he'd come to Detria's office at church only to find Skip in the office with his wife. Detria always had a good reason for Skip being there. He was helping her do this, or that or they were going over paperwork for something pertaining to the Children's Ministry. However, tonight, as he thought about the bracelet, and began adding up things in his head, he concluded that maybe there was more to Detria and Skip's relationship.

Stiles pondered over everything. *Could Skip and Detria? No way.* He shook his head, hoping to rid his mind of the crazy thoughts zooming around in his mind. He forced himself to join back in the conversation he had started up with some of the fellows about sports. *The devil is a lie,* he told himself.

All the guests had departed for the evening, and everything had been put away. Stiles and Detria went in the back yard, sat out on the lanai, partaking of a real glass of red wine, and not the sparkling juice Detria served her guests. The reason she served the non-alcoholic beverage was because she didn't want to hear the tongue-lashing she was sure to get from some of the rigid, old-timers of Holy Rock had she served alcohol.

"How did you enjoy your birthday?" she asked, her head nestled under the crook of Stiles' upper arm, as she snuggled against him on the all-weather sofa.

Stiles leaned in, took two fingers, and gently lifted Detria's face to meet his. With fervor, he began kissing his wife. "How do you think I enjoyed it?" he spoke in his deep baritone voice.

For the first time during the four years they'd been married, Stiles felt like maybe things were finally on the right track with his family, his ministry, and his marriage. So what if Skip had on a bracelet identical to the one he saw Detria buy. Skip loved flashing bling and showing off, and it wasn't like the bracelet was a one of a kind piece of jewelry. A number of men could have the same bracelet, and that included Skip. Still, there was that inquisitive part of him that couldn't help but wonder where the bracelet was that he saw Detria buy, but tonight wasn't the night and this wasn't the time to bring it up. Stiles was a firm believer that in time, all things would be revealed...good or bad.

He dismissed the crazy thoughts circulating through his mind, and in turn concentrated back on his wife. Detria was a lot of things, but stupid she was not. There would be no way, even if she did cheat on him, that she would cheat with one of his partners. No way. Plus, hadn't Detria proved that she loved him by the way she'd gone all out to make sure he had a memorable birthday? And, the night wasn't over yet. It looked like he was going to get some good loving too. What more could a man ask for?

"You ready to go upstairs?" Detria asked, stroking him in all the right places.

Stiles shook his head. "Uh uh. I don't want to waste this magical night closed up in a bedroom. I want to make love to you right here under the moon and stars." Caressing her tenderly, he eased her back down on the sofa. Tonight all he wanted to do was make love to his wife, and during the process, maybe they would make a little brother or sister for Audrey.

On the way home from the dinner party, Skip thought about Detria. She looked stunning tonight in an all-black, above the knee, strapless, wide-skirted dress, and black heels.

Stiles and Detria's new crib was like walking into a rich man's palace. Skip would never admit it, but Stiles had the life he sometimes wished he had. Fine wife, good money, a cute kid, and hardly a care in the world. Skip also knew that Holy Rock practically paid Stiles hand over fist; but in Skip's eyes, Stiles was still a jerk. Maybe no one else could see it, but Skip knew the real deal Stiles, the one from way back when.

They had been cool since middle school. Not many people other than Skip knew Stiles had a temper and could fly off the handle at the drop of a dime. Stiles used to be a ladies' man, having bedded and messed over more than his share of girls until he met Rena after returning home from Duke Divinity School.

Rena Jackson had changed Stiles for the better. She had his nose wide open. Skip laughed to himself at the memory about Rena sleeping with Francesca aka Frankie, Stiles' sister. When Stiles told him and Leo about it, they didn't blame Stiles for divorcing her. No man in his right man would want to stay with a chick after she pulled something as foul as sleeping with another woman, especially when it wasn't a threesome.

Stiles and Detria knew each other because Detria's parents had been members of Holy Rock almost since Pastor started up the church, but they never ran in the same circles. Detria wasn't a popular, stand out type of girl back then, but she was still a looker. She had long, shapely legs, and a nice round plump butt like most of the young guys liked, especially Skip.

Detria had returned to Memphis after living in Arizona for five years and resumed her membership at Holy Rock. It didn't take long for her to work her magic on the newly divorced Stiles.

Stiles fell hard for her. She was conveniently present to prepare food for him and his family, lavish him with attention, and she won over the late great First Lady Audrey Graham.

Skip had no intentions to sleep with Detria, but what man in his right mind could resist a woman like Detria Graham? She had a way of letting a guy know what she wanted, and Skip was the kind of man who you didn't have to tell twice.

When the two of them *did* do 'the do', Skip felt like he'd won the lottery because Detria was definitely no prude in the bedroom. He could see himself in a long-term relationship with her, if only he had stepped to her before Stiles. She was intelligent, smart and she didn't mind spending her money on him. He looked on his wrist at the bracelet she'd given him and smiled. She looked smoking hot tonight. He wanted her and he wanted her bad. Maybe her mouth said it was over, but Skip wasn't buying it. He wasn't about to let her go that easily. He would keep biding his time, giving her a chance to miss him, to let Stiles dig his own ditch again, and then he would fill it up and there would be no turning back. Detria would be his. All he had to do was be patient…and that would be no problem.

Hearing Detria call his name and squirm underneath his touch, intensified Stiles' desire for her. He eased up off her just enough to stare deeply into her sexy, coffee brown eyes. He increased his rhythm and Detria cried out in satisfaction as she thought about how much she missed Skip.

8

"Regardless of how hot and steamy a relationship is at first, the passion fades and there had better be something else to take its place." Susane Pieffer

Stiles preached from his heart. Sweat beads travelled across his forehead as he strolled back and forth across the plush purple carpet. "Genesis two, verse eight, says it's not good for man to be alone; I will make him a helper fit for him. And God formed woman and he said, a man leaves his father and mother; and he and his wife become one flesh. Furthermore, the Word says he who finds a wife finds a good thing." Stiles walked over to the glass podium, reached inside his suit coat, pulled out a snow-white handkerchief, and wiped his brow.

"That's why I'm grateful this morning, church. I'm thankful for my helper, my first lady. You all know I just celebrated my birthday. I want to thank God for allowing me to see another year," Stiles continued, engaging the congregation with his every word. His eyes cascaded to the second row and there sat Detria smiling from ear to ear. She loved it when Stiles publicly acknowledged her.

"I love my wife. I'm thankful that she sticks by me through thick and thin. I know y'all think I'm perfect," Stiles said, laughing, "but I'm not. Just ask her." He winked at Detria. "I just wanted to say thank you, baby." He casually walked down the steps leading from the pulpit, walked to the front pew, and stopped in front of Detria. Reaching over the pew, he took hold of her hand, guiding her as she stood up. Stiles kissed her lightly on her lips. Detria looked around like she was shy, all the time reveling in his outward show of affection.

"I'm not ashamed to let her know in front of all of Holy Rock that I belong to her." Stiles grinned, then turned and walked back up the steps to the pulpit. Behind him, he heard his congregation oohing and ahhing.

"Tell it, Pastor Graham," Hezekiah said.

Fancy, sitting next to Detria, reached over and squeezed Detria's hand when Detria sat down. "Praise God, First Lady. Bless you," she said.

After church service was over, Stiles positioned himself at the exit door so members of his congregation could shake hands with him as they left.

Detria usually stood with him, but this time she excused herself and headed to her office.

She swiftly rushed toward the back stairs, which kept her out of view of the crowd. The hallway leading to her office was empty. She was relieved because she didn't want to be held up by members of Holy Rock who wanted to chat with her. She felt like most of the people who approached her, especially the women, were fake and didn't mean her any good. She distrusted most of them, but definitely the women her age or younger. All they wanted was a window of opportunity to get next to her husband.

"Hold up," someone said as she got closer to her office.

Detria didn't have to turn around to see who it was. She knew that voice like a mother knows the voice of her kid. She kept walking, slightly increasing her pace, hoping she could make it to her office before Skip caught up to her.

"Detria." He stopped her by taking hold of her elbow. "What's up? Why you acting like I'm a serial rapist or something?"

"What do you want?" she asked between clenched teeth.

"What's wrong with you? Dang, all I'm trying to do is see how you're doing. Can't a man at least do that?"

She looked around acting nervous and paranoid. "No, you can't. I told you, I can't take the chance of anybody finding out about us."

"According to you, there is no us, not anymore. Look, let me holla at you, just for a minute." He kept his grip on her elbow and led her toward her office.

"No, Skip. We don't have anything to talk about. And definitely not here." She frowned and tried to break loose from his grasp.

"Either we can go in your office and talk or I'll say what I have to say right out here in the open." He started talking loudly and he could tell right away that he was making her uncomfortable.

The last thing she wanted was drama. She took the keychain with the office key on it from out of her handbag, unlocked the door, looked around again, and then disappeared, along with Skip, inside her office.

"What do you want? I don't have time for your foolish games. You know the business, Skip." She folded her arms and looked at him like she wanted to slap him.

"I want *this*." He stepped up on her, jerked her hands loose, and gently pushed her back to her desk until her bottom rested on the edge of it. Without saying a word, he devoured her mouth with his.

Detria twisted and turned but it made him want her even more. One hand went underneath her dress and the other hand caressed the small of her back, making it impossible for her to escape.

"Skip," she tried to speak, but he pressed his body against hers even closer. She felt his desire for her and her body couldn't deny him. She gave him what he wanted.

Afterward, Skip helped ease her down off the desk, his body still dangerously close to hers.

Detria shakily stood on her feet, steadied herself, and then stormed off to the bathroom. "I can't believe you did this," she said in tears. "Why couldn't you just leave good enough alone?"

Skip was right up on her. "Because, you know you wanted me just as much as I wanted you. We can't do without each other and you know it. You aren't going to tell me that Stiles can make your body do all the things that I make it do."

Detria bit on her bottom lip. "What do you want from me? I told you, I can't do this anymore. I love my husband."

"Bull! Who do you think you're fooling? If you loved him so much then why did we just make love?"

"Go. Leave me alone, Skip," she screamed and closed the bathroom door in his face.

Skip stood on the other side of the door listening to the running water from the faucet, while thinking about what had just happened. He couldn't help himself. He couldn't get enough of her, and from the way things had just gone down, she felt the same about him. The way her body gave in to him, there was no doubt in his mind that she was in love, and it wasn't with Pastor Stiles Graham. He smiled wickedly, then turned, and left.

"Skip." There was no answer. "Skip," Detria called out again. After there was still no response, Detria slowly turned the doorknob, opened the door, and exited the bathroom. She looked around cautiously, as she walked back to the front and out into her office. With the palm of her hand over her chest, she exhaled slowly, and sat down in her office chair to get herself together before going out to meet up with her husband.

Stiles stopped dead in his tracks when he saw Skip leaving out of Detria's office going in the opposite direction. His first thought was to stop Skip and ask him what he was doing coming out of his wife's office, but then he quickly decided against it. In due time, if something ungodly was going on he believed that God would reveal it to him.

He waited until Skip disappeared down the hall before he walked up to Detria's office. At first, he started to knock, but he thought why should he have to knock. This was his wife and this was his church. He didn't have to announce his presence to anyone. He turned the knob. Surprisingly, the door was unlocked. He walked in and immediately Detria looked up while at the same time saying, "What are you doing back here?"

"I didn't know I had to have permission to come back here."

"Oh, I...I thought." Detria stopped talking. What could she say? How was she going to explain who or what she was talking about? "Uh...are you ready to go?" she said instead.

Stiles didn't push the issue. He would find out soon enough what was really going on, if anything, between his wife and Skip. But for now, he had to keep his composure, at least until he got away from Holy Rock.

"What happened to you? You look a little flustered. You okay?"

"Yeah," she stammered. I came in here because I got nauseated all of a sudden. I didn't want to throw up my insides in front of everybody."

"Who were you talking about when I came in? Sounds like you thought I was somebody else."

"Oh, Skip saw me in front of my office fumbling with my door keys. He stopped and asked me if I needed help, which I told him that I didn't. He said I looked faint, and asked me if I was okay. I admitted that I wasn't feeling too well, so he stayed with me for a few minutes until I assured him that I would be fine. He had just left when I heard the door open, so I thought he'd come back for some reason or other." Detria stood up and walked from behind her desk.

Stiles was nobody's fool, but he was a firm believer that what's done in the dark will surely come to the light, so he took his wife at her word. "You feeling better?"

"Not really. And I don't understand, because I felt fine during service. Maybe I'm coming down with a virus or something."

"Well, let's get home. You ready?"

"Yeah. I want to get out of here, go home, and relax the rest of the afternoon. Do you think Mother Brown will take Audrey home with her for a couple of hours?"

"There's no need to ask her to do that. When we get to the house, you can relax, do whatever you want, and I'll take care of her."

"Are you sure?"

"Of course, I'm sure. She's my sweetie pie."

Detria's eyebrows raised. She picked up her purse and followed Stiles out of her office.

The ride home was quiet. Audrey sat quietly in her car seat staring out the window at the cars and trucks zooming past.

Stiles' mind was a flurry of thoughts. Skip had been his friend for years. Skip wouldn't go behind his back and try to bed his wife. Would he? No way, but then again, my ex-wife had an affair with my sister, so why would it be so hard to believe that Skip and Detria might be knocking boots? One illicit thought after another filtered through Stiles' head like a raging tsunami. The sound of screeching tires and a car horn brought him back to his senses.

"Stiles, pay attention to the road, will you," Detria shouted. "You almost hit that car."

"I saw it," he lied. "How are you feeling now?"

"What?"

"I said how are you feeling? You still feel nauseated?"

"I'm good. I guess I was just worn out from this weekend. That's why I'm going to go home, take a hot shower, and climb up in my bed and do absolutely nothing." Detria yawned and laid her head back against the headrest.

She was angry with herself. She felt like today was another huge setback for her. What was it about Skip that she couldn't resist? Somehow, someway she was going to have to get it through his thick skull that he had to leave her alone. He was treading on dangerous ground.

9

"If you're giving your all to someone, and it's not enough, you're giving it to the wrong person." Unknown

Detria's head popped up from the novel she was reading when she heard her text message notifier chime on her cell phone. She read the message from Skip and sighed heavily.

"It felt good holding u n my arms again," Skip texted.

Why was this man pushing things? Couldn't he just leave her alone? She read the text over and over, contemplating whether to reply or not. She decided to ignore him. That way he would know she was serious about not seeing him again.

She couldn't deny it. Today, it did feel good being in his arms. But she vowed to herself that it could never ever happen again. Skip needed to leave Holy Rock, go find another church to attend and work at. If he didn't, then she couldn't promise that she wouldn't fall weak to him again.

"I miss u. u miss me 2."

"Stop texting me. He is right next 2 me."

"No he isn't. If he was u wouldn't b texting me back."

"Skip stop."

"I want u."

"We hav 2 stop."

"He doesn't make u happy."

"Bye Skip."

Detria deleted the thread of text messages then turned off her cell phone. She refused to go back and forth with Skip. She sat up in her bed, placed the novel next to her, and laid back. She had to do something about Skip, but exactly what that was, she didn't know. She turned over on her side and drifted off to sleep.

Stiles came to the bedroom after playing with Audrey for hours. He had fed her, given her a bath, and read her a bedtime story until she fell fast asleep.

Stiles took his shower and climbed in the bed next to Detria. Her back was facing him. He rolled over on one elbow and used his free hand to wrap around her body. Detria didn't budge. Stiles kissed her on her shoulders, then slowly along the spine of her back.

Detria moved slightly. "Not tonight," she said barely above a whisper. "I'm tired, and I still don't feel all that great."

Stiles ignored her remarks and continued kissing her on her back. Moving up to her neck, he traced his fingers through her thick, straight hair.

Detria moved closer to the edge of the king sized bed. "I said, not tonight, Stiles." This time her voice sounded like she was agitated.

Stiles turned away from her and over onto his side. "Are you having an affair?"

Detria couldn't believe what she just heard. Why would Stiles ask her such a question? What did he know? She was too nervous to turn over and face him, so she answered him with her back still facing him.

"What kind of question is that?"

"One that I expect an answer to."

"No, of course not."

"No?" This time Stiles reached over and pulled Detria by the shoulder until she faced him.

"What is wrong with you? Stop pulling on me."

"I asked you a question, and I want an answer."

"I don't know where this sudden bout of insecurity is coming from, and right now I really don't care. I told you, I'm not feeling good, and I don't have time for stupid questions."

Stiles was hot. His face turned one shade darker. Was she brushing him off like what he thought didn't matter?

"You know what, Detria? I'm not even going to sit up here and argue with you, so let me put it like this. If I ever find out that you're cheating on me, you'll be sorry. Real sorry."

"Don't threaten me," Detria shouted, throwing the cover off her, revealing her thigh length, violet colored nightie. She pounced up from the bed, stood up, placed both hands on her hips, and stared at him like she wanted to beat him down.

Detria quickly turned the tables on Stiles. "All the women that practically throw themselves at you at Holy Rock, and you want to sit up here and accuse me of having an affair?" Detria's head flew back and she chuckled. "All night long the phone rings. I need prayer, Pastor Graham," she said mockingly. "I need a personal visit, Pastor Graham," she continued in various female voices. "I'm having problems, Pastor Graham. Can I talk to you, Pastor Graham?"

"That's part of my ministry and you know that. I'm a pastor, it's what I do. My members need me and unfortunately I can't govern when they need me."

"Oh, so that's all right for you? But me? You have to lay up here and accuse me of the unthinkable. Boy, please. You better get a life. I'm not Rena. I'm not some pushover who's going to crawl up in a corner and boo-hoo. You got the wrong one, babee."

Detria hoped she was playing a good bluff but inside she was terrified. She imagined him telling her that he knew all about her and Skip, but she had to play it off. She didn't think she'd given him a reason to suspect anything.

"You can never let things be good between us. Not ever. It's always something you're accusing me of or blaming me for, and frankly, I'm sick and tired of it." Detria folded both arms and rolled her eyes.

"You're sick and tired? You can't be serious." Stiles laughed. "You think I'm a fool or something? You actually think that I don't know about the bracelet?"

"Something is wrong with you. You sound stupid, real stupid. I don't know anything about a bracelet. You haven't given me a piece of jewelry since the time you gave me that necklace for my birthday two years ago."

"So you actually want to play me that close? The man is up in my house, wearing a bracelet that I saw YOU buy, and you want to tell me it's nothing going on between the two of you? Here I am thinking you bought me that bracelet for my birthday, and some other dude comes up in here sporting it!"

"You know what, Stiles? I'm not even going to entertain your mess tonight. You are way out of line. For your information, the only bracelet that you could possibly know that I bought was the one for my father. I don't know what in the hell else you're talking about. And why are you looking at what the next man is wearing anyway?"

"It was practically dangling in my face, Detria. I saw you that day in Zales. I even asked the sales clerk about the bracelet. So you're telling me you spent seven hundred dollars on your father? Why?"

"So now you're following me?" she was so angry, she felt like throwing something at him.

"I wasn't following you. I happened to be in the mall buying you that purse while you're buying for the next dude!"

"Look, my mother asked me to go and pick up the bracelet. In case you forgot, their fortieth wedding anniversary is coming up, and she wanted to get him something extra special. She saw it in the paper on sale and asked me if I would get it. Now don't you sound like a fool?"

He gave her a suspicious sideways squint, but said nothing else.

"You wanna call her? Huh?" She reached for the house phone on the bedside table. "Here. Call her. Go on; make an even bigger fool of yourself."

"Get that phone outta my face! Calling over there is not going to prove a thing. I hate to tell you this, but your momma's mouth ain't no prayer book." *Is she telling the truth? Did she really get the bracelet for Momma Mackey to give to Poppa Mackey?* He didn't know what to think.

"So now you wanna talk about my momma? Look, I tell you what. Since you have a problem with my quote unquote *platonic* friendship with Skip, I suggest you say something to him. But just like you have women flocking to talk to you, well for your information, Skip has talked to me about his problems a time or two. I listen because he wants someone to confide in."

"I'm his pastor and his friend. He can confide in me."

"Man, please, be for real. You know good and well that there are some things that a man needs to hear from a woman's perspective, from a Christian woman's perspective at that, but anyway, you tell him that then. But don't be up in here trying to sweat me over nothing."

"Um hum," Stiles said and turned over.

"Oh, so that's how this goes, huh?"

"You made your point. I'm through with it."

"You know what, Stiles? Good, you be through with it. But let me say this and then *I'm* through with it. Don't come up in my face trying to start some mess. I don't know what's up with you, but it's all good. Have it your way, just leave me alone. All I wanted to do was come home, chill, and enjoy my new home, but you had to ruin everything!"

"Where are you going?" He watched her put on her robe and step into her slippers.

"I refuse to deal with anymore of your crap." She stormed out of the room and with all her force, slammed the door behind her.

Dang, I left my cell phone in there. But I don't wanna go back. She threw up a hand and went into one of the bedrooms down the hall from Audrey's room. *Whew. That was a close call.*

10

"Starting all over again is not that bad. For when you restart, you get another chance to make things right." Unknown

Hezekiah had hopes that their sons would soon come to Memphis. He wished Fancy's parents would have considered moving too, but they weren't in a hurry to pick up their lives and start over in a new city and state, so Hezekiah and Fancy took the giant leap of faith and landed on their feet.

Soon after the couple arrived, they were living in their own apartment and working twelve hours, six days a week. Fancy worked the front counter at a pastry shop while Hezekiah helped manage the store. Neither he nor Fancy minded working hard. They were used to it, having spent years behind bars.

The neighborhood where they lived was the same neighborhood where Holy Rock was located. They started visiting the church, enjoyed Stiles' way of preaching and teaching the Word, and soon they joined. Almost immediately, Hezekiah became actively involved in several ministries.

Stiles noticed Hezekiah's involvement soon after the couple joined Holy Rock. He had been quite impressed with Hezekiah's knowledge of the Bible, his way of expression, and his commitment to serving God. Whenever Stiles saw him, he knew that Fancy was not going to be far behind.

"Honey, do you like the ivory or the topaz color for the accent pillows?"

Hezekiah looked up from the television and smiled. "Ivory."

"Okay, topaz it is," Fancy said and laughed. "Do you honestly think I'd take your decorating advice?"

Hezekiah joined her laughter and shrugged his shoulders. "Nothing beats a try," he responded and then resumed watching the television show.

"Baby, I want to go to Chicago. I need to see the boys. I miss them."

"I know you do, sweetheart." Hezekiah got up and walked over to his wife. Positioning his body behind hers, he wrapped his arms around her waist and kissed her on the side of her neck. "Don't you start worrying again. Remember, Khalil is in God's hands. He's where he needs to be for now. It's the only place where he can get help while serving time for his crime. If we made it through, I know he can." He kissed her again.

Fancy tilted her head upward to face her husband. "I know. It just gets hard sometimes, that's all." Slowly, she turned all the way around and faced him without moving out of his arms. "You know sometimes I wonder if God is punishing us for the stuff we did. We stole from Him, not just from some guy off the corner or some big time dope dealer. Baby, we stole from God, from the church."

"Don't do this again, Fancy."

With looming doe-shaped eyes, she slowly batted them at Hezekiah like she was seriously trying to fight back the flood of tears that desperately wanted to be released.

"God doesn't operate like that. You know that."

"Yeah, but you reap what you sow, and you know that," she emphasized.

"So you're saying that Khalil is locked up because of us? And are you saying Xavier doesn't want to come to Memphis because he knows that we're concealing the truth about our past?" Hezekiah looked down at his wife and stroked several strands of hair away from her face.

"I don't know what to think, and I don't know what they think. What I do know is that I need to see them."

"Okay, tell you what. I'll start searching for a flight to Chicago leaving later in the week. How's that? Would that make you feel better?"

"She stood on her toes, wrapped her arms around his neck, and gave him a big kiss.

"Yes! Thanks, honey. I'll go up there, stay a few days, and come on back. Seeing them, I know I'll feel much better. When I get back I can see about me and First Lady Graham getting together to talk about the marriage ministry. She told me she wanted to listen to my ideas about what we can do to revitalize it. You know Holy Rock is an up and coming church. Haven't you noticed all the young, married couples and families we have?"

"Yes, you have a point. I think a marriage ministry is a good idea."

"You know, Honey, in spite of Detria's diva-like ways, I sort of like her." Although close in age, Fancy felt ions apart from Detria. Detria reminded her of a spoiled, high society rich girl who wanted everything to go her way and wanted to have her hand in everything that went on.

"You sorta like her? Is that a good thing?"

"Yeah, but there's something about her and Pastor Graham's relationship that seems a little off balance."

"Like what?"

"I don't know. I can't quite put my finger on it, but I'm telling you, it's something that's not right. And have you noticed that most Wednesdays she's not even in Bible Study? She spends a lot of time closed up in that office of hers."

Hezekiah released his wife and walked over to the sectional and sat down. "Do I detect a little jealousy?" he asked jokingly.

"You know me better than that. And another thing."

"What is it?" asked Hezekiah.

"She and Deacon Madison seem awfully friendly." Fancy picked up the ivory pillow that was next to Hezekiah. She regarded it slowly then looked over his shoulder at the topaz colored pillow again. "If I was Pastor Graham, I'd keep my eyes and ears open, or he'll look up and he and the first lady will be a thing of the past."

"Fancy, come on. Stop speculating. Skip is the building engineer. That man is all over the place. And not only that, he's a deacon too, so there are going to be times when he and the first lady have to interact. What's wrong with that? That's how rumors get started."

Fancy shook her head and walked off. She wasn't mad, because she knew how Hezekiah detested gossip, but what he didn't know was that she had her own reasons for saying what she said. No one knew it, not Hezekiah, not Skip, not Detria, and definitely not Stiles, but one day, not long ago, she'd seen Skip and Detria going into Detria's office. She didn't think anything of it until she saw his hand touch the first lady's butt, and not in an accidental way either. It was like he was used to doing it. *What kind of building is he working on?*

she asked herself that day. She never told Hezekiah what she'd witnessed. Many times, she thought about telling Detria what she'd seen but then she talked herself out of it, saying that it wasn't any of her business.

The last thing Fancy wanted to do was interfere in somebody else's relationship. She and Hezekiah had enough skeletons in their own closet, so she kept quiet.

11

"Three things you cannot recover in life: the WORD after it's said, the MOMENT after it's missed and the TIME after it's gone. Be Careful!" – Unknown

Fancy was glad to be back in Chicago. She enjoyed spending time with her parents and seeing some familiar faces. She especially reveled in being able to have one on one time with Xavier.

Xavier acted like he was happy to see her too. She took him shopping and bought him a pair of the new Jordan's he wanted, and several pairs of pants and shirts. They had dinner together at one of the Mexican restaurants that had been featured on the show Diners, Drive-Ins and Dives. Both of them enjoyed the food.

Things were different when she went to visit Khalil. She experienced a mixture of emotions. When she saw how healthy and strong he looked, she was overjoyed and grateful to God for sparing her firstborn son's life. When he was first sentenced to the detention center, he looked like a feather could blow him away; he was just that skinny and scrawny. The heroin was killing him slowly. She was saddened every time she was faced with the reality that he no longer had his freedom. He was missing out on what should have been some of the most fun times of his young life.

When he walked into the overcrowded visiting area, Fancy spotted him right away. She got up from behind the small round steel table and rushed toward him. "Khalil, you look so handsome." She hugged him and held on to him for several seconds. He stood still, not bothering to return her embrace.

Reluctantly, she released him, stepped back, and looked at him as she walked to their table. He sat down in the chair across from hers.

"Baby, how are you?"

Khalil mumbled something, but Fancy couldn't understand him.

She had purchased several pre-packaged snack bags from the commissary when she checked in. The plastic bag filled with cookies, candy bars, two sodas and two bags of chips were on the table.

Khalil toyed with the bag. He pulled it open and got one of the sodas, screwed off the bottle cap, and put the plastic bottle up to his mouth, taking several deep swallows as if he hadn't had anything to drink in days.

"I know how much you love your snacks." She tried to laugh but found it hard. Seeing Khalil looking so unhappy hurt her to the core.

Khalil still remained quiet. Next, he pulled out a bag of the chips and a package of strawberry cookies.

"Honey, I know you don't like being here, but I hope and pray that you see that this is where you need to be for now, at least. Look at you. You're clean, you're not somewhere robbing and stealing anymore. Baby, I'm proud of you."

Khalil finally looked up at his mother. His hard stare revealed his resentment and anger. "Whateva," he responded with no excitement resonating in his voice. He couldn't understand why his mom and dad hadn't done more to keep him from coming to this God-awful place. It was supposed to be a place where he could get help and be rehabilitated, but it was nothing more than a prison to Khalil. He hated it, and he was ready to go home. He may have not been using heroin anymore, but he was still miserable.

Next, Khalil opened a bag of potato chips and grabbed a handful.

"Your father told me to tell you hello, and that he's praying for you."

"Tell 'em to save his prayers for somebody else."

"Khalil, don't talk like that."

"Why? You don't want to hear the truth? Prayer don't work, Ma. All the stuff you and Dad call yourself doing for God, and for what? Then, Grandma and Grandpa are always talking about the church is praying for me and that they pray for me every day. Well, I'm not buying it. Nothing has changed, Ma. I'm still locked up in here." Khalil poked out his lips, as he looked around the dirty, moldy smelling visiting area. "And you, Ma, you don't need to be coming up here. You living a different life now. Anyway, you know if you get caught coming up in here knowing you and dad are convicted felons, it can cause problems for you."

"Khalil," Fancy looked around and leaned in closer to him, "that's not your worry. Me and your father know what we're doing."

"All I'm saying is you living in Memphis now, so do your thing there. Don't worry about me." He got up from the chair. Khalil placed both of his hands in the side pockets of his dusty blue trousers. "Look, Ma, I gotta go. Thanks for coming, but next time, don't bother."

"Khalil, sweetheart, wait. I just got here, and we have an hour visit. Please, honey. Sit back down. Let's talk." Fancy stretched out her hand toward her son. "I want to hear about the sessions they have you going to."

"I don't wanna talk about it." He towered over his mother who remained seated. He walked over to her, kissed her on her cheek, then turned and walked away.

"Khalil."

"Bye, Ma."

Fancy stood to her feet. "Khalil, please. Don't go. We'll talk about whatever you want to talk about. Or we don't have to talk at all. Just don't leave."

Khalil turned back and looked at his mother.

Fancy could see the sadness in his eyes. She didn't want to see her son inside this place, but she knew that this was the best place for him. She prayed every day that Khalil would be healed and delivered from his addiction. If it meant he never wanted to talk to her or Hezekiah, then she would find a way to deal with it, if it meant he would be better.

Khalil succumbed and stayed for the remainder of their visit. When visiting hours ended, Fancy held Khalil's hands and began to pray, but he swiftly jerked his hands out of hers.

"I told you; don't waste your prayers on me."

Fancy stopped as tears gathered in her eyes. She caressed the side of Khalil's face. He hugged her, stood up, then turned and walked off. Fancy stood and watched him until he disappeared behind the steel doors.

12

"To know that one has a secret is to know half the secret itself."
Henry Beecher

Fancy had been back in Memphis for one week. She was glad that Hezekiah made it possible for her to go see her sons and parents, but now it was time for her to get back to living the new life she and Hezekiah were carving out for themselves. She had to trust that God would work everything out with her sons.

She finished getting dressed for her meeting with Detria, which was in a couple of hours. Spring was her favorite season because she reveled in dressing in bright happy colors.

There were tons of ideas she wanted to discuss with Detria about improving the floundering marriage ministry. For instance, she wanted couples who had been married for five years or more to mentor newly wedded couples. Another idea she had was to encourage regular date nights and short getaway marriage retreats.

Studying herself in the bathroom mirror, Fancy put the finishing touches on her make-up. Her arched brows gave her a graceful look. Equally enticing to Hezekiah was Fancy's thick, long, dark lashes that slightly curled upwards. Hezekiah would tell her often how sexy her eyes were. A slightly oval face, full luscious lips, and high cheekbones made her quite an attractive woman.

She took a last look over her shoulder at the house they'd been living in for two months. A broad smile revealed glistening white teeth. She loved their new home. They felt like they'd finally been given a new chance, and a new opportunity to make a better life for themselves.

Fancy's decorating was much like her name: *fancy*. She adored high-end items. Now that Hezekiah was associate pastor and making a pretty decent salary, he could afford to let Fancy indulge a little. He wanted his wife to be happy. She was the one who had stuck by him when he was a youngster getting into all sorts of stupid stuff like gangbanging and slanging drugs. It was only by the grace of God that he'd never been caught or worse yet, killed, like some of his friends. Sure, he and Fancy didn't exactly have a squeaky clean past, but he and Fancy loved God. Believing that it was only important that God forgive them for their past transgressions, Hezekiah saw no need to tell Stiles anything about his life before coming to Memphis. Stiles only knew that he was from Chicago, had two sons, and that he and Fancy moved to Memphis because of finances.

She turned off the kitchen light on her way to the garage. "Thank you, Father," she said, opening the door leading to the garage. She climbed in her silver Accord. Hezekiah had recently bought her the used car. She smiled as she backed out of the garage. Life was good.

Detria stood on her side of the double vanity sink in their master bath. She ran a face towel underneath the faucet, allowing the water to get as cold as it could, then she sandwiched the wet towel between her hands, gently pressing excess water out before placing it on her neck for several seconds, and on her forehead for several more.

When that didn't do any good, she walked to the other side of the bathroom, opened the private area that housed the toilet, and proceeded to lift the toilet seat and slightly lean over it. She held her tummy, but suddenly the wave of nausea left as quickly as it had come. As a nutritionist, Detria recognized when something was off about her diet or food intake. She was careful to eat healthy and choose her foods wisely, so she didn't quite know what had triggered the wave of nausea. "Thank God, that didn't last long. Must have been that salmon I ate last night. I won't get that again," she talked to herself while she finished getting dressed.

"Let's see, what shoes do I wear?" Looking at the rows of shoes that were perfectly organized in her walk-in closet, she chose a pair of signature heels and a purse that matched her jaded green maxi dress.

On her way to Holy Rock, she thought of what she could bring to the table about the marriage ministry. One of the things she wanted to implement was a program to help troubled marriages, or some type of class where women and men could come and talk about private matters. Perhaps, it was because she felt guilty about her own infidelity. She was eager to hear some of Fancy's ideas too.

In Detria's office, the two women discussed several of the items from both of their lists until they decided to implement a combination of their ideas.

"Would you like to go somewhere and have lunch?" Fancy suggested after they finished their meeting.

"Sure, that sounds good. I'm hungry. I didn't have anything but a banana this morning and a cup of coffee. Anywhere in particular you want to go?"

"I was thinking we could go to Jim and Samella's," answered Fancy.

"Jim and Samella's?"

"Yes, it's a new restaurant over on Bullington in South Memphis. I've been there twice since they opened. They have great food, and a good variety too. The staff is courteous and the atmosphere is inviting."

"Okay, sounds good. I'm game," Detria replied.

The ladies gathered their purses, and Detria put the files inside her file cabinet and got ready to leave. Just as she opened the door, Skip's hand was in a fist, like he was about to knock on the door.

"Hello, Brother Madison."

"Hello, First Lady Graham." Skip nodded. "Hello, Sister McCoy."

"Hello, Brother Madison," Fancy responded. She walked on the other side of the door and stood next to him while he talked to Detria. She paid close attention to Detria's body language.

"How can I help you?"

She looks like she's just been caught with her hands in the cookie jar, thought Fancy.

"Uh, I needed to talk to you about," he stuttered, "the two rooms over in the children's wing. You said you wanted to take a look at them to see if we can reconfigure them for the new Puppet Ministry."

"Yes, that's right, but I can't right now. Sister McCoy and I were about to go get something to eat. Maybe we can set something up for later."

Detria briefly made eye contact with Fancy like she was searching for approval. "We should be back in a couple of hours, wouldn't you say, Sister McCoy?"

"Yes, I don't see why we shouldn't."

"Okay, I'll see you when you get back. You ladies enjoy your lunch."

"Thanks, Brother Madison," Fancy replied while Detria nodded.

Fancy was no fool. She could tell by the way they looked at each other, along with the noticeable nervous twist from Detria, that there was most definitely some chemistry being generated between the two. Maybe Detria Graham needed to take heed to some of the things they discussed about the marriage ministry.

13

"For nothing is hidden that will not be made manifest, nor is anything secret that will not be known and come to light." Luke 8:17 ESV

Detria hurriedly excused herself, leaving Fancy practically standing alone on the church parking lot.

"Are you sure you're going to be okay? I'll walk to your office with you."

"No, no, I'll be fine. We'll talk later. Thanks for everything, Sister McCoy." Detria jetted off and ran inside the church. She practically ran to her office, hurriedly unlocked it, leaving the door partially open as she raced to the bathroom. She made it to the toilet just in time to throw up her insides.

"Detria. You in here?" Stiles walked all the way into her office. "Hello, anybody in here?"

Detria slowly evolved from the bathroom, looking pale and shaken.

"Honey, what is it? Are you all right?"

"I don't feel well. Me and Fancy had lunch, and before I even got to the restaurant, I started feeling a little nauseated. I ate anyway, thinking that I needed to put something on my stomach since I didn't have much breakfast. I guess that wasn't the problem. I don't know what's wrong with me. Maybe my resistance is low."

Stiles walked up to her and felt her forehead. "You don't feel like you have a fever. You're just a little clammy. Come over on the couch and sit down for a minute."

"Okay." She slowly followed Stiles to the couch and sat down.

Skip walked up and saw Detria's door open. He was on his way to see if she was back from her lunch with Fancy. He really did want to show her the rooms that they had talked about for the puppet ministry, but that was not all he had on his agenda. He was tired of Detria avoiding him at all costs. He had to talk to her again, see where her head was. He wanted to keep having his cake and eating it too. He had made up in his mind that he wasn't going to pressure her or make her feel like he was stalking her, nothing like that. But he did miss her, missed everything about her. He wasn't ready to give up on their relationship, even if what they were doing was wrong.

He was about to go into her office when he heard Stiles talking. He stood outside the door and listened as Stiles talked about taking Detria to the doctor if she didn't feel better. *What's wrong with her?* When he saw her earlier, Detria looked fine; so fine that he wanted to gather her into his arms and kiss her, but with Fancy McCoy practically breathing down his throat, that made it impossible.

"No, I'm good. I think I'll go pick up Audrey from Mother Brown's and then go home, lie down, and get some rest," he heard her tell Stiles.

"You can't get any rest with Audrey there. I tell you what, you go home. Can you drive, or do you need me to take you?"

"No, that won't be necessary. I can manage."

Skip knocked on the open door. "Hello, anyone in here?" he asked as he took a step inside.

"Skip, hello," Stiles said as he stood and greeted him. "What can I do for you?" Stiles asked, sounding like he was perturbed at Skip's untimely appearance.

"I was on my way to the children's wing, and noticed First Lady's office door was open. I was just checking to see if everything was okay."

"Everything's good." Stiles said. He was getting fed up with Skip always popping up.

Skip looked, leaned to the right, past Stiles. "You sure she's okay? She looks like she's a little under the weather. Anything I can do?"

"I got this," Stiles said, flinching his jaw line and revealing his aggravation with Skip.

Detria stood up and walked beside Stiles. Leaning against the side of his chest, she replied, "I'm fine."

"Skip, make sure everything is locked up in here. I'm going to walk my wife to her car. You and Security meet me in my office in ten minutes. I have a few things I want to talk to you guys about."

"Sure," Skip answered.

Stiles held Detria in the center of her back as the two of them walked along the corridor, with Skip watching what looked like the ideal couple.

While locking up her office, Skip thought about how it must have looked and sounded to Stiles when he asked if Detria was okay. *I have got to be more careful. Stiles looked at me like he wanted to slit my throat.* Skip shook his head from side to side, like he was trying to clear his mind.

Moments later, after Stiles returned to his office, he met briefly with Skip and some of his security staff about ways to increase security at the church and reorganize the time Stiles spent socializing with his members at the end of the church service. With the congregation in the high thousands, it was draining on Stiles to stand and talk with the droves of people who wanted him to pray for them, or tell them all about their problems, and their children's problems, and on and on. Something had to be done. After they discussed several possible solutions and scheduled to have a meeting with some of the other staff later in the week, Stiles convened the meeting, and every one proceeded to leave, except for Skip.

"Hey, I'm going to go get something to eat, unless you need me to do something else."

"Naw, everything's good. Go on," Stiles said.

"All right. I'm out then. I'll be back in about an hour."

Stiles studied the bracelet on Skip's wrist again. "Hey, man, those real diamonds?" Stiles faked a laugh as he pointed to the bracelet.

"You know I don't deal in nothing fake, bro."

"What you doing wearing it around here then? You lose that, and church or not, somebody is going to keep it for themselves."

"Believe me, it's not going anywhere. The clasp on this thing is locked tighter than Fort Knox." Skip laughed.

"Man, you're too cheap to buy something like that for yourself."

"Who said I bought it?"

"Exactly. What female you got buying you stuff now?"

If only you knew. "This ain't nothing. Just a little something-something one of my lady friends hit me with."

Stiles' mind started racing. "Who is she?" he asked, hoping he wasn't sounding too presumptuous.

"Who is who?"

"The female that bought it. Does she go to Holy Rock?"

"Man, what's with the twenty questions?"

"Hey, just asking, bro," Stiles answered.

"You know how I roll."

"Yeah, I do. You haven't changed at all."

"I can't help it. You know I'm not one to settle down with one female like you and Leo. That's just not me. I enjoy the single life too much."

"Man, you need to find you a good woman, marry her, and have some little Skips running around."

Skip laughed on the outside, but inside he was thinking about Detria. He looked at the bracelet and for a minute, just a minute, he felt guilty about sleeping with his friend's wife.

Instead of going straight home, a block from her house Detria stopped at a CVS Pharmacy. Her chime sounded on her phone just as she was at the counter paying for her items.

"U ok?" Skip texted as he walked outside to his car.

Detria read his message. *I am not going to do this, Skip. I will not talk to you. I won't. I won't. I won't.* She left the store, got in her car and drove home, ignoring Skip's text message.

"I need 2 talk to u."

Detria huffed. "Why can't he leave well enough alone?"

As soon as she stepped foot inside the house, her cell phone started ringing. Slightly irritated, she answered it. "What, Skip?"

"I'm worried about you."

"I don't need you worrying about me. All I need you to do is leave me alone."

"You looked like a ghost when I saw you. You can't blame me for being concerned."

Detria stood in the kitchen. "Like I said, I'm good. Now stop calling me!" she screamed into the phone, then abruptly ended the call.

She threw her cell phone on the foyer table as she walked out of the kitchen, up the long hallway, and into the downstairs bathroom. She sat her purse on top of the sink, opened it, and removed the small white plastic bag with the items she'd purchased from the pharmacy.

Detria lifted the lid on the toilet. Lifting her skirt and sliding down her panties, she sat down on the toilet, praying that her worst fears would not come to pass.

She finished what she dreaded having to do, then got up from the toilet, and left out of the bathroom.

Ten minutes later, she returned to the bathroom. As if in slow motion, the plastic tube fell from her trembling hand after she saw the plus symbol. With a light clinking sound, it hit the floor.

Detria's knees buckled as she slid down the back of the bathroom wall until she too was on the cold tile floor. With her head cradled in both hands, she screamed. "Oh, God, noooo, not this. Not now."

14

"The only things you give yourself when you cheat
are fear and guilt." Unknown

Detria curled up in a fetal position in the middle of the bed. Uncertain what to do, she turned over, removed the house phone from its base and called Brooke.

"I'm pregnant," she said as soon as Brooke answered the phone.

"Pregnant? How do you know? Have you been to the doctor?"

"No, but I've been nauseated for the past several days. First, I thought it was a stomach virus, then I remembered that my period hadn't started, so I stopped at CVS this afternoon and bought a pregnancy test."

"Wow, congratulations. I'm happy for you and Stiles. Girl, God is good!"

"I don't know if I would say all that." Detria sat up in the bed and held her stomach. Rocking back and forth, she started crying again. "I don't want to be pregnant, not now, Brooke."

"But why? You said Stiles wanted more children. I mean, it's not like this should be a shock to you. You aren't on the pill and obviously you and Stiles don't use—oh my gosh, please don't tell me that it could be that Skip dude's baby?" Brooke's voice shot up an octave.

Dead silence filtered through the phone.

"Detria, hello, are you there?"

"Yeah, I'm here. What am I going to do, Brooke? Suppose it *is* his baby?"

"Look, you don't even know if you're pregnant. Those tests aren't a hundred percent accurate. Make an appointment with your OB/GYN first, then worry about the rest after you find out if you really are pregnant."

"I'm no dummy. I know my body, and I'm telling you, I really think I'm pregnant. Brooke, I don't know if I can go through with this. I mean, the chance is too great. If it turns out that I am, I might have to, you know..."

"No, I don't know. What are you talking about?"

"I might have to have an abortion."

"Girl, stop talking crazy. Two wrongs do not make a right. And there is no way I am going to stand by and let you kill an innocent baby. No way. Now stop talking nonsense and call the doctor, make an appointment. I'll go with you. Until then, get yourself together. I've got to go now. The boys have baseball practice this evening. I'll call you later, okay?"

"Okay, but Brooke, don't say a word to John, or to Mom and Dad."

"I won't. I'll call you later. Bye."

"Bye." Detria put the phone back on its base, scooted up in the middle of the bed and fell asleep.

Stiles picked up Audrey from Mother Brown's but instead of going home, he went to visit Pastor. He missed the days of talking to his father about almost any and everything. Since Pastor married Josie, Stiles had backed off with his regular visits. He wanted to give Pastor and Miss Josie their space. He was glad his father had found happiness again. His mother had been Pastor's heart. It was good to see that someone, especially someone as sweet as Miss Josie, could make Pastor smile again.

"We're going to go see Paw Paw," Stiles told Baby Audrey.

"Paw, Paw," Audrey said from her car seat.

"That's right. We're going to see Paw Paw."

When they arrived at Emerald Estates, Josie greeted him at the door. Stiles was glad Pastor made the decision to move back to Emerald Estates after he got married to Miss Josie. Emerald Estates held precious memories. It was where he and Francesca had grown up.

When his mother died, Pastor moved in with him and Detria, after having had two strokes. That had been a bad idea, but after Pastor moved out from them and into the private assisted living facility, things started to turn around for him. He met Miss Josie, his health improved, and now Pastor and Miss Josie were able to enjoy a happy, healthy life together as husband and wife. On top of that, Pastor was overjoyed when Miss Josie told him she had no issue with moving back into the family house Pastor had shared with his deceased wife.

"Pastor, I don't know what to believe. I don't want to think that she's been unfaithful." Stiles shook his head in shame at the very idea that Detria really might be having an affair.

"Son, I know the two of you have seen some tough times in your marriage, but I hope that my daughter-in-law isn't so unhappy that she would go outside of her marriage."

"But, Pastor, when I look back and start putting things together, it makes me that much more suspicious. Remember that time I came home and I told you I heard her on the phone talking to somebody, and I know it wasn't Brooke or one of her other friends?"

"Yes, I vaguely remember."

"Well, I think it had to be a dude. I think that dude was Skip."

"You don't know that for sure, Son."

"There are other things. Like this bracelet that Skip is wearing. It's a bracelet I saw Detria buy with my own eyes. I'm telling you, Pastor, I think she's messing around. And I swear, if..."

"Stop. Don't swear. It will all come to the light. You know this."

"That's exactly my point. I think the light may have come on."

Stiles and Pastor had a long talk, something they hadn't done in a while. Josie entertained Audrey and then after Pastor and Stiles finished talking, Pastor played with his granddaughter, the apple of his eye. She reminded Pastor so much of Audrey. She was feisty and stubborn just like her grandmother used to be. Pastor said she was the spitting image of his dear Audrey.

When they left Pastor's house, Stiles was compelled to go to Skip's house. He didn't have proof that Skip and Detria were involved in something illicit, but he was going to confront Skip, nonetheless. It was probably all in his mind, that's what he kept telling himself. Evidently, he couldn't convince his heart to think otherwise because he continued driving until he arrived in Skip's neighborhood. Stiles neared Skip's street and it was if suddenly his spirit said, *If you go looking for trouble...*

He turned on to the street where Skip lived. Slowly, he drove along the curvaceous road, barely missing the car backing with haste from out of Skip's driveway. His mind shut down as his foot slammed on the brakes.

That's Detria's car. Stiles watched as the car barreled down the street.

Skip stood in his driveway until Detria's car was out of sight, then he turned and walked back inside, focused ahead the whole time. If Skip had simply looked to his left, he would have seen Stiles' car.

Stiles sped past Skip's house. He was confused but he was also furious. The scripture verse, 'Be angry and sin not' played in his head, but it was too late to take heed.

Instantly, another Bible verse popped into the forefront of his mind…*And Jesus answered and said unto them, Take heed that no man deceive you…* "No man or first lady," mumbled Stiles.

15

"Sometimes the person you'd take a bullet for is the person behind the trigger." Taylor Swift

Stiles tried catching up to Detria, but as he sped out of Skip's neighborhood, he didn't see her car anywhere. He drove directly home. When he let up the garage door, Detria was getting out of her car.

Stiles opened the driver's door with such force the door swung back and immediately jerked forward, slamming hard against his right shinbone. He yelped, bit his bottom lip, and grabbed his aching leg with one hand, using the other to push the door back off him. This time he held the door, then jumped out of his car without taking Audrey out of her car seat. When she started wailing and reaching for him, he turned around, unbuckled her, and got her out.

"Where have you been?" His nostrils were flared and his head was pounding.

"I stopped at the drugstore to pick up a few items." Detria frowned. "What's with the attitude?"

"You expect me to believe that?"

"What are you taking about?" Detria looked at Audrey and reached for her. Audrey reached out to her mother and Detria took her out of Stiles' arms.

"Hi, pretty girl," she said to the toddler and kissed her on her forehead, before she placed her on the ground. She took hold of Audrey's hand and led her inside the house.

"You think you can just tell me anything and I'll believe it, huh? You're no better than my ex."

Detria entered the kitchen, and then turned around and gawked angrily at Stiles. *What's got him this mad? He doesn't know about the pregnancy. He can't know about me and Skip.*

"Look, fool!" Detria yelled. "I don't have time for your mind games. Don't come at me like I'm some trick off the street, Stiles. I don't know what you're talking about, and frankly, I don't feel like dealing with your insecurities today. And another thing, don't you ever compare me to your ex-wife, or *any* female for that matter!" Detria rolled her eyes, threw up her hands, and proceeded to walk from the kitchen toward the back stairs.

Stiles followed. "Don't you walk off from me, and don't you act like you don't know what I'm talking about," he screamed at Detria until Audrey started crying. She reached up for her daddy, and Stiles looked at his daughter, then picked her up.

"I *said* I don't know what you're talking about. If you have something to say, then say it. I am not going to engage in some senseless argument with you. Dang, you can be so childish and stupid acting!" Detria bolted past him. Rather than go upstairs, she turned around and went toward the family room.

Her text message chime sounded. She looked back to see if Stiles was behind her, before she quickly read the message. "I saw a car pass by here after u left. Looked like Stiles," the text message read. Detria read it over again. Her heart started beating fast. Had he seen her?

"U think it was him?" she texted Skip back as fast as she could.

"Not 100 percent but think it was."

"No wonder he's actin a fool."

"What r u talkin bout? What is he doing?"

"Goin' off. Actin stoopid. I'll call u latr."

"I'm coming ova—"

"Don't. I'm good. I'll call u."

"Dude bet not lay a hand on u."

"You're talking to him, aren't you?" Stiles roared.

Detria jumped and turned around. Her eyes grew so big they looked like they were about to pop out of their sockets when she heard Stiles behind her.

Stiles rushed up to her and abruptly snatched the cell phone from out of her hand.

"What are you doing?" she screamed. "Give me back my phone." She reached up toward Stiles. Her petite stature was no match for his towering frame, plus he had the hand that he held the phone in, up in the air. He began reading the text messages.

"So this is what you've been doing all this time. Screwing my friends, huh?"

Poor Audrey was standing next to her daddy. She ran up to him, grabbing hold of his leg. Tears were pouring down her angelic face.

"Give me my phone!" Detria yelled again, still trying her best to get it out of his hands. "You don't know what you're talking about."

"You have me pegged for a fool! Well, I'm nobody's fool. You got me wrong." Stiles slightly leaned to the side of Detria, scooped up Audrey, and abruptly sat her on the sofa before turning his focus back on Detria.

"I said, give me my phone, Stiles. Give it to me, now!" she demanded, crying and screaming profanities while shaking like a leaf.

Stiles elbowed her, pushing her away from him.

Audrey was screaming to the top of her lungs by this time, but neither one of them did anything to console her.

"You're nothing but a slut. A Jezebel. You screwing my friends, and using my money to buy presents for the next dude!"

Detria prayed that Stiles would not see the fear on her face.

"Don't try to play me. I know you're screwing Skip, and I know you bought that bracelet for him. And dude had the nerve to wear it up in *my* house and at *my* church! But you know what? I don't blame him…I blame you—"

"Look, I don't know what kind of little game this is supposed to be, but it's not funny. I told you already, I bought that bracelet for my mom to give to my dad," Detria explained, while cautiously moving toward the sofa where Audrey was sitting and still crying.

"So you wanna go there? That's the way you really want to do this? Since you don't know what I'm talking about, maybe you'll remember this--I just saw you, Detria. I saw you leaving his house. How do you explain that?" Stiles folded his arms. "How do you explain these text messages?"

His intense stare made Detria feel like she was being raked across a pile of hot coals.

"It's not what you think. I can explain." She leaned over closer to her little girl, like Audrey could shield her from Stile's verbal assaults.

Stiles began laughing, sounding like a mad scientist.

Detria became even more fearful. She had to get away from him before he really lost it.

"There's nothing to explain. The text messages, seeing you leaving his house, the bracelet....there's nothing you can tell me except the truth. So, let's hear it. How did the first lady hook up with the deacon?"

"For the last time, I'm telling you that I did not—"

"Shut up! I can't stand yo lyin', two dollar, wanna be..." A long rant of expletives burst forth out of his mouth, until suddenly Stiles stopped his angry tirade just as quickly as he had started it. He walked to the sofa and stood in front of her. Audrey was crying loudly and reaching for him, but he ignored her, something Stiles never did. He catered to Audrey like she was Princess Kate. To let her cry uncontrollably was evidence that he was infuriated.

"Let me see what your lover boy has to say about all this." He read another one of the text messages out loud while Detria reached up, trying to snatch the phone out of his hand again.

"You think he wants you? Huh? Don't you know Skip by now, Detria? Why do you think he isn't married? Why do you think he won't settle down and commit to one woman? I'll tell you why; because he enjoys making a fool of ignorant women like you. How much money have you spent on him? That little bracelet, I'm sure is just one of many gifts you've given him, other than your body. No wonder you don't want me to touch you."

"Please, it's not true. I told you, I'm not sleeping with Skip, or anybody. I swear."

"Shut up! You're lying and you know it. You make me sick." He started walking off. "I'm going to kill 'em."

"Stiles," Detria pleaded, jumping up from the sofa and running behind him. This time she lunged at him. Hopping on his back, she tried to jerk the phone out of his hand again. Stiles abruptly turned around. A snarl on his face, he grabbed hold of her wrist. Raising his hand to strike her, he suddenly stopped as he looked at his little girl and heard her screams. Instead of hitting her, he violently pushed Detria off him with more force than the first time.

The push caused Detria to stumble backward, and she fell hard. The front of her face hit the edge of the wood coffee table, immediately causing a deep gash underneath her eye. Blood spewed out.

Crying and screaming profanities, Detria tried to scramble and get up off the floor. She was shaking like a leaf and her feet wouldn't gain enough traction for her to get up.

Audrey was screaming to the top of her lungs by this time, but neither one of them did anything to console her.

When she tried to get up again, Stiles stood over her, one leg on each side of her body. Detria didn't move.

Stiles took a step backward when Detria tried getting up off the floor a third time. She finally got up. Rubbing the side of her face, and feeling and seeing blood, she screamed, "You hit me. You hurt me. You tried to kill me. I hate you!" Her heart felt like a nuclear blast was about to go off.

"Cut out the theatrics. You did that to yourself. If I hit you, you'd definitely know it 'cause you wouldn't still be talking smack like you're doing."

Stiles looked down at her. Standing still, the expression on his face revealed his anger and disdain toward her. His eyes appeared glazed over like he was in another place.

Detria was hysterical. Hollering and crying, she quickly grabbed up Audrey from the sofa and took off upstairs. She rushed to their bedroom, closing and locking the door behind her. She used the house phone to try to call Skip to warn him that Stiles might be coming over there. He didn't answer his phone. She was in a panic. What was she going to do? She cried until she heard Stiles rushing up the stairs. He sounded like a tidal wave. He turned the doorknob.

"Open this door," he yelled while simultaneously pounding on it. "I said open this door now, Detria, or I swear, I'll kick it in!"

Detria panicked. The house phone started ringing. She grabbed it. It was Skip.

"Hey, why are you calling me from the house phone?"

"Oh, my God; he knows, Skip."

"He knows? Baby, are you sure?"

"Didn't you hear me? I said Stiles knows about us," she said. "He's gone crazy, I'm telling you. Oh, Lord, please don't let him kill me. Please..."

"I'm on my way," she heard Skip say before the phone went dead.

Boom. Boom.

Stiles was beating on the door so hard it felt like an earthquake had struck. Was the door about to pop off its hinges? Audrey was screaming and crying, and so was Detria.

"Detria. You better open this door." Stiles kept getting louder and louder.

Detria picked up the phone again and dialed 9-1-1. "Please send the police right away. I think my husband, Pastor Stiles Graham, is going to kill me!"

16

"Be careful of who you trust; the devil was once an angel." Unknown

Skip drove as fast he could. He tried to remember which street to turn down. He had been to their new house only once, and that was the day of Stiles' birthday dinner. If Stiles had hurt her, Skip had made up in his mind that he was going to do something bad to the dude. He wished he had listened to Detria when she said she wanted to end things between them. He didn't mean her any harm. Unlike most of the other women he fooled around with, he actually cared about Detria.

This whole thing was because she had called him earlier, after leaving Holy Rock. She told him she had something urgent she needed to talk to him about. He left work early and told her to meet him at his house. She did, but he wasn't prepared for what she had to tell him when she got there.

"Skip, I took one of those over the counter pregnancy tests. It came back positive."

"What are you saying? You're pregnant?"

"Yes."

" Is it mine?"

"I...I don't know for sure. It's definitely a possibility."

"Are you sure you're pregnant?"

"Pretty certain, and my period is late. I told you that I wanted to break things off with you, but you wouldn't listen," she cried. "And that day, in my office, when you, when we...that may have been—"

"When you got pregnant?" Skip finished her sentence.

Detria nodded, placing her head in her hands. "Skip, what am I going to do?"

"What you aren't going to do is panic. Everything will work out. If it turns out that you are pregnant, and it's my child, then I'm just gone handle my business."

Detria looked startled. "What do you mean by you're just going to handle your business?"

"Just what I said. If it turns out that there's a chance this kid is mine, I'm handling my business. Which means, forget Stiles. My child is going to know me."

"So you would be willing to see my marriage destroyed? You can't be serious. If I am pregnant, then Stiles can never know that you might be this baby's father."

"I'm not going to go there with you, Detria. I tell you what," Skip told her, *"make the doctor's appointment. Find out if you're pregnant for sure, and how far along you are first. But, let me tell you this. Stiles can kick rocks if that child ends up being mine, because I'm going to be a part of my child's life."*

Skip looked at the speedometer. He was going 95 miles an hour on the expressway, but he had to get to Detria and Stiles' house. He was going so fast that his GPS even sounded confused. "Turn right...make a u....do three quarters of a mile," the mechanical woman's voice instructed without hesitation.

Skip's heart felt like it was about to burst out of his chest when he turned onto Stiles and Detria's street and saw blue lights flashing. Hastily, he parked the car as close as he could to their house, turned it off, jumped out the car, and ran toward their house.

The blaring sound of sirens caused him to turn around. He saw an ambulance approaching. Neighbors were standing outside and others stood in their doorways or on their porches. Skip ran toward the house until a police officer told him to stop.

"Hey, hold up. You can't go up there," a burly looking female officer told him.

"What's going on? Why is there an ambulance?"

"I said, step back, sir, before I haul your butt off to jail."

Skip placed both hands on his waist and gritted his teeth. With his head hung low, he paced the sidewalk, until he saw the ambulance pull up in the long driveway. Paramedics rushed out and one of the police officers led them into the house. The front door was open, but Skip could see nothing.

He didn't know what made him look, but he did. He looked at one of the squad cars lined up in front of Stiles' house. He bit his bottom lip, shook his head, and started yelling when he saw Stiles sitting in the back of one of them.

"If you hurt her, I'm gonna kill you, man. I swear I am," Skip ranted.

Stiles watched and listened to Skip cussing him out and threatening to kill him. He hadn't meant to hurt Detria. Didn't mean to kick in their door, didn't mean to lose it like he had. But she had pushed him, pushed him to the point that he snapped. He sat in the back of the car and thought about Rena, of all people. Rena was the first woman to crush his heart. She'd just about broken his spirit, but then Detria had come along and he allowed himself to love again. He didn't love her in the same way that he once loved Rena, but he loved her nonetheless, and he really wanted their marriage to work.

How did things get out of hand so fast? Detria and Skip? How long had they been secret lovers? Was Baby Audrey even his daughter? He didn't know what was true and what was fabricated.

What was his congregation going to think when they found out that he had been arrested and thrown in jail for domestic violence? Hearing Skip cussing him made the situation that much worse. Police or no police, Holy Rock or no Holy Rock, if he could get out of that squad car, he would have beat Skip until there wasn't a breath left in his body, and the way he felt now, if he had his way, Detria would be lying right next to him.

17

"It takes no time for a small drama in life to become a wide screen cinema with big blown music for only others to enjoy." A. Somejoy

Hezekiah and Leo went to the downtown courthouse Monday morning for Stiles' arraignment. They had contacted the church's attorney, Barry Whitlock, who was in the courtroom too. They made Stiles bond, and he was released.

"The media has already gotten wind of this, so your picture has been on the news and in the newspaper," Whitlock informed him as they led him out the courtroom.

Stiles kept his head down. He didn't want to face Hezekiah, Leo, not anybody. All he wanted to know was if his daughter was all right.

"She's fine. She's with Mother Brown," Hezekiah assured him. When Fancy heard about what went down, she went and got her from the hospital."

"What did you say?" Stiles questioned. "Why was Audrey in the hospital? What had Detria done to his little girl?"

"Don't worry. Audrey's fine. It's just that when...," Hezekiah paused.

"When they took Detria to the hospital, they took Audrey to have her checked out too," Leo finished Hezekiah's sentence.

"How is she?" Stiles asked. "Detria, I mean."

"She's okay, except for a few bruises and a deep cut or gash underneath one of her eyes. But thank God, the baby is fine."

"I wouldn't hurt my little girl for anything in this world. You know that."

Hezekiah looked strangely at Stiles. *He doesn't know Detria is pregnant?* "I'm not talking about Audrey. I'm talking about the baby your wife is carrying."

Stiles stumbled and almost collapsed at the car. "Baby? She's pregnant?"

"You didn't know?" Hezekiah asked, opening the front passenger door to Whitlock's black Chrysler 300. "Get in the car, Pastor Graham," Hezekiah instructed.

"Of course I didn't know. Man, that girl is so foul." Stiles fumed. "But you said the baby is good?" He rubbed his forehead nervously.

"Yeah, the baby is good," Hezekiah answered.

"Man, it's going to be all right. Just maintain your cool," Leo replied, looking just as stunned as Stiles to hear that Detria was pregnant.

Stiles got in the car in slow motion like his feet were embedded in concrete. *Pregnant?* He couldn't believe it. All the time he longed for Detria to get pregnant and now she was? Why now?

"Explain to me again what caused all of this," Attorney Whitlock said as he drove through downtown Memphis.

"Like I said, she's sleeping with one of my friends. His name is Skip Madison." The anger swiftly returned as soon as the words came out. "That low down, trifling, son of a—"

"Calm down, Stiles," Leo told him.

"Skip Madison? Deacon Skip Madison?" Hezekiah asked.

"Yeah, none other than Mr. Romeo himself," Stiles exclaimed, hitting the armrest with his fist.

"Are you sure, man?" asked Leo.

"Yeah, I'm sure. Man, I caught her leaving his house, and I read text messages in her phone between him and her. I don't know how long they've been sleeping together. The baby in her belly could very well be his and not mine."

Stiles' voice finally broke and when Hezekiah looked at him, it looked like Stiles was about to cry. Hezekiah couldn't blame him if he did. This was a lot for a man to handle. Being in the position of leadership, especially the senior pastor of a big church like Holy Rock, well, let's just say this could be pretty bad for Stiles. Hezekiah already felt it in his gut.

"Why don't you come stay with me and Fancy? I don't think it's a good idea for you to go back home right now."

"He's right," agreed Attorney Whitlock.

"Or you can stay at my crib," offered Leo. "I know Crystal won't mind."

"Naw, take me to the Hilton on Ridge Lake Boulevard. I'll get a room there. I don't want to bring you all into my mess. I mean, I guess I've already done that, but I don't want to get you any more involved than you have to be."

"We'll drop you off at the hotel first, then after I get my car from Attorney Whitlock's office, I'll go pick up some of your clothes from the house," Leo offered.

"Thanks, man." Stiles looked back at Leo and Hezekiah, then over at Attorney Whitlock. "Thanks. I can't believe I let the devil get me like this. I mean, what was I thinking? My God," Stiles cried out.

"It happens to the best of us. There's nothing you can do about it now but try to rectify the situation," advised Attorney Whitlock. "Domestic assault is a serious charge. I don't think I have to tell you that, but I'm going to see if we can get this squashed without you having to go before a jury of your peers. Since you have no prior record, not even a traffic ticket, and you have a stellar reputation in the community and this city, I should be able to get you probation with no time served, and diversion after your probation ends. Now, tonight, I want you to go to the hotel and get some rest. Do not contact your wife. Do you understand?"

"Yeah, I understand," Stiles answered reluctantly.

"You heard the judge tell you that your wife has secured a temporary protective order against you. So, if you don't want to get in any deeper than you are, you'll take heed to my advice. That goes for this Mr. Madison fellow too. Do not call or try to confront him."

"You don't have to worry. We'll make sure he doesn't do anything rash or stupid," said Hezekiah.

"Yeah, you hear that? You have to lay low, man," Leo warned. "Brother to brother, I'm telling you to keep your head together, man. You hear me?"

"Yeah, sure. I hear you."

18

"A half-truth is the most cowardly of lies." Unknown

Detria lay on the couch downstairs in the family room. Her body ached, and it was sore like she'd been in a terrible car accident. She still found it hard to believe that Stiles had become so irate to the point that he had almost broken her wrist when he grabbed her. It was his fault too that she'd hit her face on the table. The cut underneath her eye required stitches. A millimeter closer, and she could have put out her eye. She had fallen just that hard. Detria told anyone who would listen that Stiles had beaten her, and that he threatened to kill her and Skip.

Pastor called and talked to her and told her how sorry he was for what Stiles did. He was upset and disappointed that his son had allowed the enemy to manipulate him into abusing his wife. He told Detria that no matter what had transpired between her and Stiles, that his son had no right to strike her.

Detria had already been crying and now she cried harder and louder into the phone with Pastor on the other end. She thought of the time she physically abused Pastor when he was helpless and defenseless after having suffered his second stroke. Pastor forgave her and to this day, he treated her like a daughter.

"Pastor, I can't believe he did this. And Audrey was in the room too. I was so scared. I've never seen him so angry. It was like he was a different person."

Brooke sat across from her in an oversized chair, listening to her sister talking on the phone. Brooke also hated what Stiles had done, but she also understood how a man like Stiles could snap. Stiles loved her sister, and Detria was wrong, dead wrong for cheating on the man. She also knew how cynical Detria could be. Her mouth had gotten her into trouble more than once while they were growing up. That didn't give Stiles any right whatsoever to hit her sister but Brooke looked at the situation from both sides. She didn't say it aloud, but she thought about the story Detria told her. She didn't know if she believed her sister. Had Stiles really hit her?

"Thank you, Pastor. Yes...okay...I will. Goodnight."

"So, what did Pastor have to say?"

"He said that he couldn't uphold Stiles because what he did was wrong. He said he still wanted me to pray and ask God to give me a forgiving spirit."

"And?" said Brooke.

"And what?"

"Are you going to forgive him?"

"I can't think about forgiving him right now. I just got from the hospital from the man beating the brakes off me. He could have made me lose my baby, and you want to sit here and talk about forgiving him? I don't think so."

"Are you sure he beat you, Detria?" Brooke looked at her sister. One eyebrow rose, like she didn't quite know what to believe.

"What kind of question is that? Can you see?" Detria eyed herself, pointing to her face. "You think I did this to myself?"

"Of course, I can see. And I'm not taking up for him, I'm just asking. You're my sister. I know you."

"Obviously you don't if you think I would make up something like this."

"I'm just saying, it's not like your record is squeaky clean. I mean, the man found out you were cheating on him. And not only are you cheating on him, you're doing it with one of his best friends, and one of the deacons at the church. Come on, now. Be for real. What would you do if the shoe was on the other foot?"

"I wouldn't do what he did to me, that's for sure. I would have just left his butt, divorced him, and got everything I could, including this house! I will not allow any man to abuse me and get away with it. Stiles is going to pay. You best believe that."

"I said he was wrong, Detria."

Detria rolled her eyes at her sister before she stood up and started walking toward the open designed, chef-styled kitchen.

"Does he know you're pregnant?" Brooke stood up and followed her.

"No. I was going to wait until it was confirmed by my OB/GYN. But after everything that happened, and I went to the ER, I told the doctor that I might be pregnant, so they gave me a pregnancy test. They said I'm about eleven weeks." Detria rested at the kitchen island. Nervously she ran her hands through her hair. "This can't be Skip's baby. It just can't."

"My God, Detria. How could you do this? You had a good marriage, a great husband. You have a beautiful daughter, and look at this house." Brooke looked around the enormous kitchen that was bigger than both of her sons' bedrooms put together. "I mean it's like stepping into one of those houses for the rich and famous. And you want to throw it all away for some building engineer, wannabe player like Skip Madison? Come on, now."

"Look, I don't need you judging me. You don't know what goes on behind closed doors."

"No, you're right. I don't. Why don't you fill me in? What exactly has Stiles done that you had to go and cheat on the man?"

"I guess whipping on me is not a good enough reason, huh, my high and mighty sister." Detria was fuming. She couldn't believe that Brooke was coming to Stiles' defense the way that she was. "Honey, Stiles is not Mr. Perfect. Look how he dumped Rena at the first sign of trouble, and what about when he was going behind my back emailing and calling her long after they had been divorced. Oh, and let's not forget that he's raised his hand at me before. I guess you forgot all about that, huh, Brooke?"

"No, I haven't forgotten, but it still does not justify committing adultery. For Christ sakes, Detria, you're the first lady. What kind of example are you setting? What kind of role model are you for young women in the church?"

"That's just it; I'm not a role model. I don't want to be one either. I'm human. I'm me! I made a mistake. So what if I'm the first lady. I'm not the first woman to cheat on her husband and I most certainly won't be the last. Now, if you ask me if I regret what I've done, yes, I do. But it's done now. I can't change what happened. And," she lowered her voice and placed her hand on her belly, "if it turns out that this baby *is* Skip's, then I'll have to cross that bridge when I get to it. And, if it's Stiles' baby, then I still have to come to a decision about what I'm going to do. I do know that I can't see myself staying with a man who would do to me what Stiles has done."

"I hear you. And I'm sorry. I didn't mean to come off like I was accusing you or blaming you for what Stiles did. As a man of God, he should have been able, in my opinion, to exercise more self-control."

"Exactly," agreed Detria.

"So what happens from this point forward?"

"I know he's made bond. You know Crystal, Leo Jones' wife?"

"Yeah, I remember Crystal."

"Well, she texted me and told me that he's supposed to be staying at a hotel. She didn't know which hotel. She said Leo wouldn't tell her."

"Have you talked to Pastor McCoy yet?"

"Yeah, for a minute. He called earlier this morning. He said that he and Sister McCoy would be over here sometime today to check on me."

"That's good. What about Audrey? Have you heard from Mother Brown?"

"Not since she called and told me that Sister McCoy dropped Audrey off over there. As far as I know, Mother Brown doesn't know that I'm home from the hospital. I guess I'll call her now."

"When you call, tell her that I'm going to come and get Audrey and take her home with me. You know I don't mind and John adores that little girl. If he had his way, I would be pregnant with baby number three." Brooke laughed.

"See, that's what I'm talking about."

"What?" Brooke's eyebrows raised.

"You and John have the perfect marriage. A blind man see that."

"That's because me and John work hard at our marriage. You think we don't fight? You think we don't disagree at times? And you know for yourself that I put that man through some things in my marriage before the boys came along."

"Yeah, but that was a long time ago. Other than that, I've never seen John say a cross word to you, and come to think of it, I've never heard you say anything remotely offensive to him either."

"You'd be surprised, but it's just that John and I try to do like the Bible instructs, and that's not to let the sun go down and we're angry at one another. We make it a point to resolve our differences before we go to bed. And it works. But like I said, it isn't always easy. We've been together for eleven years, and it's taken every single second of every day, working to make our marriage strong."

"In other words, what you're telling me is that you would never do what I did? You would never cheat."

"I don't think I even have to answer that. Look, let's drop this for now. Why don't you call Mother Brown while I whip us up something sinfully delicious to eat."

"Sounds good to me. And Brooke?"

"Yes, Sis?"

"Thank you."

19

"If a relationship has to be a secret, you shouldn't be in it." Unknown

```
    I want 2 see u."
    "I can't do that."
    "I'll b careful no one sees me. hav to
make sur u r ok"
    "I'm good, Skip."
    "Just let me com ova for a few
minutes."
    "No. leave me alone."
```

The phone rang. It was Skip. Detria exhaled slowly, allowing the phone to ring several more times before she pushed the button to answer it.

"Why are you doing this? Haven't you caused enough trouble?"

"Trouble? Me? I think you have the wrong guy, baby. This is me, Skip, not that crazy preacher boy you're married to."

"What do you want?"

"I told you. I want to see you. I want to see for myself that you're okay."

"And I told you, no. You have to take my word. I'm good."

Detria stayed on the phone trying to convince Skip that she was good. Right now her mind wasn't on him. She didn't want to see him, didn't want anything to do with him. She realized that she shouldn't have let things between them go on for so long. When she first flirted with Skip, she hadn't expected anything to come of it, but some kind of way, one thing led to another and she found herself in bed with him. After that first time, it was like she became addicted to Skip Madison. The more she tried to tell him that they had to end things, the more she clung to the guy.

She loved Stiles but she felt like he wasn't exactly attentive to her needs. It was always about that *daggone* church. She thought about First Lady Audrey. How had she endured being the first lady all those years? How did she put up with Pastor putting the church ahead of her and their children? *No wonder you cheated on Pastor.*

You went through the same thing I'm going through now. And like you, I may be carrying my lover's child. First Lady Audrey, what do I do?

"Detria, are you listening to me?" Skip asked.

"I've got to go. I'm tired, Skip. I'll call you later."

"Promise?"

"I said that I would. Bye."

"Bye, sweetheart. Take care of yourself and my baby."

"You don't know if it's yours yet, so I wouldn't go there if I were you."

"I know, but something tells me it is."

"Bye, Skip." Detria ended the call and returned to thinking about what her next step would be.

20

"Whatever is begun in anger ends in shame." Benjamin Franklin

Stiles sat alone in his office at Holy Rock. It had been two and a half weeks since the incident between him and Detria. After his picture was blasted all over the news, Internet, and God only knows where else, Stiles realized he had some tough decisions to make about his marriage, his pastoral position, and his life overall.

He was due back in court the following week. His lawyer believed that everything would be resolved, and he would be able to move on with his life.

He had prayed, talked to Hezekiah, and absolutely sought his father's guidance, but he still wasn't any closer to knowing what he should do. Should he give it all up? This was the church that his father had built and now because of him and Detria's dirty laundry being aired all over the city, he was between a rock and a hard place. The last thing he wanted to do was destroy everything Pastor had spent his life building.

Stiles rubbed his hand over his head, then put his elbow on his mahogany desk, made a fist, and rested his tilting head against it. He began praying out loud.

"Father God, what am I to do? I need you. I need you now. Give me direction." A tear formed in the crest of his left eye. "I was wrong. I didn't practice self-control. I let my flesh bring me down and now look at me." He looked up toward the ceiling and tears flowed down his face. Lifting both hands upward, he kept praying, pleading with God to show him the way.

A light knock on the door came and Stiles slowly lowered his head and hands. Reaching to his left, he opened the top drawer and pulled out a hand towel and began wiping his tear streaked face.

Knock, Knock.

"Pastor Graham. You in there?" Hezekiah stood outside Stiles' office. He felt bad for the guy. What Stiles and Detria were going through made him and Fancy's problems seem miniscule.

Hezekiah understood what it felt like to become enraged, to get so mad and angry that you lose all sense of reasoning and for a moment, that nano second, you could very well cross over to the 'no return' zone. Only by the grace of God do the angels of the Lord hold you back and give you clarity of mind. Just in the nick of time. Yeah, Hezekiah understood that, but Hezekiah never exhibited that unbridled anger toward Fancy. That type of anger was once reserved for whoever he had to fight off when he lived in Cabrini-Green. Back then, he had to do whatever it took just to survive and come up out of those projects alive.

God had been faithful, and he heard the cries of Hezekiah to save him. Since that day, he believed in God, but the streets of Chicago didn't care what he believed. The streets kept calling his name. When he first met Fancy, almost right away she became a ride or die girl, totally faithful and ready to stand by him, at any costs.

"Umm," Stiles cleared his throat, got up, walked from behind his desk, and to the door. He opened the door and nodded at Hezekiah,

"Come on in," he said somberly, taking a half step backward. He turned, walked back to his desk, and sat back down.

"How are you, Pastor Graham?" Depending on where the two men were, what they were talking about, and what they were doing, determined how they addressed one another. If they were talking about the Grizzlies or something that was going on in the city, they definitely addressed each other like buds, calling each other by their first names. Otherwise, they addressed one another by their ministerial titles.

Today, things were more serious than Hezekiah could ever imagine, especially coming from Stiles, who he and countless others at Holy Rock, and in the community, respected as a stand-up man and a dynamic preacher. In Hezekiah's eyes, Stiles remained that same person, no matter what the first lady had accused the man of doing.

Hezekiah, having come from the streets, considered himself wise to the game, meaning he could see right through *Mizz Detria 'The First Lady' Graham*. Stiles was blind to the fact, but right from the beginning, when he and Fancy first officially met her, Hezekiah had told Fancy, "Don't let her get too close. Something about her isn't right. Something about her spirit."

His spirit of discernment rarely led him wrong. Hezekiah wasn't aimed on getting Stiles off the hook for what he'd done to Detria. His mission was to help Stiles get his name cleared. If that meant stepping up and becoming interim Senior Pastor until the dust settled with Stiles, well, he would just have to do that. Hezekiah relished at the thought: *Hezekiah McCoy, Senior Pastor Holy Rock Church and the lovely First Lady Fancy McCoy.* He pulled himself out of his daydream and refocused on Stiles.

Stiles fumbled with the pages of the open Bible on his desk then looked up at Hezekiah. "I can't say how I'm doing. You tell me. What's the latest poll? How many members want me out of here?"

Hezekiah pursed his lips, closed the door, entwined his hands behind his back, and stepped further into Stiles' office.

"All I can say is that it seems like the church is torn. Half of the members want you to stay. They say that it had to be a good reason for you to snap the way you did. Then you know there're the other ones who say you should go to jail for what you did, and you need to step down as pastor."

Stiles looked at Hezekiah with sad eyes. "I messed up. I really messed up."

"You're human. Sure, you're the shepherd of this church, and you are held to a higher standard than most, but that's part of what we sign up for when we accept our calling into God's ministry."

Hezekiah pulled out one of the brown leather high back chairs in front of Stiles' desk and sat down. "Sitting in here beating up on yourself is not going to help things. Have you made up your mind about what you're going to do? Are you going to address the congregation?"

Stiles shook his head, then rested his head on top of his hands. "I owe Holy Rock that much. This coming Sunday will make three weeks since I've been MIA from the pulpit. It's time I say something. I'm grateful that you've been willing to fill in."

"No problem. But the fact remains, I'm not you. Holy Rock wants to hear from you; they want to see you. I can't tell you what to do because I don't know what I would do if I were in your shoes. What I *can* tell you is to keep seeking God like I know you've been doing. He's the only one who can give you clear direction."

"Yeah, you're right, and I have been praying." Stiles pushed his chair away from his desk with his long legs. Slightly leaning back in, he looked up at the wall that showcased the picture of Pastor and First Lady Audrey Graham."

"My mother would be so angry about everything that's happening. I miss her, and this might sound, well, sound crazy but in a way, I'm glad she's gone to glory. I wouldn't want her to see the mess I've made of things."

"Don't do that. I didn't know your mother, but I'm sure I can safely say that she would understand. Do you think me and Fancy see eye to eye about everything? Do you honestly think Deacon Jones and his wife have the perfect relationship?"

Stiles looked seriously at Hezekiah as if he was really tuned in to what he was saying.

"Nobody has the perfect anything. Nobody. I don't care how many sermons you get up there and preach every Sunday. I don't care how long a couple has been married; how many wonderful anniversaries they've celebrated, or how many times you see people acting like everything in their lives is all hunky dory; the fact is, we all fall short. You know the Word, Pastor Graham. I don't have to tell you," Hezekiah said with conviction.

"Yeah, I know the Word, but right now, I'm just being truthful, I don't feel the Word."

"Your faith is not based on feelings and emotions. You know what God can do. One thing I know about you is that your belief in what you do is real. I respect you a lot, and I honestly believe you when you say that you didn't beat your wife."

"And I didn't. I won't deny that I pushed her up off me. I can't deny that I was rough, real rough when I did it. But I was so mad." Stiles bit down on his bottom lip and got up from his seat. "Did I want to hit her? I have to admit that I did. I wanted to hurt her for what she did to me."

"But you didn't. Yeah, you lost it. You pushed her and she injured herself in the process, but was that really your fault? I would say it wasn't, but it's not the same as what she's saying. Remember, it's her word against yours, and she's got the bruises to show it."

"You're right. She's going around telling any and everybody that will listen that I beat her up The nerve of that woman! Why is she trying to destroy me? If her and Skip want to be together, then I'll gladly give her a divorce. She can have the house, the car, whatever she wants. But I won't let her have Audrey or the baby she's carrying...not unless."

"Unless the baby is Skip's?" finished Hezekiah.

"Yeah, unless it's Skip's. I can't see myself raising another man's seed, not in a situation like this."

"I understand."

"What about Skip? What's he saying?" asked Stiles.

"I gave that dude his walking papers. Told him to get to stepping and don't look back."

Stiles' eyes seemed to sparkle for a second. "You fired him? When?"

"Last week. We can't have someone like him working at the church and knowingly having an affair with the first lady. We definitely can't have him on the deacon board, so basically, Skip Madison is history. I can't bar him from Holy Rock, but I haven't seen him during any of the services since I let him go."

"How did he react?"

"He wasn't a happy camper. Not at all, but he didn't buck me too much. I could tell he wanted to take a punch at me, but he must have realized that I would have jacked him up so fast he would have thought he was on a zip line sailing over Holy Rock." Hezekiah reared back in his chair and started laughing.

Stiles laughed right along with him. The thought of Hezekiah pounding Skip was worth laughing about, unlike the situation Stiles was in.

21

"Never use your failure of yesterday as an excuse for not trying again today." Unknown

Detria left the doctor's office and drove to meet Brooke for lunch at a cafe in the Cooper-Young district known for restaurants that served scrumptious comfort food. Right now Detria could use some comfort in whichever form she could get it.

While they ate, Detria and Brooke talked about what they'd been talking about for the past few weeks: Stiles, the baby, Holy Rock, and of course, Skip. Detria was still no closer to making up her mind what she was going to do about the state of her marriage. Did she even want Stiles back? And supposed she did, and it turned out that he didn't want her back? What then? Question after question raced through her mind.

Today the doctor told her she had to stop stressing so much or she could put the baby's health in danger. She had to take better care of herself, but how, when everything that could go wrong had gone wrong.

Detria continued to pray that the baby belonged to Stiles. That way, Skip would be out of her life, certainly not at Holy Rock ever again, and she and Stiles could have a new slate. They would have two precious, beautiful children. Detria told herself she would be more patient, act more like a mother, and a doting wife – she just needed another chance.

Stiles had to be back in court the next day, and she and Brooke planned to be there. The prosecutor told her that Stiles and his attorney had entered a plea deal. He would plead guilty to simple assault and in return would be given probation and a fine.

"Would you be satisfied with that?" Brooke asked.

Detria shrugged. "I mean, what he did was wrong, dead wrong." Detria paused, slowly twirling the small portion of remaining pasta on her fork.

"Can you forgive him?"

Detria nodded. "I think I can. If I'm ever going to be able to move forward, I've got to let go of the past. I can't put all the blame on Stiles. I have to let go of the old me, the selfish, self-centered me that I was. I have to be better, Brooke." She spoke with a slight hesitation. "You know what I mean?"

"Yes, I know. And I'm proud of you. I've been praying real hard for you, and for Stiles, too." Brooke reached across the table, took hold of her sister's hand, and squeezed it. Smiling at Detria, she encouraged her by letting her know that she supported her decision and would do anything she could to help her.

Brooke accepted that she would probably have to do more in the way of helping Detria out with Audrey and the new baby. Like Detria, Brooke was also praying that the baby Detria was carrying belonged to Stiles.

Stiles was not a bad guy in Brooke's book. He, of course, had his ways, but she still didn't think that he deserved to be booted out of a church that his own father founded. But that's exactly what was happening. Detria had told Brooke that the congregation at Holy Rock was torn over whether they wanted Stiles to remain as senior pastor.

Brooke paused for a moment, as if hesitant about saying her next thought. "I'll be praying for God's will. That's all I know to do."

"I'm going to let my lawyer know that I want the protective order lifted. I don't think Stiles is going to be fool enough to try anything crazy."

"You *still* have a protective order?" A hard pinched expression appeared on Brooke's face.

"Uhhh, yes."

"Okay, so tell me, why the change of heart?"

"I've been reevaluating my marriage, my life, everything. If there's any chance of me and Stiles reconciling, then I have to try to move forward. The first step for me is to get that order lifted. The rest is sort of up to him."

"That makes sense. What about the baby? How are you dealing with being pregnant?"

"As for this baby, Brooke, let's be real. You know I never was too keen on having a houseful of kids."

"Yeah, I know."

"Stiles, on the other hand, always wanted at least two or three, maybe more. That's one reason, though this pregnancy is bad timing, that I really want this baby to be his. Even if we don't get back together, I know that he will be a good father just like he is to Audrey. Skip, well, Skip would make a good father too, I think, but there is too much drama when it comes to Skip and me." Detria sighed deeply. "I don't know what to do. I'm confused."

Detria looked down at her belly. Resting her hands on top of it, she thought, *God, please, let Stiles be my baby's daddy.*

22

"We may not be able to undo damages,
but we can always make a fresh start." Unknown

Stiles stood before the judge and listened as she tongue lashed him before sentencing him to twelve months' probation. He would have to complete a thirteen-week anger management class as well. She reminded him that he was to keep his distance from his wife and from Skip Madison. He would have to make arrangements to see his daughter.

Detria and Brooke sat quietly in the courtroom next to Detria's lawyer. Detria listened intently as the judge chastised Stiles. The judge talked about him so badly that for a minute, Detria felt sorry for him.

At the end of the hearing, without saying anything to Detria or Brooke, Stiles walked out of the courtroom. He was happy that he hadn't been sentenced to any jail time, but still felt somewhat dejected because now he had a criminal record. Knowing that it would be expunged after he served his probationary period still did not make him feel one iota better. Thanks to his cheating, scheming wife he may as well have been some abusive thug off the street because that's exactly the way the judge talked to him.

Attorney Whitlock, Leo, and Hezekiah walked beside Stiles and made small talk amongst one another, while Stiles was bombarded with thoughts about his future and his position at Holy Rock. The fact that it was possible that his pregnant wife may be carrying another man's child was not what he wanted to deal with right now. It was too much and if he pondered on it long enough, it may do him good to attend a class to get his anger in check, because he wanted to annihilate Skip Madison.

Arriving at Leo's car, Stiles bid his lawyer goodbye. "Thanks for everything, Attorney Whitlock."

The attorney patted Stiles on his back. "Remember, keep your cool. Lay low for a minute. And think about what I suggested."

"What? Finding another place to live?"

"Exactly. You can't keep staying at hotels, you know."

Stiles tilted his head, and his eyebrows perked up like a dog's ears. "The couch in my office isn't so bad. Actually, it's rather comfortable," Stiles tried to joke.

"You need somewhere more stable for your visits with your daughter."

"Yeah, I know, and you're right. I can't let anything else jeopardize my relationship with that little girl. She means the world to me."

The attorney half-smiled, patted him on the shoulder again, and walked in the opposite direction toward his car.

"Where to?" Leo asked when Stiles got in the car and closed the door. Hezekiah sat in the back.

"I want to stop somewhere and grab a bite to eat, and then go back to Holy Rock to get my car. I need to take care of a few things."

"I'm off work today, so I'll be glad to take you wherever you need to go."

"Thanks, but I can manage." Stiles briefly glanced over his shoulder. Hezekiah, who was sitting in the back seat, was busy talking on the phone. Stiles turned back and started talking to Leo again.

"I'm going to contact Riley Hollingsworth to see if she can help me find a spot to lay my head. Somewhere that I can be to myself, just me and God." Stiles rubbed his head back and forth with his hand. "I'm telling you, this feels like a nightmare. I know God won't put more on me than I can bear, but it sure feels like this burden is more than I can take."

"It's going to be all right," Hezekiah spoke up.

Stiles looked back over his shoulder again. Hezekiah was off the phone. "Thanks, Hezekiah. I'm glad you think so."

Stiles called Riley Hollingsworth and arranged to meet with her so she could take him around to see a few rental properties.

Riley was an attractive, but sort of reserved looking woman in her early forties, with a professional demeanor.

Stiles parked in front of the first rental property where they agreed to meet. Right away, from the outside, the cottage style house didn't suit his taste, but he was willing to look at it and see how the layout was on the inside.

Riley pulled up and Stiles swallowed deep when he saw her get out of the car and stand up. Something about her was different. Her long locks of blonde hair were pulled back in one ponytail that trailed to the center of her back. Large, gold, hoop earrings kissed the side of her high yellow skin. The berry colored dress she wore rested well above her knees, but was tasteful at the same time. And when she walked, the dressed swayed with her every stride.

Walking up to Stiles, she extended her hand and shook his, then led him up the steps to the house.

The inside was not to his liking. It was too drab, felt cramped, and needed quite a number of repairs. He wanted a move-in ready place.

For the next several hours, Riley showed Stiles several houses and townhomes. Stiles decided that a townhome in downtown Memphis would be an ideal spot. It was centrally located to Holy Rock, which was definitely a plus.

"So, let's say we celebrate. I'll buy you lunch. What do you say?" Stiles asked Riley as they exited the townhome.

Riley glanced at her cell phone before replying. "That would be nice. My next appointment isn't until later this afternoon, and I could use something to eat."

"Good, then let's see what we can find downtown. I might as well get used to living down here."

They found a restaurant and for the first time in a while, Stiles felt himself relaxing. He learned that Riley had an identical twin named Miley who lived in Nashville. Riley was engaged but she said her fiancé wasn't a member of Holy Rock. They laughed and talked while they dined.

While they ate and talked, Stiles wondered if Riley was one of the church members who wanted him gone or was she one of the more understanding and sympathetic members who wanted to keep him. From her demeanor and the easiness in which they got along, Stiles got the feeling that Riley was not the judgmental, unforgiving type of woman. He could be wrong, but at this point, it really didn't matter because he had come to the realization that his days as Senior Pastor of Holy Rock were numbered.

He had no inkling of an idea what he was going to do. He had made the decision that on Sunday morning he was definitely going to address his congregation. He would be open with them and let them know that he was sorry for his actions, sorry for disappointing his flock, and sorry that yet another marriage had fallen apart. How had everything come to such a bitter end? He had been duped by yet another woman and he started to feel that something was wrong with him. Was he a weak man? Was he too easy going or was he too controlling like Detria often accused him of being?

He walked Riley to her car, then on the walk back to where he had parked, he thought about his life and how it had gone from sugar to stank. He felt like a total fool for not seeing that his wife was truly unhappy. He thought the trip they took to Myrtle Beach had been good for the both of them. They had made vows to work harder on their relationship. Obviously, it all had been a bunch of talk on Detria's end. No telling how long her and Skip's affair had been going on.

Stiles got in his car, put his foot to the floor, and sped off, heading to Holy Rock.

His phone rang. He pushed the hands free button in his car. It was Pastor.

"How are you, Son?"

"I'm good. I found a place to live. It's downtown. I'm leaving from there now headed to Holy Rock."

"I'm close by the church. Why don't I meet you there?" Pastor suggested.

"Sounds good. I should be there in a few."

"Okay, Son."

"Bye, Pastor."

Pastor hadn't said a lot to Stiles about his future at Holy Rock. But Stiles felt that Pastor had to be hurt by everything that was going on. There was no way around it. After all, Stiles could probably lose Holy Rock; the one thing Pastor had spent his life building.

23

"True love isn't about being inseparable; it's about two people being true to each other even when they are separated." Unknown

Rena packed the last of her clothes in her suitcase, closed it, and put it down on the floor next to her bed. Her flight to Memphis was scheduled to depart later that afternoon. She had mixed emotions about returning to Memphis. It held so many unpleasant memories. She had promised that she would not look back on her past, and she really hadn't. Yes, there were times she thought about Stiles and Francesca, but the two of them were just that, in her past.

When she heard the news about Stiles and Detria, Rena's heart immediately softened for Stiles. She knew all along that Detria was bad news, but then again, Rena told herself 'you reap what you sow' and that meant Stiles too. It's not that she wished bad karma on him for the way he treated her when he found out she had slept with his sister, but that happened way before she hooked up with Stiles. Yes, she was probably wrong for not telling him about the relationship, but she honestly didn't think it was his business. Rena was sure he hadn't told her about all the women he had bedded before they got together either. But again, the past was the past and she hated that he could lose his pastoral position at Holy Rock because of his actions. That had to be tearing Stiles apart.

She would be in Memphis for the funeral of Mr. Bolden, her former library supervisor. The two of them had remained friends after she moved to Andover. He had passed away in his sleep from natural causes. When his wife called and told Rena, she knew she wanted to go back to Memphis and pay her respects. What she didn't know was if she was going to try to see Stiles while she was there.

"You about ready?" Robert asked as he walked up on her, grabbing her waist from behind, and nibbling on her ear lobe.

Rena giggled and slightly turned around.

Robert met her lips with his for a tender kiss.

"I guess so," she replied, easing out of her husband's arms. She then sat down on the side of their bed.

Robert remained standing. "What's on your mind? Or should I say, who's on your mind?"

Robert had an uncanny way of knowing when something was bothering her. It was one of the things Rena loved about him. He was understanding, never put her down, and he always, always listened to what she had to say. He was a special man in her eyes, and she was grateful that God had brought Robert Becton into her life.

"You need to leave it alone, Rena. There is nothing you can do or say that can change things. Stiles is no longer part of your life. Let it go."

Rena looked at her husband, still truly amazed at how well he knew her.

"I don't know what you're talking about. Stiles is the last person on my mind. I was thinking about Mr. Bolden's wife and kids. You know how much that man loved his family, and knowing that his kids have to grow up without him in their lives, it's just horrible, Robert. I can't imagine if, if our..." Rena shook her head like she was trying to shake the thoughts out of her mind.

Robert sat down next to her. "Look at me."

Rena did.

"I know you're upset about Mr. Bolden's sudden passing. But, this is your husband you're talking to, and I know you. This is more than just about Mr. Bolden. I know that when you read about the fall of the one and only Stiles Graham, you were shocked and devastated. But, baby, he's not your concern anymore. There is absolutely nothing you can do for him."

"I know that," she responded, hoping that he couldn't detect that she was uneasy about talking to him about her ex-husband. "Stiles made his bed, and that's his problem. What's going on in his life is my least concern. I love you. I love our kids. I love what we have here in Andover, and I wouldn't jeopardize that for anything in this world."

Rena leaned in and began kissing her husband until their oldest little girl, Isabelle, bolted inside their room, tattling about something her brother, Robbie, had done.

On the airplane, Rena rested against the headrest. *Don't even think about seeing him while you're in Memphis. You're going for one thing, and one thing only, to pay your respects to Mr. Bolden's family. Nothing else, and no one else.*

24

"The weak can never forgive. Forgiveness is the attribute
of the strong." - Mahatma Gandhi

Francesca sat in front of the computer reading different online news articles about her brother and his fall from grace. For her, it was another drama-filled episode in the life of the Graham family. Would it ever stop? *We should have one of those family TV reality shows.*

Unfortunately, news about Stiles didn't take Francesca by surprise, because her family reminded her of everything God didn't like. She wasn't trying to be condemning toward them because she was part of their dysfunctional, damaging ways and deeds. She had played her role, and all too well. She had to admit that she used to flaunt her lesbian lifestyle and hood chick ways in front of them every chance she got. She used to boast about being in and out of jail, and rebelled as a young girl against her family, her church, and God.

Francesca sat in front of the 23-inch computer screen, succumbing to the thoughts of her messed up past filtering through her mind. She thought about the horrid molestation she endured at the hands of her cousin, Fonda. She thought about being rape by Pastor Travis, one of Holy Rock's former youth pastors. She had kept silent about the rape because she felt like no one would be on her side. Her mother would always make sure of that. All Audrey Graham cared about when she was alive was her precious Stiles. As for Pastor, Audrey had him wrapped around her wicked little finger too. First Lady Audrey Graham could do no wrong in Pastor's eyes.

Francesca's mind continued to replay her past, step by step, frame by frame, until she couldn't take it anymore, and transferred her thoughts to Detria. She always had an unsettling feeling about Detria. Detria, before Audrey died, had been a constant presence around the Graham family, at least that's what Francesca heard. When she attended Audrey's funeral and the repast, she had the chance to see Detria in full effect, prancing around like she was *soooo* concerned about Pastor and Stiles. It turned out, she had been concerned all right. Concerned about finding a way to get next to Stiles, and she did. Francesca shrugged at the thought of Detria and the way she had finagled herself into Stiles' life.

How could he stay with a woman like Detria? This was the same woman who beat down Pastor like he was a thug on the streets, yet he forgave her and stayed in the marriage. Now, this same conniving, slick woman, Detria Graham, had managed to get her brother in a world of trouble.

Stiles could get angry, really heated; Francesca knew of it firsthand, but she didn't know whether to believe that he had attacked Detria in the manner the news reported. From what she had been reading, he had beaten Detria so bad that she had to be hospitalized. Now he was on the verge of losing his ministry, his livelihood, perhaps even his little girl, all because he couldn't keep his hands to himself.

Francesca shook her head and proceeded to read one more article about her brother before she clicked off the Memphis newspaper website.

She picked up her cell phone lying next to the computer. Scrolling through her Contacts, she stopped at her brother's number. Should she call him? She wasn't sure if it still belonged to him or not. It had been way over a year since they last spoke and frankly, Francesca had not missed talking to him or Pastor. She had her husband, and his family to replace her messed up one. What exactly would she say to him anyway?

Should I call him? Or should I leave well enough alone. I don't want to resurrect my past. Maybe I'll just pray for him, ask Tim to have the church to lift him up in prayer. Yeah, that's what I'll do.

Francesca changed her mind again, picked up her cell phone and found Stiles phone number. She stared at each number *9 –0 –1 –3 – 4*....stopped, placed the phone back over on the computer table, turned and walked out of the office. *I can't do it. Let your past stay in the past Francesca, and that means your family.*

25

"Sometimes I wish I could go back to before we met. Not because I want to forget you or what we had. But, because it would be so much easier than knowing what I don't have, now that you left." Unknown

Rena, along with a flock of other church going people, drifted inside Holy Rock for the second worship service of the morning. She walked inside and was pleasantly surprised at the stellar beauty of the church. It looked nothing like the old Holy Rock. From the time she walked inside and stepped into the vestibule, all the way to the sanctuary, she was impressed. The church had been totally remodeled. Rena thought about how proud Stiles must have been to know that Holy Rock was growing rapidly.

The massive sanctuary was almost full. Rena went to the end section of a row of pews and found a seat mid-way the sanctuary. Part of her was a little nervous. Being inside Holy Rock, brought back memories; some good and some not so good, and she hoped she wouldn't regret being here. It went against everything she said she wouldn't do, but her heart wouldn't let her stay away from. She promised herself that she wouldn't say anything to Stiles. All she was going to do was sit through the service, see how he looked just to make sure he was okay, and then she would slip out at the end and go back to her hotel room until tomorrow morning when her flight left for Massachusetts.

An usher came to her row and passed out the church bulletin. Rena looked through it but stopped and focused on the Praise Team when she heard the music start.

She enjoyed the progression of the service, but swallowed deeply when Stiles walked up the steps leading to the pulpit. He looked just as handsome as ever. Like she thought he could see her out of all the thousands of people in the sanctuary, Rena looked away from him and down at her bulletin, but when he spoke, she couldn't help it. She looked up and found herself being drawn into Stiles Graham.

"Let me start by saying, God is good all the time and all the time God is good," Stiles said.

Rena listened as Stiles shared with the congregation, without going into deep detail, his sorrow and hurt over what had gone on in his marriage.

"My marriage and my personal life should be just that, personal." His voice seemed to tremble as he asked that his family be given privacy and time to work on their problems. "Do not believe everything you hear on the news or read in the paper. Contrary to what is being said, I want to assure you that I would never intentionally hurt my wife. I love her. I love my family, and I love you, Holy Rock." Stiles looked out in the congregation. His eyes drifted to the pew where Detria always sat. It was empty.

Rena listened and watched as Stiles bared his soul. She hadn't seen this side of him in a very long time. On the one hand, he was a fiery, bold preacher but he usually tried to keep his family life private.

"Again, I ask that you respect me and the first lady's privacy during this time. I solicit your prayers. To those of you who feel I don't deserve to be standing up here, then I respect your thoughts and opinion but I am on assignment by God, not man. I won't leave this church, won't step down from this pulpit, unless God says otherwise."

Rena looked around as droves of people stood up and started clapping. She watched as Stiles stood in the pulpit, shoulders back, head up, and a serious but satisfied look on his face.

After several seconds of applause, Stiles raised his hand. The applause tapered off and people took their seats.

He took his text and began his sermon.

Rena used to love hearing him deliver the Word, and today was no different. Stiles preached about Joseph. He told of how Joseph's brothers were jealous and went so far as to want him dead. He talked about how they wanted to see his life destroyed, but God had other plans for Joseph.

"The devil wants to destroy me, but I'm here to tell you that I'm not up for defeat. God has other plans for me. I will not be moved," Stiles preached.

By the end of service, Rena was glad she had come. Hearing him deliver such a powerful message, she felt like Stiles would be fine She stood up after church was over and looked over her shoulder toward the exit, and saw that hundreds of people were already lined up to speak to him. Her eyes locked with his.

Rena found it impossible to look away. She stared at him staring at her.

"Excuse me," someone behind her said, waking Rena from her dreamlike stance.

"Oh, I'm sorry." Rena moved to the side to allow the woman and kids to move past her.

Stiles couldn't believe his eyes. He thought, *Is that Rena? No, it can't be. It has to be someone that looks like her.* It was like time had stopped. He couldn't move, he maintained his gaze on the Rena lookalike. *It is Rena. What is she doing in Memphis? And what is she doing at Holy Rock?*

Rena turned and headed toward an alternate exit, leading out of the church, when she heard her name called and felt someone's hand on her shoulder. Her heart raced as she expected to turn around and come face to face with Stiles, but it wasn't him.

"Yes?" she answered the man.

"Aren't you Rena Graham?"

"Becton. Rena Becton," she corrected the man, still unsure as to what he wanted.

"Pastor Graham wanted me to tell you that he would like to say hello. He wants me to direct you to his office. That is, if you have the time," the young man who appeared to be in his early twenties, stated.

"I." She looked back over her shoulder to see if she could still see Stiles among the crowd. Once again, her eyes locked with his, and he nodded, like he could read the apprehension in her mind. "Sure," she said as she turned to face the man again.

"Right this way, ma'am."

Rena followed the polite man down a winding corridor, up a small flight of about seven steps, and down another corridor. She was in constant amazement because Holy Rock was entirely different, in a good way. It was so much larger and just as elegant. She felt happy and overjoyed for Stiles, but also sad about his present dilemma.

"Right in here, Mrs. Becton," the man pointed as he opened the door to a large office that was decorated just like she imagined Stiles' dream office would be.

Stiles always had impeccable taste, much like his deceased mother, Audrey Graham.

"You can have a seat," the man said.

"Thank you." Rena slowly nodded and went to sit down in one of the chairs positioned in front of Stiles' desk, while studying all the pictures, certificates, and accolades lining the walls.

"Can I get you some water, coffee, anything?" the man offered. "No, but thank you for asking."

"No problem. Pastor Graham should be here soon." The man left, closing the door behind him.

Left alone, almost immediately, waves of guilt started to surface. What was she doing here? She should have left well enough alone. She chastised herself for being at Holy Rock and now she was sitting here in Stiles' office. What if Detria came in? What if someone recognized her, or saw her being led to Stiles' office. What if Robert found out where she was?

Rena swiftly got up, grabbed her purse, and walked toward the door. She looked back in the office again, stared at the picture of Stiles on the wall dressed in his robe, and another picture of him, Detria and Baby Audrey, before she flung open the door and ran out.

Stiles couldn't believe it was Rena. What was she doing in Memphis? But more important than that, what was she doing at Holy Rock? When he saw her, his first instinct was to stop shaking hands, kissing babies, and hugging old folks and take off toward her, but he couldn't, so he did the next best thing and that was to tell one of his armor bearers to ask her to meet him in his office.

Detria hadn't been coming to church since the big blow up they'd had. Stiles wasn't too shocked that she wasn't coming because he felt like she may have been somewhere following up behind her *not so secret* lover. At this point, he was at a crossroads. He wanted to possibly work things out with Detria. They could go to marriage counseling, and try to put the past behind them, but that was only for the sake of Audrey and the baby she was carrying. If the baby turned out not to be his, Stiles hadn't thought about what he would do next. As a man of God, he knew he had to forgive Detria, but as a man period, he didn't know if he could.

Stiles shook hands one last time and darted off to his office, only to open the door and find it empty. He looked around. He could smell the sweet fragrance of her perfume. He went to his bathroom. No Rena. He looked in the small private meeting space adjoined to his office. No Rena.

Stiles inhaled and then exhaled heavily. Where had she gone? Frank, the armor bearer who escorted Rena to his office, had assured him that she was waiting for him.

He walked up and down the hall then rushed outside. A long line of cars was still exiting the parking lot while some other cars remained parked. He looked around hoping to see Rena appear out of nowhere. No such luck.

Stiles turned back around, and was immediately flanked by several churchgoers who wanted to stop and talk as he made his way back inside the church. When he finally made it back to his office, he sat down in his chair and thought about Rena.

She looked more beautiful than ever. She was stylishly dressed and from what Stiles could see of her, she seemed to have a radiance about her that probably meant she was happy with her life. But if she was so happy, then why was she at Holy Rock? And why did she agree to meet him in his office? Was she in Memphis alone or was her husband and kids with her and she had left them behind at a hotel or something? He didn't have her phone number anymore, so it wasn't like he could call and find out why she decided not to wait to see him.

Rena, what are you up to?

26

"A dad's love is the gift that keeps on giving." Jude Larbes

"Detria, it's time for you to own up to your mistakes. I've told you before, recognize that two wrongs don't make a right. When you and Stiles got married you acted like you were the happiest bride on earth. What went wrong?"

"How many times do I have to tell you that Stiles is not the perfect man everybody seems to think he is."

Brooke's sons were playing with Audrey in the little girl's playroom while Detria and Brooke talked. Detria rarely ventured out of the house since everything had gone down. She hadn't been back to Holy Rock even after Skip told her that he had gotten fired. The truth of the matter was she wouldn't have gone back to Holy Rock even if they hadn't fired him. She couldn't face seeing the church members smiling and grinning all up in her face while they were probably talking behind her back.

Part of her felt bad for things getting so out of control like they had, but Stiles had brought a lot of what happened on himself. The night that they got into it Detria was terrified, that much was true. The way Stiles looked at her, the way he pushed her off him, his hand raised in the air poised to hit her, all of it was frightening. Had it not been for their little girl, Detria believed Stiles would have hurt her really bad. She felt like she had no choice but to call the police. She had told herself repeatedly that she did it to protect her and Audrey.

"Detria, I never said Stiles was perfect. I don't know what goes on in your marriage, and to be honest, that's the way it should be between a married couple."

Detria tried sitting patiently and listening to her sister, but she found it hard to do. She thought about the phone call she'd made to Stiles right before Brooke came over. He had sounded like he was unsure whether he should come over or not. Detria tried to assure him that contrary to what he may have thought, she was *not* trying to set him up. She called him because Audrey had been asking for her daddy. The little girl was old enough to miss having him around and Detria didn't want to say it, but she sort of missed Stiles too.

Brooke continued talking but it sounded like she was a voice in the background, and Detria was oblivious to what all her sister was saying.

"Detria, do you understand any of this?"

"Of course, I understand where you're coming from. And I'm praying about what to do." Suddenly, she said, "I didn't tell you, but I called Stiles."

"You did what? Why?"

"Audrey has been asking about him. She misses him being around every day."

"But I thought you two had made arrangements for him to see her on a regular basis. What happened?" asked Brooke. "I know you are not like these baby mamas who keeps the child away from the father because she's mad at him." Brooke frowned.

"You should know me better than that. He visits her over at Mother Brown's house. He doesn't come over here because of the protective order. And before you have something to say about that, I did have the order lifted, only I didn't tell him that I did, at least not until today." Detria flipped her hand. "Anyway, I take her over to Mother Brown's as much as possible. When she gets over there, Mother Brown calls Stiles and he goes over to her house to see her, which is fine with me. But it's not the same. You know what I mean?"

Brooke's tone expressed her surprise. "You actually called him?"

"Yep."

"When? What did you say?"

"I called him right before you got here. I didn't say much. Just told him that Audrey was asking for her daddy. He asked about the protective order. That's when I told him I had it removed."

"What did he say?"

"At first he sounded like he didn't trust me. He was full of questions. I started to tell him to just forget I even called, but then I thought about our daughter and realized that it wasn't fair to keep her away from him. I know we're skating on thin ice, but I know he loves that spoiled little brat."

Brooke looked at her sister's protruding belly. "Speaking of Audrey, how do you feel? You've been under a lot of pressure and stress. It certainly can't be good for the baby you're carrying."

Unlike with Audrey, where she gained a small amount of weight, Detria was gaining weight rather rapidly. She was 24 weeks pregnant and huge. The doctor warned her to watch her sodium intake, and told her to keep her stress levels down as much as possible.

Keep her stress levels down? When her doctor told her this, Detria almost laughed out loud. Not because it was funny, but because it was easier said than done.

The doorbell rang, and Detria's head popped up before she looked over at Brooke.

"You want me to get it?"

Detria shook her head. "No, I'll get it. It's probably him."

"Okay. You answer the door and I'm going to go check on the kids. Do you want me to get some things together for Audrey in case he wants to take her out for a while?"

"If you don't mind."

"Of course, I don't mind. I'll be back." Brooke got up and left the room.

Detria got up, held her belly, and started walking from the family room toward the front of the house. This was her dream home, but she felt like she was living anything but a dream. She had the material trappings that any woman would be more than thrilled to have, yet she wasn't happy. How had things turned out the way they had? Where was the love, the real love that a wife should have for her husband, and when had her feelings changed? Even she didn't know the answer to that million-dollar question.

As she got closer to the door, Detria gave pause and thought, *sometimes it's not the letting go, it's making the decision to stay and try to start over that's the hardest.* Did she want to start over, especially if it turned out that this was Skip's baby in her belly.

She opened the door. "Hi," she said, standing in front of the man she thought she once loved with all her heart. He looked good as heck, so why wasn't her heart racing and beating for him like it used to? And why was she looking at Stiles but almost without fail, thinking about Mr. Wrong?

27

"All married women are not wives." Japanese Proverb

"Come in," Detria said. No smile. No real expression, and far from sounding like she was happy to see him.

Stiles felt her indifference toward him. Why was he here and why did Detria even call him in the first place if she was going to act all brand new. He reminded himself of the real reason he made the decision to come to *his* house; it was for his daughter, not Detria.

He looked at her round belly and fought against the anger brewing within. The anger management classes were designed to help him curb his anger. Right now he felt like he could explode at the thought that not only had his wife been sleeping with another man, but the child in her belly could belong to that punk. *Think before you speak. Don't say something you might end up regretting.*

"Hi, where's my baby girl?" Stiles asked, but didn't take one step further into his own castle.

"Daddy," Audrey appeared from out of nowhere and rushed into his outstretched arms.

"I *said* you could come in, Stiles."

Stiles scooped up Audrey and held his baby girl in his arms as he walked inside the house. He noticed Brooke standing several feet away with a slight smile on her face.

"Hey, Brooke."

"Hi, brother-in-law. It's good to see you."

"Yeah, good seeing you too." He focused his attention back on Audrey. "How is daddy's princess?" he asked the little girl, kissing her on her forehead. "Daddy missed you. You know that?"

Audrey bobbed her cute little head up and down, while holding Stiles tightly around his neck. Then, out of the blue, she kissed him on the side of his face.

Tears immediately formed in Stiles' eyes but he willed them to stay back. He squeezed his little girl even tighter.

Detria forced herself to ignore the heart-wrenching scene of father and daughter playing before her eyes. "Are you going to stay here and visit or do you want to take her out for a while?" She glanced quickly over her shoulder at her sister.

Brooke looked like she was about to cry too, so she hurriedly turned around and walked away, forgetting to give Audrey's backpack to Detria.

"Since it's such a beautiful day, I think we'll go to the park. Would you like that, Audrey? You want daddy to take you to the park and then we can go get some pizza and ice cream," he said, lightly tickling her tummy until Audrey started giggling.

"Yaaay, I want to go to the park. I want pizza, Daddy." She hugged him tight around his neck.

"Okay, let's go then." Stiles put her down.

"Let me go get her backpack," Detria told him with her arms folded across her chest and resting on top of her belly. "Are you going to just stand there?" she asked him before turning and walking off.

"I'm cool. Thanks."

"Come on, Audrey. Let's go get your backpack so you can go with Daddy." Detria reached out for her little girl's hand and Audrey quickly obliged by running up to her mother and taking hold of her hand.

Stiles stood in the middle of the foyer surveying his surroundings. He had worked hard to buy this house for Detria. He wanted her to be happy, wanted to give her some of the desires of her heart. He longed to fill it with the pitter-patter of little feet. Never in a million years did he think the pitter-patter could possibly belong to another man.

28

"Everyone can be a father, but it takes a lot to be a daddy." A Geddes

Stiles sat Audrey down on the playground horse. She giggled which made him smile, but his smile turned into a dismal look as he thought about the direction he was headed. How had he gotten to this place in his life? Was God trying to show him something? If so, what was it? Stiles pondered one question after another in his mind until he heard Audrey's screams, yanking him back to what he was supposed to be doing: having fun with his little girl. When had he released his hold on her? She had fallen off the horse, landing face first on the mound of hard, dry earth.

Stiles immediately saw a big lump appear on her forehead. It was already red and blood oozed from the open wound. He grabbed her up swiftly, as kids and a couple of parents gathered around to see what all the commotion was about.

"Is she all right?" he heard a lady standing nearby ask.

"Baby, it's going to be all right." Stiles tried to calm her down, but she was crying loudly, and totally out of control.

She fell off of that." A little boy pointed at the horse like he was the only one privy to what had happened. Stiles disregarded the child, dashed from the park and ran to his car. The knot was growing bigger, and the blood spilled out faster, flowing down her face and some even in her eyes, Stiles tried to keep himself from panicking. He jumped in the car with Audrey still in his arms and frantically searched for something to wipe the blood off her face.

"Hold on, sweetheart. Daddy's got you." After finding some tissue in the glove compartment, he placed several pieces on Audrey's head. Blood soaked through it. At that moment, Stiles realized Audrey was probably going to need stitches. Against her will, he placed her in her car seat while she continued to bawl.

After getting her securely strapped in, he jumped in the car, and took off in the direction of the hospital.

Fighting through the mounting traffic while listening to his daughter scream, Stiles prayed openly while using one hand to reach in the back seat and soothe his child and the other hand to maneuver the steering wheel. He found a side street he was familiar with that would lead him to the hospital. Thank God, it wasn't too far away.

Within fifteen minutes of leaving the park, he arrived at the hospital. Favor was with him because he spotted a parking space directly in front of the ER Department. Jumping out of his car, he opened the back door, unbuckled Audrey, and quickly lifted her into his arms while kissing her hair and her bloody face. Holding her tightly, he ran up to the double doors that opened as he approached them. He dashed to the front desk. A nurse, seeing the little girl's bloody face, came from behind the desk, opened the door leading to triage, and ushered him inside.

The nurse cleaned her wound, taking a closer look at the knot on her head.

"Come with me." She took them to one of the ER beds.

Audrey held on to her daddy's neck. She refused to let Stiles put her down on the bed.

The doctor will be in here shortly," the nurse explained. "Please, just keep calm so she'll be calm," she advised Stiles.

The ER doctor, along with another nurse, came to the room. He studied Audrey's injury, talking to the small child in a calm voice, gently stroking her hair back from her face.

Audrey began to quiet down some but her body jerked occasionally from having cried so hard. "You say she fell off a gym horse in the park?" the doctor asked.

"Yes. It happened so fast."

"Believe me, I understand. I have three-year-old triplets. I know how quickly they get into stuff. Don't beat yourself up. She's going to be fine. She *is* going to need a stitch or two, and I want to do a CAT scan just to make sure she doesn't have a concussion. That's just to be on the safe side; nothing to worry about."

Nervous and feeling awful that he'd allowed his problems to make him neglect his daughter, Stiles nodded and said, "Thanks, Doc."

Audrey had stopped crying, but it didn't take long for her to start up again, this time screaming for her mommy as they wheeled her off for the CAT scan.

Stiles' cell phone started ringing. He looked at the display screen. It was Detria. He hadn't been gone that long, or had he, for her to be calling already. "Hello."

"Hey. Where are you? I didn't know you were going to be gone this long. It's been almost three hours."

Stiles didn't want to tell her what happened but he really didn't have much of a choice. She was going to find out either way. It would be after he took Audrey home with a bandaged head and then he would really have to listen to her go off, or he could tell her now. Telling her over the phone was something he didn't want to do because more than likely Detria would panic. Nevertheless, he sucked in his breath and told her where he was.

"You're where? Oh, my God. What happened?"

He told her how Audrey fell off the gym horse. "She's fine though, Detria. She had to get a couple of stiches."

"Stitches, oh, Lord," she screamed into the phone. "I'm on my way."

Stiles heard the phone click. Detria had ended the call. He rubbed his head and paced the floor. "God, what is happening?" he mumbled.

Audrey returned from her CAT scan with a clean bill of health. The doctor told Stiles to follow up with Audrey's pediatrician in the next couple of days to check on the stiches and clean the wound.

Stiles, holding a sleeping Audrey in his arms, was met by his wife as soon as he opened the exit doors.

Detria walked up on him and tried to take Audrey out of his arms. "How is she?"

Stiles stepped back. "She's good. She's too heavy for you to be carrying." He looked down at her swollen belly.

Detria walked around him and looked at Audrey's face as she lay sleeping soundly with her head on her daddy's shoulder. Detria smoothed back the little girl's hair, stood on her tiptoes, and kissed Audrey on top of her head.

Surprisingly, Detria didn't blame him for their daughter's accident.

"You drove here by yourself?"

"Yes, I'm pregnant, Stiles. I'm not an invalid."

"I didn't mean it like that. I know you can drive. But Brooke was at the house and I, well anyway, you're here and I'm glad you aren't upset with me."

"Brooke left right after you did."

Detria stopped walking and stood in front of Stiles as they exited the ER and approached her car, which was only a few cars from where he parked.

"Look, Stiles. No matter what *our* issues are, one thing I know is that you would never do anything to hurt our daughter. Kids have accidents all the time, and it doesn't always mean someone else is at fault. You're a good father. Our daughter is going to be fine. That's all I'm concerned about." With that, Detria opened her car door then she opened the back door.

"Thanks," he said.

"It's the truth. Now, if you'll put her in her car seat, I'd appreciate it."

"Are you sure? She was pretty upset after that fall and having to get stitches. If she wakes up on the drive home, she might have another one of her tantrums."

"She'll be fine, but...," Detria paused, "if you want to follow me home, you can. If that'll make you feel better."

"Thanks, I'll do that. Oh, do you want me to stop and grab something for her to eat? I never got the chance to get that pizza I promised her."

"Yeah, that would be nice. When she wakes up, I'm sure she's going to be starving."

"Okay. See you in a few."

Stiles waited until Detria was safely inside her car. He double-checked to make sure a sleeping Audrey was securely latched in her car seat before he turned and walked to his own car.

He drove behind Detria until he made it to the street where the pizza restaurant was located.

Detria continued the drive home and Audrey didn't wake up. *God, I wish I could say I love my husband. I really do wish that I could.*

She turned on to their street, pushed the remote button built into the car and the garage door opened. Her cell phone started ringing just after she pulled in. She ignored it, but right away it started ringing again while she was trying to unlatch Audrey from her car seat. She ignored the call again.

When she unlatched Audrey, the little girl woke up. She stared at her mother like she was still half-asleep but then quickly started crying and reaching for her.

"You're going to be okay, Audrey. Daddy's going to get you some pizza. You want some pizza, don't you?"

Audrey whined, but she nodded her head too.

"Okay, come on then. Stand up like a big girl. I can't hold you because Mommy's tummy is in the way. So hold my hand, and we're going to go in the house and wait for Daddy."

For the third time the phone started ringing. This time Detria had made it inside the house. She pulled the phone from her purse and looked at the number. "Dang, Skip. You have a weird sense of timing," she said aloud, while at the same time pushing the button to answer his call.

29

"There comes a time when silence is betrayal." M. L. King, Jr.

Skip pulled up into Detria's driveway. He was sick and tired of her putting him on a back burner like he didn't matter. And to make matters worse, the broad had hurried him off the phone – again by talking all crazy. No way was she going to push him off like he was some *okie-doke* kinda dude. He wasn't one to be played with; he was always the one to call the shots. A female like Detria would never control him or kick him to the curb. Women like Detria came a dime a dozen and his motto was, *he didn't chase 'em he replaced 'em*. That was his motto. If it hadn't been for the fact she might be carrying his child, he would have been glad to call it quits. She was the one who went after him in the first place.

Detria hadn't been shy at all about letting him know that she was attracted to him. That day when Audrey was still just a baby, and Detria exposed her supple breasts in her office at Holy Rock on the premise that she had to feed her child, Skip knew what time it was. Detria wanted him, and he wasn't one to back away from a female, especially one as hot as Detria Graham.

He didn't especially like that the years of friendship between him and Stiles was over but in his book, Stiles must not have been doing something right, or Detria wouldn't have stepped his way in the first place.

Now, here he was, about to knock on Detria's door, unannounced. But it is what it is. He knocked on the door repeatedly until Detria answered. She looked like she could have been bought for a dime when she saw him standing there.

"What are you doing here? Turn right back around and leave." She tried to close the door, but Skip pressed the palm of his hand against it, halting her attempt.

"Look, all I want to do is know how you're doing." He reached out and touched her belly.

"Skip, you need to leave."

Skip ignored her and walked up on her. Gently pushing her inside the house, he closed the door behind them. He pulled her into his arms and began kissing her passionately. His hands visited her familiar curves and mounds as his breath grew heavy with desire.

In return, Detria tried to push him away but her desire for him was greater than what her mind was telling her she needed to do. When it came to Skip, there was no turning back. This was the very reason she tried to ignore him, tried to get him out of her life.

"Momma." Audrey appeared and started crying. "Momma," she said again.

Skip stepped off. Detria moved slowly from against the wall and looked down at her daughter like she was irritated that the little girl had walked up on her and Skip.

"What happened to her?" Skip asked, looking at the bandage on Audrey's head.

"She was with her daddy earlier and she had an accident in the park."

Skip stooped down until he was face to face with the toddler. "Hi, there, sweet girl. You all right?"

Audrey stopped crying and looked at Skip.

Skip reached for her tiny little hand. "You're going to be all right. You're a big girl, you know." He continued talking to her, and before long, Audrey was practically giggling.

Detria stood back and watched the scene as it unfolded before her. She imagined how good a father Skip would be to their son. That was another secret she had kept from both Skip and Stiles. She had an ultrasound and found out she was carrying a boy. She only confided in Brooke, and had sworn her to secrecy.

Detria used to have several women friends that she worked with when she was a nutritionist, but those friendships she had severed long ago. It was hard for her to trust other women because she knew how conniving women could be, especially women in the church who practically preyed on men like Stiles. A handsome, young, charismatic preacher like Stiles...women practically threw their panties up in the pulpit on Sundays.

Detria's mother had cautioned her more than once about having too many women friends. And when First Lady Graham was alive, she had told her to watch out for church women because they were only out to steal her man from underneath her nose. Detria was not going to have that.

Skip wrapped his arms around her rapidly expanding waist, and used his other hand to rub her belly while Audrey stood next to them.

"Stop, boy. You see Audrey," she whispered, as the little girl was busy trying to open the stick of gum Skip had given her. "You have to go. Stiles will be here any minute. He stopped to get some pizza for Audrey, and then he's on his way."

Skip acted like Detria hadn't said a word as his hands traveled below her belly, sending shivers of excitement up and down her spine.

"I'm not going anywhere," he whispered hoarsely. He kissed her again and caressed her tenderly in her intimate spot.

"I told you," she stuttered.

"If you want me to go, tell me the sex of our child."

"I don't know. I haven't had an ultrasound yet," she conveniently lied.

""Feels like a boy," he said, kissing her again.

"Quit it," she said in short, almost gasping breaths as she moved his hand off her belly.

The doorbell rang. Detria swiftly shoved him away. "I told you to go. Now Stiles is here. Oh, God!"

Skip appeared unfazed. "That fool knows what time it is. Anyway, he doesn't live here anymore, and I'm here to check on you."

"You should have left like I told you," Detria shouted as the doorbell rang a second time, followed by a third.

Detria rushed to the door, but by the time she got there, Stiles had used his key and bolted inside.

"I know this nee...I know you ain't got him up in my house around my daughter," Stiles yelled, dropping the pizza to the floor and rushing up the foyer.

Audrey ran to her daddy and reached for him. Stiles picked her up and then turned and gave Detria, who had followed behind him, a nasty look. "You got him around my daughter?"

"Don't blame her," Skip said in a harsh voice as he appeared from around the corner and faced Stiles. "She wanted me to go but like I told her, I have every right to come check on the mother of my child."

"Get her out of here," Stiles barked at Detria, putting Audrey back down on the floor.

Detria stepped between them. "Stiles, look...why don't you just go."

"What did you say? Me? Go? Are you out of your freaking mind? This is *my* house," he barked. "You need to tell him to go!" Stiles pointed at Skip. "Better yet, I'll tell him. Get out of my house, now!"

Without warning or saying another word, Stiles lunged at Skip and the two men began fighting, knocking over the bronze finished console table in the foyer. The mirror above it came crashing down to the floor next, shattering in pieces, followed by the two sconces that framed the mirror.

Audrey was crying and Detria was screaming for the two of them to stop. She took hold of Audrey's hand and practically dragged her to the family room and sat her down in one of the chairs.

"Stay here." Audrey shook her head and cried even louder, refusing to be still. "I said stay here!"

Audrey buried her head in its soft cushion and cried her little heart out, while Detria turned and raced back into the foyer.

When she got back to the foyer, she was blood was all over the hardwood floors. Both hands flew up against her face as she yelled and screamed. "Stop. Stiles...don't. You're going to kill him. *Pleease,* stop!"

Stiles pounded Skip mercilessly. Skip struggled to get up off the floor, only to have Stiles kick him in the ribs again and again.

"I'm calling the police," Detria warned but Stiles still didn't stop. He was acting like a lunatic, like he'd gone out of his mind.

Skip managed to get up. His face was bloody and swollen. It was like a tag team match or something because now Skip was pounding Stiles. Stiles fell back and landed on the box of pizza. Now there was sauce and pepperoni pizza mixed with blood all over the floor.

Detria, in her haste to separate her husband and lover, slipped, and fell hard. Her belly hit against the broken table. She hollered in pain but the men didn't seem to notice or hear her.

She held on to her cell phone, and slowly managed to get to her feet, though she was wobbly. She called 9-1-1. While listening to the operator on the other end, without warning, she collapsed onto the floor again. This time she screamed even louder like she was in excruciating pain, causing both men to stop fighting as she begged for help.

"Detria." Skip staggered like a drunk man over to her side, falling down on his knees beside her.

"Ohhhh," Detria cried. "My baby, I think my baby is coming."

"It's too early," Stiles yelled as he rushed to her other side and glared with evil eyes at Skip. "Get away from her. Get out of here."

"I'm not going anywhere," Skip screamed back, cussing violently. His left eye was swollen shut and blood dripped down on his clothes and onto the floor from his busted lip and nose.

Audrey came in the foyer crying so loud that Stiles had to leave Detria's side and go to his daughter.

"Ohhh, God, nooo! It's too early." Detria held her stomach. "Hang on, Detria. I'm calling 9-1-1 now," Skip told her and proceeded calling, unaware that Detria had already put in the call. "Just hang on."

Within minutes, sirens could be heard as squad cars rode down on the Graham house.

Stiles, with bloody clothes and a bloody face of his own, rushed to the door and opened it. Leaving poor little Audrey crying inside, he ran outside to meet the police.

Next, an ambulance pulled up, and paramedics got out, followed by another squad car. Neighbors started gathering outside their homes and along the sidewalks in the prestigious neighborhood, while still others peered through their picture windows.

"My wife, Officer. She's pregnant, and I think she's gone into labor."

30

"Nothing takes the taste out of peanut butter quite
like unrequited love." Charles Schulz

Hezekiah was at home, in his office, on the Internet, finalizing travel arrangements for Xavier's visit to Memphis, when Fancy burst into the room.

"Baby, I just got off the phone with Sister Kastleberry." Fancy sounded panicky. "She said Pastor Graham and the first lady were involved in some kind of altercation. They were taken by ambulance to the hospital! She said Pastor Graham is in critical condition, and the first lady lost their baby."

"What? Are you sure? You know Sister Kastleberry is the church gossip, Fancy."

"I know, honey. But it sounded like she knew what she was talking about. Anyway, I think it's worth checking out."

"Yeah, I guess you're right."

Hezekiah called Stiles' phone several times, but it kept going to his voicemail. Next, he called Leo and repeated what Fancy told him.

"Deacon Jones, I've been trying to reach Pastor Graham, but his phone keeps going to his voicemail. Have you talked to him today?"

"No, not today."

"I'm starting to get worried," said Hezekiah.

"Man, I hope he hasn't done anything stupid," Leo mouthed.

"Why don't you try to get in touch with the first lady? Me and Fancy are going to drive over to Pastor Graham's apartment. I can't dismiss Sister Kastleberry, because as much as I hate to say this, that woman always seems to have the inside scoop on the going-ons at Holy Rock."

"How she manages to find out stuff so quickly amazes me too," Leo responded. "I'll try calling the first lady before I head over her way."

"Cool. Let me know what you find out."

"Will do," answered Leo."

"I'll talk to you in a few," said Hezekiah and they ended their call.

When the couple arrived at Stiles' apartment, Hezekiah knocked until he was confident that Stiles wasn't home. He and Fancy left there and headed straight over to Stiles and Detria's home, praying that the call Fancy received wasn't true and was just another ridiculous rumor circulating. So many untruths had been told about Stiles and First Lady Graham ever since news of her affair with Skip went public.

Leo called Hezekiah and told him what he found when he arrived at the Graham's house. "Man, me and Cynthia are at their house now. Someone just told Cynthia that Stiles and another man got into a big fight, so I take it Stiles wasn't at his apartment?"

"No, he wasn't there." Hezekiah's voice revealed frustration mixed with uncertainty. "Jesus," Hezekiah swore before realizing it. "You think it was with Skip?"

"I don't know, but more than likely it was. Anyway, that's not all."

"What else?"

"There's nothing but chaos. Cops are everywhere. The news and media are out here too," Leo told Hezekiah.

"This means that what Sister Kastleberry said is probably true. What could Pastor Graham have been thinking?"

"Who knows, but there's a big crowd gathered outside their house."

"And you don't see the first lady? Pastor Graham? Skip? Anybody?"

"Nope, I'm afraid not."

Suddenly the phone quality was muffled. Hezekiah could hear people talking but he couldn't' understand what was being said.

Leo returned to the phone. "One of the cops out here just confirmed to the media that several people were injured and had to be hospitalized. They didn't give the names or their conditions."

"God, no. Not this."

"What is it?" Fancy asked but Hezekiah ignored her.

"They probably took them to Methodist Germantown. That's the closest hospital to here," Leo said.

"Okay. We were headed over your way, but we'll go to the hospital instead and see what we can find out."

"Okay. I'll meet you there," Leo said. "But first, me and Cynthia are going to see if someone can tell us where Audrey is."

"Oh, Lord. I pray that little girl didn't witness anything tragic."

"Lord, have mercy." Fancy suddenly looked like all the blood had been drained from her face.

"Leo, I'll call and let you know what I find out. In the meantime, wait before you contact the First Lady's family and Pastor Graham's father. We need to confirm how much of this stuff is true."

"Yes, Pastor McCoy." They ended the call and Hezekiah and Fancy took off in the direction of the hospital.

Hezekiah and Fancy were stationed in the ER waiting room, waiting to hear news about the condition of Stiles and Detria.

Cynthia located Audrey at one of Detria's neighbors and carried the traumatized little girl home with her. Leo told her to go on and call the Mackey family and tell them what had happened.

Cynthia called Brother Mackey, told him the unfortunate news, but assured him that Audrey was safe with her and that she would take care of the little girl while they went to the hospital to see about Detria.

"Leo is on his way to the hospital. So are Pastor and Sister McCoy," Cynthia further explained to Brother Mackey over the phone.

"Thank you, Sista Cynthia."

"No problem. I'm praying for your family, Brother Mackey."

"Thank you, we're get to the hospital right away, and God bless you, Sista Cynthia." Brother Mackey hung up the phone, and rushed to call and tell Brooke the tragic news.

"Any news yet?" Leo asked Hezekiah upon arriving at the hospital.

"No, not yet. Did you call Brother and Sister Mackey?"

"Cynthia called them, and I called Pastor. They should be here soon."

It didn't take long before Pastor, Miss Josie, Brooke and the Mackey family arrived. Hezekiah, Fancy, and Leo gathered around them, assuring both families that they were praying for them.

They stopped talking to each other when the receptionist asked, "Is the family of Stiles Graham here?"

"Yes, right here," Pastor spoke up, as he, Josie and the Mackey's walked up to the front desk.

"Only two of you can come back to the patient area," the nurse explained.

"I'll wait out here," said Josie.

"Okay, thanks, baby." Pastor kissed Josie on her cheek.

"We'll wait out here too," said Brooke, looking at her mother for her to agree. She did.

Pastor and Brother Mackey walked up to the double doors. Pastor pushed the button. The door opened.

A nurse greeted them. Are you looking for Mr. Graham?"

"Yes," Pastor answered.

"Follow that blue line until you get to ER15." The nurse pointed at the blue line on the floor.

"Can you tell me how my daughter is doing too?" Brother Mackey asked.

"Your daughter?" The nurse looked puzzled.

"Yes. She was brought here too. She's married to the patient. Her name is Detria Graham."

"I'll see what I can find out," she said, as she prepared to walk away. "You can go ahead to Mr. Graham's room."

"Thank you. God bless you," Pastor responded.

"How are you, Son?" Pastor asked when they walked into Stiles' room.

"I'm good," Stiles answered, looking and sounding like he was embarrassed when he saw his father-in-law enter the room with Pastor.

The ER doctor arrived soon after they entered Stiles' room. He was short in stature, sported a thick beard, and was somewhat on the chubby side. It was easy to tell that he was of Indian descent by way of his complexion and thick black hair.

"What's the verdict, Doctor?" Stiles asked, grimacing as if he was in pain.

"The x-rays show you have two fractured fingers on your left hand and some internal bruising around your torso." His accent proved that he was indeed of Indian descent. "You're going to be sore for a few days. The good news is you'll survive," the doctor said jokingly. "I've written you a prescription for pain along with an anti-inflammatory medicine. When the nurse brings your script, you're free to go. Follow up with your doctor in one week."

"And my daughter? How is she?" Detria's father asked as he stood next to the doctor, not bothering to acknowledge Stiles or anything the doctor said about his son-in-law.

"Yes, the nurse told me you were inquiring about, uhh." He looked down on the clipboard he was holding, "Detria Graham?"

"Yes. Where is she? How is she doing?" Brother Mackey asked.

"Yes, how is my wife, Doctor?" asked Stiles.

"It says here that she was transported across the street to the Women's Pavilion. They should be able to tell you something over there. I'm sorry, I don't know any more than that."

"Thank you, Doctor." Mr. Mackey turned and starting walking off, but then as if he suddenly remembered something, he stopped, turned back around, walked, and stood at the side of Stiles' hospital bed.

"Brother Mackey, I'm sorry. I didn't mean to...," Stiles began trying to explain.

"I swear, as God is my witness, if you hurt my daughter again, or my grandbaby she's carrying, I'll spend the rest of my life making your life miserable."

"Brother Mackey, I understand how you feel, but please be careful. Don't use the Lord's name in vain," Pastor warned.

"Don't you get all sanctimonious with me. That son of yours is the one who's hiding behind the Lord. He can run all he wants, but he can't hide. And I'm telling you," Brother Mackey said, pointing his finger at Stiles, "you're going to pay for what you've done to my baby girl. You're going to pay dearly."

Brother and Sister Mackey and Brooke left the hospital where Stiles was and rushed across the street to the Women's Pavilion to check on Detria and the baby. When they inquired about Detria, they were told that she was on the third floor in Labor and Delivery.

When they got to Labor and Delivery the doctor was still making rounds, so the Mackey's were able to talk to him about Detria.

"Your daughter is a little dehydrated. Due to the stress of a premature labor, her blood pressure is somewhat elevated but that's nothing to be overly concerned about," he explained. "We're giving her fluids and monitoring her. We're going to keep her for a couple of days since we had to perform a C-section."

"And what about my grandbaby? Is my grandchild going to be all right?" Brother Mackey looked at the doctor like he was expecting to hear the worse.

"All I can tell you is that we were able to save the baby, but I can't say if the little one will survive. He's fighting but he's in bad shape because he was born so early. The pediatric neonatologist will have to tell you more about that. I'm sure he'll be here as soon as he can. I'm sorry."

"A boy? She had a little boy." Mr. Mackey tried to smile but his pain was too great.

Brooke hugged her mother and father. "Everything is going to be fine. You'll see. Just keep the faith."

31

"People are such great mysteries. Just when we think we have understood them, a wonderful new aspect shows in them." Eucharista Ward

Skip tried sitting up in the narrow hospital bed, but fell backward from the stabbing pain that hit him in his ribs. The bandages made it even harder for him to move. "Ughhh."

"Baby, lay back. Relax. Your ribs are fractured, so don't try to move."

Skip looked on the left of him, and Meaghan Perkins got up from the cold green leather chair and stood next to the bed. She rubbed the back of her hand along his swollen face before leaning over and kissing him on his forehead.

"You need to take it easy. Are you in much pain?"

"Yeah. I guess I'm not the prize fighter I thought I was," Skip said and tried to chuckle but instead winced in pain.

"The pain medicine will take effect soon. Try to be quiet and just chill."

Unlike other women who'd come and gone in Skip's life, Skip and Meaghan had been in an on again off again relationship for three years. Skip called her his 'bed buddy' but Meaghan wanted more.

Meaghan seemed to understand, or rather accept, his insatiable desire for women, including his fascination with the first lady. However, she was still curious to find out how serious he was about Detria.

Meaghan was a member of Holy Rock too. She and Detria knew each other from the women's focus group meetings they attended monthly at the church. That was the extent of their interaction with one another.

One evening when she was over at Skip's place, Meaghan went through his phone while he was in the shower. She found a string of sexual text messages between him and Detria. *Some men can be so stupid,* she thought. *He doesn't have a password on his phone, and he doesn't have sense enough to delete his messages.*

She kept quiet for several weeks, not wanting Skip to know that after they made love, she made it her business to find out who else he was messing around with.

On several occasions, she thought about confronting Detria, but always told herself to keep quiet and let the affair play out. Meaghan thought about the whole scenario with Skip and Detria. Instead of Detria realizing that she was just another one of Skip's casual flings, the stupid woman had fallen hard for Skip and now Detria was pregnant, possibly with his love child.

"So I have busted ribs, a broken nose, a couple of missing teeth, and what else?" Skip tried to be humorous but inside he was seething. Stiles had gotten the best of him, and Skip wasn't happy about it. Here he was, laid up in the hospital all whipped up like he'd been in the ring with Floyd Mayweather. And for what? All because Stiles couldn't stand the fact that he couldn't keep the hot little First Lady happy in the bedroom.

"That's it, honey," Meaghan said, trying not to sound like she was worried.

"When is the doctor coming? I want to know how long they plan on keeping me up in here."

"I wish you would try to relax and let the medication take effect, Skip. You're going to be in here for at least a couple of days so there's no need to get yourself all worked up. Plus, the longer you stay here, the more time your lawyer can work on building an airtight case against Pastor Graham for assaulting you."

"Good, because I'm the one laid up in here on my back. Preacher boy is the one who walked up on me, not the other way around. I was Detria's guest and he came barging up in there like he was Iron Man or somebody. Everybody knows that he and Detria are separated. That dude has some serious issues. So, whatever he gets he deserves."

"Look, baby, there's no need to dwell on any of that now. Close your eyes and rest." Meaghan lightly pecked him on his swollen lips as Skip's eyes slowly closed. The medication had finally kicked in.

Meaghan quietly stepped back and sat down on the hospital sofa, folded her arms, and laid her head against the cold leather. She had a thousand nasty, evil thoughts racing through her head, and every one of them was about Detria Graham. It was high time Detria got a taste of her own medicine. Meaghan believed she was just the woman to give it to her.

32

"Not all scars show." Unknown

Skip was released after spending three days in the hospital. He still had some physical healing to do, but as for his wounded ego, it would probably take quite some time before he felt better.

Detria hadn't been as fortunate as Skip and Stiles. Within hours of arriving at the hospital after the brawl between the two men, she had gone into labor. Giving birth at 24 weeks proved to be quite dangerous for her baby. Her baby boy entered the world weighing barely over one pound. Detria was heartbroken and terrified. She prayed that her little boy would be okay.

The neonatologist explained to her that babies born between 23 and 24 weeks have a good chance of survival. Detria was relieved to hear this bit of good news, but he warned her that her son still was not out of danger. Babies like her son who were born months before the due date, faced a long time in NICU. The baby was also at risk for serious disabilities, although some extremely premature babies grow up with no long-term effects of prematurity. Her precious little boy faced a bevy of possible health concerns. The doctor was especially worried because her baby showed signs of respiratory distress syndrome, also known as RDS. RDS babies lack a protein called surfactant that keeps small air sacs in the lungs from collapsing. Another concern was IVH, or bleeding in the brain, which usually occurs near the ventricles in the center of the brain. He was on oxygen, needed mechanical assistance to help him breathe, and his body systems were underdeveloped.

Detria sobbed. Was her child going to have to pay for her mistakes? Would her little boy suffer because she had exercised poor judgment in her marriage, her relationships, and her life?

Her parents and Brooke had come to the hospital to be with her, but they had left to take Sister Mackey home.

Sister Mackey's health was unstable. Not wanting to chance her having a lupus flare up, Brother Mackey insisted that the two of them go home so his wife could get some rest. He assured Sister Mackey that he would bring her back to the hospital the following day to see Detria and check on the newest addition to the Mackey family.

After a few hours, Stiles was released from the ER. Assuring Pastor, the McCoys, Leo and Cynthia that he was all right, he insisted they all go on home. It had been enough drama for one night, he told them. He was going to go across the street to check on Detria.

On his way to the Women's Pavilion, Stiles decided to call Brooke first. He wanted to know if the Mackey's were still visiting with Detria. Stiles understood that Poppa Mackey was upset with him, and he didn't want to cause more friction between himself and Poppa Mackey. His father-in-law already looked like he wanted to cause him harm when he came with Pastor to see him in the ER.

Stiles was relieved when Brooke answered her cell phone. Surprisingly, she didn't sound like she was upset with him. If anything, she sounded like she felt sorry for him. Brooke told him that they had left the hospital. She also told him that Detria had a baby boy. Stiles was overjoyed to hear that she'd given birth to a son, but saddened when Brooke told him that the little boy was in a medical dilemma. He released a heavy sigh as he ended the call and headed to see his cheating wife and newborn baby.

When Detria saw Stiles enter her hospital room bruised and swollen, instead of feeling sympathy toward him, she became angry. She almost hated him. She felt that because of him, she had gone into premature labor and now her son's life was at risk. Detria pressed the Call button and begged the nurse to come and make Stiles leave.

The nurse came in and insisted that he allow Detria to rest. Sadly, Stiles turned and left, not wanting to cause Detria any more discomfort, or get himself in deeper trouble.

With everyone gone, Detria lay in the hospital room all alone to face her demons.

33

"It hurts the worst when the person that made you feel so special yesterday, makes you feel so unwanted today." Unknown

Stiles stood outside NICU peering through the glass window separating him from his one-week old son. Stiles still had a number of bruises on his body. His nose and eyes were still slightly swollen, and his broken fingers were encased in splints.

The NICU nurse had rolled Elijah's tiny incubator close to the window so Stiles could see him for the few minutes he was allowed. She remained next to the incubator while Stiles watched the newborn. Elijah was still in guarded condition and even Detria was not allowed to see him, except through the glass partition.

From what the doctor had said, Elijah could grow up to be a normal kid despite his difficult and premature birth, of which Stiles partly blamed himself for. If he hadn't lost his temper, if he had practiced self-control, if he hadn't let Skip get under his skin then Detria would not have gone into premature labor. Sadly, there was nothing he could do to change any of that now.

He looked at the infant and prayed for his little boy to survive. He prayed that God would forgive him for the hardship he had already brought on Elijah's life because of his uncontrolled anger. Lastly, he prayed that Elijah shared his DNA. It would be days, if not weeks, before he found out.

Detria's infidelity had caused him to be uncertain about everything they shared. He felt that she further betrayed when she named the little boy Elijah James Graham, knowing full well the two of them had agreed early in their marriage that if ever they had a son they would name him Stiles Chauncey Graham. Stiles was crushed. It felt like the ultimate sense of disloyalty. Did she really hate him that much? Not only had she not named the boy after him, but Detria didn't give him Pastor's name either. Stiles didn't know what to think anymore. The only thing he was sure of was that his life was in shambles and he didn't know where to turn. Tears silently flowed down his cheeks as he placed both hands flat against the window. His faith was shaken. For the first time in years, he felt disconnected from God.

He had stood in the pulpit of Holy Rock just weeks ago and assured his congregation that he was not going anywhere. Now, he was having second thoughts. He didn't know how he could lead the congregation when his own life was so messed up, so disoriented. Stiles turned and walked away from the NICU.

The ringing cell phone startled Stiles as he drove toward his townhome. He answered it. It was his administrative assistant, Sister Gloria Wooten.

"Hello, Sister Gloria."

"Hello, Pastor Graham. How are you? I've been so worried about you?"

"I'm going to be fine. How can I help you?"

"Pastor Graham, your ex-wife called."

"What did you just say?"

"Sister Rena Graham called you," she repeated.

"Rena? Are you sure it was Rena?"

"Yes, Pastor. It was her."

Stiles rubbed his head back and forth as he made a right turn at the light. "What did she say?"

"Only that she wanted to talk to you."

For a minute, he was without words. Did Sister Wooten just tell him that Rena had called? Was she back in Memphis? Had she ever left? And why didn't she wait to see him in his office when she was here not long ago? It didn't make sense, but then again, lately nothing in his life made sense.

"Uh, look, Sister Gloria. Did she," he paused, "did she leave a number where I can reach her?"

"Yes, she did."

Gloria became his administrative assistant weeks after he became Holy Rock's Senior Pastor. She had witnessed the fall of his marriage to Rena and here she was again, watching him go through drama with his second wife.

Gloria voiced her dislike for the First Lady on several occasions throughout his marriage to Detria, but her opinion fell on deaf ears. Maybe that was the way it was supposed to be, because Stiles was a man of God, and as a man of God he did not want to entertain gossipy opinions about who he was married to. Gloria came to the conclusion that it was not her place to give him counsel, so she had long since stopped acting like a second mother to him and tried to remain in the role of his administrative assistant.

"I'm driving, so if you don't mind, will you text me her phone number? I'll save it in my phone."

"Yes, Pastor Graham."

"Thank you, Sister Gloria. Is there anything else I need to know before we hang up?"

"No, not really. Oh, yes, wait; there is one more thing."

"Yes, what is it?"

"Are you planning on preaching at midweek service tomorrow night, or do you want Pastor McCoy or one of the other ministers to do it?"

Stiles drove in silence for a second or two before he responded. "Call and tell Pastor McCoy to be prepared to deliver the Word."

"Yes, sir. Goodbye," responded Sister Gloria, and ended the call.

Stiles arrived at his townhome, parked his car, and went inside. It was quiet, almost too quiet. The silence reminded him of how alone he truly was. He thought about Rena. His heart picked up its pace as memories of the love he once had for her resurfaced. If only he had been a big enough man to forgive her and keep their marriage intact, then maybe, just maybe he wouldn't be in the mess he was in now. He and Rena could have worked through the mistakes of the past. It wasn't like he was the perfect man himself. *We all fall short...He who is without sin let him cast the first stone.* Scripture after scripture flooded his mind.

He sat on his sofa and studied Rena's number. Finally, he inhaled then slowly dialed it. After five rings, she answered.

"Rena, it's Stiles. I got your message. Is this a good time?"

"Yes, sure. How are you?" She sounded like the same sweet Rena he had fallen in love with.

"I'm good. How's your family?"

"Everyone is great. The kids are growing up like wild fire. How's your little girl?"

"She's good."

Silence infiltrated the phone lines until Rena cleared her throat and spoke up.

"Look, how are you really doing? I mean, it's like every time I read the Memphis newspaper, there's something about you, and it's not good. What's going on?"

"Why are you concerned?" Stiles tone went from welcoming to highly irritated. "As I recall, it wasn't that long ago when you came to Holy Rock and then up and disappeared as quickly as you came without so much as a hello. Now you're asking me how I'm doing? I'm a little confused, Rena." Stiles didn't have time to play games, not with Rena, not with anyone. He was going through enough with Detria and her drama.

"I left that day because, well, because I felt guilty."

"Guilty? Guilty about what?"

"I came to Memphis because my former boss and friend, Mr. Bolden died. I don't know if you remember him or not. At first I planned to come here, attend his funeral, and fly back home the following Monday. I wasn't going to come to Holy Rock, but I realized that I couldn't come to Memphis and not see you, or at least come hear you preach."

"I don't know, something doesn't sound right. You were supposed to wait in my office so we could at least say hello to one another. But when I got there, you were nowhere to be found. What was up with that? Your hubby stopped you or what?"

"I came to Memphis alone, Stiles. But, in a way I guess you're right. I got cold feet, had second thoughts, because I wouldn't want to do anything that would give Robert a reason to distrust me."

"I guess you have a point. Showing up at your ex-husband's church or being caught in his office would definitely cause him to distrust you. I'm glad you followed your mind. Although you know, that he wouldn't have a reason to be jealous. You're married to him, you've given him babies, and you've moved on with your life. Good for you, Rena."

"Okay, enough acting like you're so hardcore. Tell me, how are you doing for real? I read in the paper that you could face jail time for assaulting Skip Madison, who's supposed to be Detria's lover. It sounds like something straight off of TMZ."

He was getting fed up with people judging him when they didn't know what was going on. He was tired of the media portraying him as the bad guy. "Look, if you called to get the inside scoop, then you need to go somewhere else because it's none of your business."

"I'm concerned about you. That's all."

"I don't need you or anyone else to be concerned about me. I'm okay. And I don't want to talk to you about my marriage, and I sure don't want to talk about the garbage they're writing about me in the newspaper. I'm cool. Everything is fine."

"Stiles, don't do this. Remember, I know you. I know you've got to be hurt by everything that's been happening. And I want you to know that I—"

"That you what, Rena? That you care about me? Please. Don't tell me that you're here for me, because you and I both know that's a bunch of crap. Be concerned about your husband. There's nothing you can do for me."

"Stiles, please. Don't shut me out. I really am worried about you."

Stiles chuckled. "Please. Worried? So what are you going to do, Rena? You coming back to Memphis? You coming to nurse my wounds?"

"No, you know that's not what I'm saying."

"Then what are you saying? Look, tell you what, why don't you concentrate on your marriage, your own family and your own life. Now, I've got to go. I have a ton of things I still have to do before calling it a day. Thanks for your concern, and God bless."

"I...okay. Fine then. Have it your way, but I didn't mean any harm, and I didn't mean to upset you. I just wanted you to know that you and your family are in my prayers. I hope everything works out."

"Yeah, whatever. Bye, Rena." Stiles pushed the End button on his phone. He had to be blunt with Rena. He wasn't about to let her know the effect she still had over him. But there really was no reason for her to be trying to see how he was doing when in all actuality there was nothing she could do for him now. He was glad he told her to concentrate on her own family. He had enough problems without adding her into the loop.

He went upstairs to his bedroom and undressed. While in the shower, he wept. He wept for all the mistakes he had made. He wept over the possibility of his newborn son not being his. He wept over the loss of his mother. The estranged relationship between his only sister, Francesca bothered him too, but most of all, he wept because he finally understood and accepted what he had to do. It was inevitable. It was his fate. His lot in life because there was no way he could forgive Detria. He had forgiven her for physically abusing Pastor, but this was different. Her adultery was too much and he wasn't that strong of a man to turn the other cheek. He knew it and God knew it. He was human first, a man whose heart had been broken *again*, and it hurt to be hurt. Rena had hurt him but Detria had hurt him more than anything.

According to the neonatologist, it would be at least a few more days before they could do the DNA swab test on Elijah. The newborn was still too weak. But if all went as planned, soon enough, he would know if Elijah belonged to him. But whether he did or whether he didn't, it wouldn't change the decision that tormented his spirit - maybe it was time for him to leave Holy Rock.

34

"The world is round and the place which may seem like the end may also be the beginning." Ivy B Priest

Xavier had been in Memphis for a few days but he had already decided that it was not where he wanted to live. He had barely had a chance to spend any time with his dad since arriving. Hezekiah had been busy running here and there, back and forth, with stuff going on at Holy Rock.

Xavier toyed with his iPhone while he sat outside on the backyard deck. It was March, and the temperatures hovered around sixty plus degrees. Xavier enjoyed the mild weather, compared to the frigid temps of the Windy City, but it wasn't enough to make him want to remain in Memphis.

"Honey." His mother appeared. "Your father should be home soon."

"What does that mean?" Xavier looked at her like she'd committed a cardinal sin.

"It means that the three of us can finally spend some time together. We're going to take you to eat barbeque since you said you wanted to taste some Memphis barbeque." Fancy smiled and walked out on the backyard deck. "Would you like that?" she asked, walking up to Xavier and patting him on the back like she was burping a baby

Xavier hated it when she talked to him like he was a little kid. When was she going to look at him and realize that he was practically a grown man.

"Xavier, honey. I asked you a question."

Xavier looked up from his phone. "What?"

"I said, would you like to go eat barbeque tonight when your father gets home?"

"I don't care." Xavier shrugged his shoulders. "I guess so."

"Okay, good. Then change clothes and we can leave when he gets here.

"Change clothes? What's wrong with what I have on?" He frowned, looked at his attire, then looked at his mother like she had lost her mind.

Fancy shook her head and smiled. "Okay, I guess what you have on is fine. But no sagging pants. You need to eat more, so your clothes will fit you better. Now that you're here, I'm going to take care of that. Everything is going to be fine."

"Mom, you know I'm not staying here. I want to go back to Chicago. That's my home. I don't know why you and Dad had to move here in the first place. This place sucks. It's boring." He said all of this without taking his eyes off his iPhone. He was busy texting and wished his mother would leave him alone.

"It's all in what you make it, Xavier. All I'm asking is for you to give Memphis a try. I know we haven't been able to take you around, show you the city and all, but I promise you, you'll like it here. And Sunday when we go to church, I'll introduce you to the youth pastor. You can connect with kids your own age. It's going to be fun."

Xavier shook his head. "Whatever, Mom." He focused back on the task at hand: texting.

35

"You can't run away from trouble.
There ain't no place that far." Unknown

"Son, I want you to be sure that this is what God is telling you to do. We all make mistakes. God knows I've made plenty of them, but God is a forgiving God."

"Yes, I know that, Pastor, and believe me, this is what I have to do. I can't stand up in that pulpit Sunday after Sunday, week after week, preaching the Word, trying to lead others to Christ, not when I've messed up the way that I have."

"That's no excuse for leaving the church. God can use anybody. He uses the broken to carry out his plan. He uses the weak. He uses the imperfect." Pastor sat across from Stiles in the church office. He looked around at the walls that were lined with pictures of when he was senior pastor of Holy Rock. Slowly, he stood and walked over in front of the oil portrait of himself and First Lady Audrey Graham, and smiled.

"Your mother was so proud of you. She was the happiest she's ever been when you took on the role of Senior Pastor." Pastor turned and looked at Stiles sitting behind his desk, his chin resting on the insert of his hand. "I thought after my first stroke that I was going to lose everything I'd worked hard to attain. Building and growing this church was my life. When I could no longer stand in that pulpit and preach God's Word, I wanted to die. I felt my life was over."

Stiles turned in his office chair, got up and walked over and stood next to his father. He draped his arm over Pastor's shoulder.

"I never knew you felt like that. Don't get me wrong, I knew this church was your life, but not to the extent that you didn't want to live after you couldn't preach again."

"God showed mercy and favor when He blessed me with you. Don't get me wrong, your sister is a big blessing in my life too, but you, you took hold of the reins. You stepped up and accepted the call on your life to lead this great congregation. Now look at it.

It's grown from 500 to over 7,500 members, and it's still growing. Now you're telling me that God wants you to leave?"

Stiles was silent momentarily. "I'm not strong like you."

"What do you mean?" Pastor turned and looked at Stiles, moving back from his embrace. "You can do all things through Christ who strengthens you.

"How did you stay with Mom after you learned that she cheated on you? How did you find it in your heart to not only forgive her, but you accepted Francesca as your own? I don't understand." Stiles shook his head and lowered it, as if he was in shame.

"I loved your mother then and I love her now. God rest her soul. The day she strolled into Holy Rock with you by her side," Pastor smiled, "was the day my life changed. I saw my mate; the woman God had for me. And the double blessing was that He blessed me with a son through you." Pastor faced Stiles, smiled, and laid one hand on top of Stiles' shoulder.

"I can't be like you, Pastor. I don't have the strength. I didn't have the strength to forgive Rena for sleeping with Francesca, and I can't forgive Detria. I just can't. That's why I have to leave; I won't be a hypocrite. I won't lead my congregation to believe that I have it all together and that I'm such a strong, Godly man when I'm not. I can't even control my anger. I'm practically labeled as a woman beater, and that fight with Skip, well it shows the magnitude of what I'm dealing with."

"Listen to me, Son. You've made mistakes, costly mistakes; but it doesn't discount who you are to God. The Word says that we all fall short. Your strength comes from God, Son. You know the Word. Not by might, nor by power, but by my spirit, saith the Lord of hosts. For my grace is sufficient for thee; for my strength is made perfect in weakness. I will glory in my infirmities that the power of Christ may rest upon me." Pastor stepped closer to his son and embraced him.

Stiles held on to his father, and allowed himself to finally exhale before he stepped out from under Pastor's embrace, and looked at him. "I'm not strong like you, Pastor. I'm just not." Stiles walked away and returned to his chair, placing his head in his hands.

36

"The saddest thing about betrayal is that
it never comes from your enemies." Unknown

Monday afternoon, and the paternity test results were in. Detria and Stiles were to meet in the doctor's office at one o'clock.

Elijah was three weeks old and was still in the hospital. Every day, Detria visited her little boy while Mother Brown and Detria's family helped her out with Audrey. Elijah now weighed two pounds. He was still on oxygen and unfortunately, the bleeding in his brain was hindering the little boy's health.

"There is a silver lining in everything, if you look for it," Pastor told Detria one day when he went to visit her and Audrey. "Think about it. Elijah could be much worse. From what I understand the specialists said that the IVH falls into four grades. Right?"

"Right," Detria said.

"And the higher the grade, the more severe the bleeding. Am I right?" Pastor asked.

"Yes."

"Well, Elijah's grade is a two, which from my understanding means that there is just a small amount of bleeding and it usually does not cause long-term problems."

Detria teared up. "That's right, but my baby. My baby is sick, Pastor, and it's all my fault."

Pastor held her in his arms, allowing her tears to freely land on his starched white shirt.

"Shhh, Elijah is going to be fine. The doctor and nurses are keeping him as stable as possible, and he hasn't had to have a blood transfusion, like so many other babies born like him." He held Detria's hand and caressed it, hoping that she would be calm. "He hasn't had to have a tube or shunt in the brain to drain fluid. That's God, Detria. God has your son. He is not punishing you. He loves you and He loves that little boy."

Detria arrived at the Professional Doctor's Building across from the hospital at twelve thirty. Standing in front of the elevator, waiting on the doors to open, she texted back and forth with Skip. Reading his text messages was a too late reminder that she should have kept quiet about today's appointment. Telling Skip was the last thing she should have done because he was going to do just like he always did, which was pressure her until he got his way.

"I want 2 know the results as soon as the dr tells u."

"I told u. Elijah belongs 2 Stiles."

"I don't care what u say. I want 2 know what the tests says."

"Yeah, sure, Skip."

She turned off her phone to avoid any more of his harassing texts or phone calls, which were sure to follow.

Detria didn't notice that Stiles had walked up and stood next to her.

Stiles watched as she texted on her phone, but did not say anything. *I bet she's texting him. God, let Elijah be my son. Don't give Skip the satisfaction of having a son.*

The doors opened and Detria looked up from her cell phone and walked toward the doors. She looked surprised when she saw Stiles get on the elevator too.

She looked at him, obvious tension was evident all over her face. "Hi."

"Hello, Detria."

"Stiles, whatever the results are, I want you to know that I'm sorry. I'm sorry for everything. I never ever meant to hurt you," she said, glad that they were the only two on the elevator.

"It's a little late for that, don't you think?"

The doors to the fifth floor opened before Detria could answer. She was more than glad. She quickly stepped off the elevator, strolled ahead of Stiles, and walked to the doctor's office.

Showtime.

Detria's crocodile tears could have easily measured up to the quarter sized raindrops pelting her car like mini meteors. A booming, almost guttural roll of thunder announced the bolt of lightning that pierced the threatening skyline, and matched the beat of her heart. Detria accelerated, perhaps hoping that the speed of the car could outrun the hurt and embarrassment she felt.

She avoided Skip's constant calling and ignored the text message notifier. She needed time to think, to sort the doctor's words out in her mind. Nothing made sense. *Elijah is not Stiles' son? Lord, no. No, no, no.*

Arriving at her house, she immediately called Brooke.

"What are you going to do?" Brooke asked her sister. "What was Stiles reaction?"

"I don't know what I'm going to do. Believe it or not, Stiles didn't say one word to me afterward. I can't explain it."

"What do you mean?"

"He just looked so, like he was spaced out or something. He just got up and left. I'm scared. Suppose he comes here and tries to do something to me?"

"Stiles is not going to do anything to you, Detria. The man is just crushed. What do you expect? I wish you would tell me what you were thinking about when you had the affair with Skip, of all people. Where was your mind?"

Detria lashed out over the phone. "For the millionth time, I do not need you condemning me! Don't act so holy like you've never done anything that you're sorry for. I guess you forgot about your skeletons, huh?"

"This is not about me, so don't even go there," Brooke yelled.

"Yeah, you don't want anybody to know that you had an affair too. Only yours wasn't with a man now, was it?" Detria said in a condescending tone.

"I will not let you make this about me. And if you listen to yourself you'll realize what you said. You said *I used to be*. That means, I'm not that person anymore. That was before the boys were born. And I will not let you try to take the blame off what you've done."

"Yeah, you don't want anybody to know that you were a prescription drug junkie, do you? You don't want folks to know that you almost lost your husband because you were busy downing Xanax like candy. So don't get all self-righteous on me, big sister."

Click. Air filled the space of silence and then Detria heard the dial tone as it buzzed in her ear. She fell on to the cold concrete floor and sobbed.

Stiles couldn't identify his feelings. It was beyond pain, beyond hurt, beyond a broken heart. It ran deeper than a jagged edge knife puncturing the very center of his being. To know that Elijah did not share in his DNA was the ultimate betrayal.

"Pastor McCoy," Stiles spoke matter-of-factly. His voice was elevated to a fever pitch.

"Yes, Pastor Graham?" Hezekiah sounded like he could detect the frustration in Stiles' voice.

"I want you and Deacon Jones to meet me in the boardroom at Holy Rock in thirty minutes."

"Are you sure about that? It's fierce out there." Hezekiah warned.

Blaring tornado sirens and roaring rounds of thunder caused the skies to vibrate in a show of power and authority.

"Quite sure. Be there." Stiles ordered.

The three men sat at the oblong oak table in the boardroom. Hezekiah and Leo were anxious to hear what it was that Stiles had to tell them. They knew today was the day that he was supposed to find out if Elijah was his; from the dejected look on Stiles' face, they already guessed the answer.

Stiles looked broken. His eyes were bloodshot red. His brows were drawn together in an angry frown. The tensing of his jaw betrayed his frustration.

"I want you to be the first ones to know, other than my father, that I've made a decision."

"A decision?"

"Yeah, what kind of decision?" asked Leo with clasped hands and a furrowed brow. Leo was almost afraid to hear what Stiles was about to say. Whatever it was, he felt like it was going to be a doozie.

"First, let me tell you that Elijah is not my son." With a deep sigh, Stiles formed a bridge with his hands and rested his chin on top of it. He chewed on his bottom lip, pausing before he continued. "I can't tell you how angry I am. I feel like doing something bad to both of them, something real bad."

"Come on now, man," Hezekiah interjected. "Don't let the devil make you go there."

Stiles gave Hezekiah a stern look of disapproval. "I think it's a little late for that advice."

"I'm just saying. I understand how you feel, but no matter how bad things are, it's still no reason for you to let the devil have the winning hand."

"You have no idea how I feel," Stiles bit back. He got up from his chair and rubbed his head while he paced around his office. "When you hear a doctor tell you that the baby, the son you always wanted, is not yours, then maybe you can tell me you understand."

Leo spoke up. "Look, you have to keep your cool, man. I don't blame you for wanting to hurt somebody but that won't change a thing."

"I'm leaving Holy Rock."

"You're what?" Leo jumped up from his chair and positioned himself in front of Stiles. "You can't be serious."

Hezekiah remained seated. *Leaving Holy Rock? Did I just hear him right? God, I know you answer prayers but I didn't know you were going to do it like this.* Hezekiah turned off the rush of thoughts in his head and tuned back to what Stiles was saying.

"I cannot effectively lead this congregation anymore. I just can't do it. I've been thinking about this for some time now, and today, well, today I finally understand what God is telling me. Maybe that's why I've avoided going to jail not one time, but twice. I could have been charged with assaulting that punk since I'm still on probation. Maybe it's God's way of telling me that I need to leave this town and this church."

"So you're saying God told you to leave this church, to leave your congregation, to just give all of this up?" Hezekiah countered.

Stiles zeroed in on Hezekiah again with a hard, focused glare. "Don't even pretend like you don't want to be the shepherd of this church. You're ambitious, and you've never tried to hide that. Every chance you get, you jump at the chance to stand in my place. Well, you can have it. It's yours, Hezekiah. It's all yours."

"Don't you think you're being a little hard on Pastor McCoy? It's not like he made this choice. You're the one who's jumping the gun. Man, just chill."

"Chill?" Stiles chuckled loudly. "How do you suppose I *chill* when my whole life has been a lie? How can I *chill* when my wife has been screwing one of my best friends for God knows how long?"

"I can't believe that you honestly think I would glory over your trials," Hezekiah spoke up. "And the last time I checked, being ambitious wasn't a crime. But since you think I'm rejoicing over your situation, why don't you stay in the position you were called and then you wouldn't have to worry about whether or not I want to take your place." *You just don't know how I would love the chance to lead Holy Rock. This would be the best thing that could happen to me and Fancy,* he thought.

Stiles remained silent, like he was suddenly in deep thought, perhaps pondering the things he'd just said. Out of nowhere, Stiles balled his fist up and hit the wall, leaving a gaping hole.

"Hold up, man," Leo yelled and ran up and restrained Stiles. "Calm down. Get it together."

Stiles jerked away from Leo then swiftly turned and walked toward the door.

"Get everything written up. Get the paperwork done, whatever you have to do, just as long as you do it. Pastor McCoy, unless this congregation says otherwise, this is your baby now. Tell the church what you want. I don't care anymore."

"Hold up, Pastor Graham. Why don't you—"

"Why don't I what? Wait until the congregation votes me out? I guess you forgot that it wasn't that long ago when the church was torn in two about whether I should stay or leave. So I'll make it easy for everybody, I'm out of here."

Stiles opened the door and stormed out before Hezekiah could finish his sentence.

Leo looked at Hezekiah. Their silence spoke volumes.

Stiles sped through the blinding tornado-like thunderstorm, disregarding cars that had pulled over to the side of the road, and others that had all but stopped in the middle of the street. In some areas, the streets were flooded, but Stiles kept his foot pressed down full force on the pedal. Driving with reckless abandonment, he almost collided with several of them. There certainly must have been angels encamped around his speeding car. It could be the only explanation why he didn't kill himself or someone else, with his dangerous driving.

Sirens wailed throughout the city. Thunder, lightning, and the rushing sound of the mighty wind was nothing compared to the storm raging on the inside of him.

He made it to his townhome safe and sound by the grace of God, though God was the last thing on his mind. He packed as much as he could in one of his upright suitcases before sitting down in front of his computer to search for airline flights. He wasn't exactly sure where he was going, but one thing was certain: he had to get out of Memphis, Tennessee quick, fast and in a hurry or he wouldn't be responsible for his actions.

37

"Some of us think holding on makes us strong; but sometimes
it is letting go." Hermann Hesse

"Hold up," Stiles hollered while making his way to answer the
constant knocking on his front door. "What fool is this beating on my
door?" he muttered.

He opened the door with force. Standing on the other side was
Leo.

"What's wrong with you, man, knocking on my door like you
wanna break in or something?"

Leo walked inside the townhome and Stiles closed the door
behind him.

"What's up?"

"You need to stop acting weak, man. That's what's up."

"Weak? Man, don't come up in here talking all crazy to me like
that. You better step back before I show you weak."

Leo waved a hand in the air, dismissing Stiles' remarks. "Look,
don't come to me with that bull, man. You know good and well what
I'm talking about."

"Naw, enlighten me, because I don't know what your problem is."

"My problem is that all this confusion going on between you and
your woman, you acting like some weak-as-water type of man. You
walking around here practically whining like you ain't got no spine.
Okay, the girl messed off on you. Back in the day, think about it, bro.
What would you have done? How would you have handled a female
back then who even thought about cheating on you?"

Stiles stood motionless.

"I tell you what you would have done. You would have dismissed
her so quick, man. Just like yesterday's trash."

"The difference is, Detria is not some female, she's my wife. I
can't just dismiss her like that."

"The woman cheated, man. What is wrong with you? Not only
that, she got a baby that ain't even yours! She got a son by Skip,
man. Look, I know you're a man of the cloth, or whatever you wanna

call yourself. I respect that, which is why I've been by your side since day one. When you appointed me as a deacon then Chairman of the Deacon Board, I fully accepted my role. You know for yourself that I have not stepped out of my lane since then, but now I can't hold back. I got to come to you as your friend, road dog. We go too far back and have come through too much for me to let you be taken under by some female, wife or no wife, first lady or no first lady. You walking around like some sick puppy dog, talking about giving up everything you've worked hard for? And for what? Some woman? A woman who can't be straight up with you?"

Stiles walked past Leo and went into the living room and sat down. Leo followed but remained standing.

"Man, you're like a brother to me. Ain't no way I'm going to let you go out like this. I know you're hurt, and I'm hurt for you, but just like you cut all ties with Rena when you found she was swinging both ways, then hey, this is even worse, man. Detria sleeping with your friend. She got a baby with dude and you sitting over here like you about to lose your freaking mind. I'm telling you, let this crap go."

"You don't understand." Stiles shook his head.

"What is it I don't understand? Tell me."

"The dynamics are different. We are not in high school or college anymore, Leo. We're men; grown men. And I'm the leader of thousands of people. People who look to *me* for guidance, direction and to lead them to God. How can I do that when my life has been spread across the newspaper, the television and in the church? Everybody knows my wife committed adultery. Everybody knows that Rena slept with Francesca. People think I'm a woman beater. You think they don't question my ability to lead them after all of this?"

Stiles stood up, rubbing his head like he always did when he was frustrated or stressed. "I hear what you're saying, Leo, but I'm so messed up right about now. I need to get away, man. I need some time to clear my head; decide on what I'm going to do next. Not only that, this broad got me doubting if Audrey is even mine. I don't know what to think. I mean, I'm praying and asking God for direction." Stiles began pacing. "It's like I can't hear God, so much noise is filling my head."

"First of all, you're human man. Newsflash, my brother, you're not God. This crap is serious, but you got to get it together. If you know you can't get past this, then you have to make a decision. Move on, let it go. Let *her* go. Then again, if you're worried about what other folks are thinking and saying about you and you want to stay with Detria to make yourself look like you're some kind of perfect guy, then go for it. But you're the one who has to suffer behind that. I remember you were the one who always used to say that the one thing you would never tolerate from a female was infidelity, and that was when you weren't married. Remember? You were playing women like we used to play Spades. Now, here you are about to lose your freaking mind over one woman? Come on, man, you're the senior pastor of Holy Rock. You can have any woman you choose, and I'm sure you'll find plenty of them who will be faithful to you."

Stiles was silent.

Leo walked into the kitchen, opened the fridge, and looked inside and got a bottled water. Opening it, he turned and looked back at Stiles.

"I understand if you need to get away from Memphis for a minute. Maybe that's a good thing. You do need to clear your head. Maybe a week, a couple of weeks out of this city will do you good. That way you can hopefully get your mind right, bro, but stepping down? Naw, man. That's crazy."

Leo took a deep swallow of the cold water. Walking over to where Stiles had sat down again, Leo looked at him. "Man, you look like you've been shipwrecked on a deserted island or something. It's time for you to man up, make a decision about what it's gone be and then just do it. And I don't mean irrational decisions like stepping down from your pastoral position. That's something you really need to think about and pray about. You don't make a serious decision like that on impulse."

"Yea, you're right." Stiles looked at Leo. "Thanks, man."

"You know I'm going to tell you like it is. Now, what's it gone be? Where are you going to get stuff sorted out?"

Stiles hunched his shoulders. "I don't know. I guess I should check with my probation officer, let him know my plans first. I'm thinking maybe I'll go to Houston or DC. I got frat brothers in both places, and a few preacher friends."

"So, here's what you do. Figure out where it is you want to go, and I'll do whatever I can to help you get there. Anything to get you somewhere so you can clear your head. I need the old Stiles back, man. No more Mr. Nice Guy. No more head tucked between your shoulders. You hear me, bro?"

Clenching his jaw, then pushing his bottom lip forward, Stiles replied, "Yeah, I hear you."

38

"There is a smile of love, And there is a smile of deceit, And there is a smile of smiles, In which these two smiles meet."
William Blake

"You know, baby, just because that kid isn't Stiles' doesn't mean that he's yours," Meaghan whispered in Skip's ear as she laid up in the bed curled underneath his arm.

Skip eased up in the bed and looked over at her. "What is that supposed to mean?" His voice revealed that he didn't quite like or maybe understand what Meaghan was talking about.

"Hold up, don't get mad. I'm just saying, have you ever considered taking a paternity test yourself? Who knows if you were the only one the she was sleeping with? I mean, you never know."

As much as Skip wanted to dismiss what Meaghan was saying, he couldn't. Suppose she was right? Suppose Detria had been sleeping with somebody other than him? Why would it be so hard to believe when she was the one who came on to him? He never would have thought twice about sleeping with her, not because she wasn't desirable, but for the simple fact she was married to Stiles, his road dog, his longtime friend and his pastor. But Detria Graham made it hard, no downright impossible to resist her. And like just about any man in his right mind would do, he jumped on it when she practically offered herself to him. He couldn't believe that their affair had lasted this long.

Detria wasn't the only female he was sleeping with, of course. Meaghan was proof of that, but there were also a bevy of other women who shared his bed whenever he wanted, and however he wanted. The only thing about Detria Graham was he had given her too much credit. Surely she should have known not to go and get pregnant, knowing that they rarely, if ever, used protection. That was another story altogether. Yeah, he should have used a condom, and most times he did, but Detria could be wild and freaky. There were numerous occasions when she refused to let him use protection, *and* she'd obviously lied when she told him she was on birth control. The girl was someone to write a novel about now that he stopped to think about things.

He was more than shocked when Detria told him that Elijah was his. *What if he isn't? What if Meaghan is right? Shooot, these females be straight up cheating and sleeping around like it ain't nothing. If she gave it up to me, who knows who else she gave it up to. Yeah, I need to think about getting that DNA test.*

"I can help you get a DNA test if want me to, and she doesn't even have to know."

Skip's ears connected with the words coming out of her mouth. He wanted to hear more.

"You know she's not going to do another paternity test. And, if you tell her you want one and she gets mad and refuses to do it, then that's a sure indication that she's not sure if you're the baby daddy either."

"So what do you propose I do, *Miss I Have All the Answers.*"

"I propose you get one of those DNA test kits. You can go to the hospital and see the baby. Now that it's been proven that the little boy doesn't belong to Stiles, surely you can see him, right?"

Skip shook his head. "Naw, legally I am still not his father, so I can't see him, and he's still not out of the woods yet. From talking to Detria, little dude still has a long way to go. He's gaining weight and she said he's been eating more, but she said the doctors say he won't be coming home for at least a few more weeks."

"Can't you get her to give you permission or a clearance of some kind to see your son? She shouldn't have a problem with that unless, like I said, she has something to hide."

"Clearance? I don't think so. Hell, it's like pulling teeth to get her to tell me how my son is doing, and she won't even let me come see her in the hospital, not that I really want to, but she barely takes my calls. The bottom line is I just wanna see my boy, that's all."

Skip slowly got up out of the bed. Meaghan's eyes hungrily raked over his naked body as he walked past her and went into the bathroom. She watched him as he stood over the toilet and relieved himself. Skip was so dang hot and fine in her eyes, and she wanted him all to herself. If she could do something to cause that conniving, cheating Detria to slip up, then the better her chances of getting Skip to realize that she was the one and only woman he needed – not Detria Graham.

Skip flushed the toilet, washed his hands, then stood in the door of the bathroom, looking in his bedroom at Meaghan. "Keep talking," he said.

"I was thinking that we go get one of the DNA test kits from the drugstore. According to what I've heard about them, all you have to do is take a cotton swab and rub it inside your mouth and the baby's mouth. That's supposed to be enough DNA for the test."

"Then what, since you know so much about this."

"You know my friend, Pat?"

"Yeah. What about her?"

"She said her brother took one because this girl was saying he was her baby daddy. He said he couldn't be because he always used protection. Anyway, since neither one of them could afford to get tested through the court system, they went and got one of the over the counter kits. She said it took two days for the test to come back. You go to a confidential website and get the results."

"Still, I bet they're not accurate."

"Let's see." Meaghan got up from the bed in her birthday suit. This time it was Skip's turn to lust after her smooth naked skin.

"Where are you going?" He watched her every move, feeling his excitement building.

She noticed his growing desire and said, smiling seductively, "Hold up, partner," she teased. "Let's check this out before we play again." She walked over to his laptop that was sitting on top of his dresser. Meaghan googled, 'How accurate is an over the counter DNA test?' She started reading one of the sites she clicked on.

"See, listen to this. Over the counter DNA tests are 100 percent accurate if the child and the dad's DNA are collected. See, I told you," she said, her voice ringing with excitement. "Oh, wait, get this, Skip."

"What?" Their naked skin kissed as he moved in close so he could read the article.

"You can test the baby with or without Detria. All you have to do is wait until the doctor clears the poor little thing to come home."

"Yeah," Skip mumbled like he was already devising a plan so he could somehow see Elijah at the hospital and do the test.

"Anyway, regardless of the results, you'll have something to go by. If it turns out that he's yours, then I say you should petition for sole custody. Think about it. What kind of decent mother will she make? From what I hear, she doesn't even want the little girl she has. And you said yourself that some old lady at church keeps her more than Detria does. What does that tell you?"

Skip's eyebrows raised in question.

"On top of that, Detria is one of the most talked about, probably most despised women at Holy Rock and maybe the entire city."

"I guess that makes me the most hated man, huh?" Skip chuckled.

Meaghan put the laptop back on the dresser, and smiled at Skip before she stood up and pressed her body against his. Standing on her toes, she looked up at him and began kissing his face all over while her hands expertly explored his body.

Skip didn't deny her. He grabbed hold of her hand and led her back to his bed.

"No one could ever hate you," she whispered. "No one."

39

"Love and Death are two uninvited guests, when they will come, nobody knows but both do the same work, one takes heart and the other takes its beats." Nishan Panwar

Stiles sat on the front row of his frat brother's church and listened to him preach the Word.

"Do you hear me?" Pastor Wallace preached to his flock. "I tell you my brothers and sisters; God is able to keep you while you're going through, no matter how big the problem. Listen to me!"

Wallace and Stiles attended Duke School of Divinity together and both pledged Kappa at the same time. Wallace's church, Church With No Borders Ministries, was an up and coming church in Houston. Wallace founded the church less than four years ago and it was growing at a steady pace.

"We are pressed on every side by troubles, but we are not crushed. We are perplexed, but not driven to despair. We are hunted down, but never abandoned by God. We get knocked down, but we are not destroyed."

"Amen," Stiles shouted in agreement along with much of the congregation.

Stiles had been in Houston for less than a week but he already felt that he'd made the right decision to leave Memphis for a while. The realization that Elijah was not his son sent him into a dark place. He had to find a way of escape. Leo's talk really helped him. Because of what he'd said, Stiles told Hezekiah to inform the congregation that he was on sabbatical rather than stepping down totally from his ministry. It made more sense to do it this way once he sat down and really thought and prayed about it.

Before he left for Houston, he had received clearance from the courts to leave Memphis. He was grateful that he had once again avoided jail time. His criminal lawyer had suggested a good attorney and Stiles was definitely going to divorce Detria.

Being a man of God, he understood and accepted that he would have to forgive her, but forgiving her didn't mean that he had to stay in a marriage where the trust had been irretrievably broken and the marriage bed defiled.

He clapped his hands and stood to his feet, praising God as Pastor Wallace broke out singing Bishop Paul Morton's, "You Ain't Seen Your Best Days Yet." *You may think that it's over, that your life is done…your battle is already won.*

Stiles leaped for joy as the words of the song reminded him that with God everything would be all right.

"I know your game. You think you just gone put that baby off on Skip? Well, first lady or no first lady, I'm telling you that you ain't gonna get away with your scheming. Not as long as I'm around."

"Look, I don't know who you think you're talking to, Meaghan, but the best thing you can do is to get up out of my face."

"And if I don't?" Meaghan snapped back, using one hand to swiftly throw back her Brazilian weave from off her face.

Detria pushed her grocery cart past Meaghan as quickly as she could. She and Audrey had come to the grocery store to pick up a few items, and of all people to run into, it had to be none other than Meaghan Perkins. Detria knew that Skip used to mess around with Meaghan. He told her himself, but he also told her that it had been over between them since he and Detria started sleeping together. Obviously, somebody lied. From the way Meaghan was going off on her, it appeared that she was still sharing Skip's bed. Detria tried to hide her feelings, but she was having a hard time. Meaghan was dogging her footsteps all through the store, getting louder and louder.

Detria pushed her cart as fast as she could, trying to avoid a confrontation with the irate Meaghan Perkins. The faster she moved, the louder Meaghan seemed to get.

"And you call yourself a first lady. Please, you are pathetic, a hypocrite. Skanks like you are the very ones that give Christian folks a bad name. You're nothing but a ghetto chick, straight from the hood. Why don't you crawl back into the hole you came up from?"

Audrey sat in the grocery cart trying to open some of the food packages. She seemed unmindful of what was going on around her.

Meaghan stayed on Detria's heels. "I hope you don't think Skip is just going to accept what you say. He may want a baby, but like I told him, that baby could easily belong to some other dude you've slept with. God knows you've probably been on more wieners than Heinz ketchup."

Detria wanted to turn around and slap the taste out of Meaghan's mouth. It took everything in her not to do it. She could not afford to be out in public making a spectacle of herself. There were enough people already gawking at them and listening to Meaghan's tirade. All Detria wanted to do was pay for her items and get out of the store and away from Meaghan as fast as she could.

While Detria hurriedly walked to the front of the grocery store with a basket full of groceries, Meaghan continued her rant. She went to the express lane, paid for her items while Meaghan posted on the other side, near the door, waiting on Detria.

"Look, I'm warning you, Meaghan. If you don't get up out of my face, I'm going to..."

"You're going to what? I tell you what you're going to do. Nothing, because you know I'm telling the truth."

"Get outta my face," Detria yelled this time when Meaghan followed her and Audrey out to her car.

One expletive after another exploded from Meaghan's mouth. She called Detria everything but a child of God, totally dismissing the fact that the woman had her daughter with her.

Detria hurriedly put the last of the groceries in the car, got Audrey out of the cart, put her in her car seat, then turned toward Meaghan one final time before she got inside the car.

Underneath her breath, and looking around the parking lot Detria told her, "You're just jealous that Skip doesn't want you. If he did, don't you think he would have committed to you by now, Meaghan? You're nothing to him. He loves me. I have his child," Detria pointed at herself, "not you. Don't fool yourself, you will never ever be me, and don't you forget it."

Detria opened the door and hurriedly got inside her car. "Women like you kill me. You out here making a total fool of yourself over a man who doesn't care a thing about you." Detria cracked a smile. "And as far as my baby's daddy goes, that's none of your business. But, baby, at the end of the day, I will tell you this, Skip is going to take care of his, and the only way he'll be in your bed is if I give him up. Then you can have my sloppy seconds."

Detria started the car, put it in gear, and sped off, leaving Meaghan standing in the parking lot spewing another round of cuss words.

"Witch," Detria said as she sped down the street. She didn't realize until now that Skip had still been messing around with Meaghan, of all people. Here she was thinking that she was the only one rocking his world but to hear Meaghan talking, Skip had to have been talking to her because Meaghan was saying stuff that only Detria and Skip had talked about. This infuriated Detria. The nerve of Meaghan to put in Skip's head that Elijah was not his son. She may have cheated on Stiles, but she knew who her baby daddy was and it was Skip Madison.

Detria sat at the intersection waiting on the light to change. She reached over on the passenger's seat and started fumbling inside her purse for her cell phone so she could call Skip and tell him that he needed to put his little side chick, Meaghan, in check. She found the phone and started pressing the keys to unlock it but then Audrey started crying.

The light changed and the car horn behind her blew for her to go.

"Look, don't start all that unnecessary crying," she yelled at the little girl as she drove into the intersection. "I cannot deal with your hollering tail today. Now shut yo' mouth before I give you something to cry about!"

The look on Detria's face reflected the horror unfolding in front of her eyes. A horror that she instantly knew she could not avoid.

"OH, GOD, NOOOOO!"

40

"Sometimes moving on with the rest of your life
starts with goodbye." Unknown

Stiles lay in the full size bed at Wallace Dodson's tri-level home. He was grateful for friends like Wallace that God had strategically placed in his life over the years. When he made the decision to go to Houston, Wallace was the first person that came to mind for Stiles to contact. He encouraged Stiles to stay with him and his family for as long as he needed because he had plenty of space.

"Lord," Stiles prayed. "I need your guidance. Am I doing the right thing by cutting ties with Detria? You know my heart. You know that I want to do your will. I don't want to get divorced again, but, Lord, I would be lying if I tell you that I can look past my wife's infidelity. So, please, help me, Father. Show me where to go and what to do. Show me if it is your will that I leave the church I've come to love and the family I thought I would have forever."

Stiles turned over in the bed, resting both hands behind his head and on top of the fluffy, soft down pillow. He continued to have one on one time with the God he wanted to serve for the rest of his life. Suddenly, he felt deep anguish in his spirit and an unrest overtook him almost as soon as he finished his petition.

His cell phone rang, momentarily distracting him. He ignored it. It started ringing again. Stiles sighed heavily, picked up the phone from next to him on the bed, and then looked at it. It was Leo.

What's up, Leo? How's it going?"

"You need to get back to Memphis right away." Leo's voice conveyed an unsettling urgency that immediately caused Stiles to partially sit up in the comfortable bed, propping his body on one elbow.

"What is it? What's wrong, man?"

"Man, I don't know how to tell you this."

Stiles got up and stood to his feet. "Tell me what? Is Pastor all right?" His mounting tension escalated as he rubbed his head back and forth.

Knock. Knock.

Stiles looked toward the door.

"Stiles, it's Wallace. Open up." Wallace sounded wild too, just like Leo. What was going on? Had Pastor had another stroke? Was he dead?"

Stiles hurried to the door, opened it, and Wallace bolted in.

"Is that Deacon Jones on the phone?" he immediately asked.

Stiles nodded and kept talking to Leo. "Look, Leo, tell me what's going on? Is it my father?"

"Naw, Pastor is good. It's Detria. She's been in a pretty bad accident. You need to get home, man. Your flight arrangements are already made. Your plane is leaving at three. It's a nonstop flight, so you'll have only an hour and a half flying time. One of the deacons will be waiting on you at the airport. We're already at the hospital, and we aren't going anywhere, so Detria and her family are not alone."

"How is she?"

Leo was silent on the other end of the phone.

"Did you hear me? How is she?" Stiles asked again.

"She's in surgery."

"Where is my daughter?"

"Don't worry about all that right now, man. We got this. You just get here," Leo answered, avoiding a direct answer to Stiles' question. There was no way he was going to tell him over the phone that Audrey had been in the car with Detria.

Stiles hung up the phone. Pushing past Wallace, he grabbed his suitcase and threw in the few clothes that he'd unpacked. It took him less than ten minutes.

"Let's go," Stiles practically ordered Wallace.

Wallace hurriedly locked the door behind him as Stiles bolted down the steps ahead.

On the way to the airport, Stiles called Leo again to get as much detail about the accident as possible. All Leo was able to tell him was that an eighteen-wheeler rear-ended Detria while she was stopped at an intersection not far from their house. Detria had no time to react or get out of the truck's path.

"God is able," Wallace told Stiles after he hung up from talking to Leo. "Keep the faith. Everything is going to be all right."

"Yeah, it is. You know, man, I had just been praying, asking God for His guidance, then this. I don't know how to explain it, it was like a sense of dread came over me. Then the phone rings and it's Leo telling me Detria's been hurt. Here I was talking about divorce and now this. Is this some kind of sign? Am I supposed to stay with her? What?"

"Look, man, this is not the time to be thinking about whether you should divorce your wife or not. This is not some sign. Concentrate on getting back to Memphis and being by her side. Let tomorrow take care of itself."

They arrived at the airport and Wallace prayed with Stiles before he got out of the car. "Keep me posted, man. And, hey," Wallace said as Stiles started to walk toward the entrance of the airport, "I'm praying."

Stiles stopped, turned back, and looked at his friend. "Thanks, Wallace. I appreciate it, man. I really do."

Wallace and Stiles hugged and Stiles took off running inside the busy terminal.

The impact of the tractor-trailer forced Detria into the dash of the car, pinning her body between the front and back seats, crushing almost every bone in her legs and one of her arms. A chest tube was inserted into the space around her lungs to help drain the air and allow the lung to re-expand.

Detria was taken to the Regional Medical Center Trauma Unit and Audrey was transported by medevac to Methodist Le Bonheur Children's Hospital. The Mackey's remained at the hospital with Detria, while The McCoy's, Brooke, and Leo's wife went to Le Bonheur.

Stiles' flight arrived on time. Just like Leo told him, one of the newer deacons from the church was there to take him to the hospital. Stiles questioned him, but the man told him he didn't know the extent of Detria's injuries, so he couldn't be of any help.

When he arrived at the hospital, Leo met him downstairs in the Trauma Unit waiting area.

"How is she?" Stiles asked Leo.

"They just brought her out of surgery a few minutes ago. She's in Recovery. Come on, I'll take you to the Critical Care Waiting Room. You can talk to the receptionist up there. She'll make sure the doctor knows you're here. Brother and Sister Mackey are up there and some of the church members too."

"Thanks, Leo."

"Man, you know I got your back."

"Hello," Brother Mackey said when Stiles approached his in-laws in the waiting room. If Brother Mackey had any lingering animosity toward Stiles, it didn't show. Only a sadness was heard in his eyes and worry was evident on his wrinkling face.

Stiles kissed Mrs. Mackey on the cheek and several other women from Holy Rock.

One of the trustees approached Stiles and hugged him. "We're praying for y'all, Pastor Graham," the trustee told him.

"Thank you, Brother. I stopped and talked to the receptionist. She told me the doctor should be calling soon to let us know how Detria's doing," Stiles told the small crowd gathered in the waiting room.

"Yes, that's what they told us too," Mrs. Mackey responded. "They also said that she made it through the surgery okay."

"Praise God," one of the church members said.

"Now, if I can just find out how my precious grandbaby is doing," Mrs. Mackey cried. "I'm worried about her. Brooke still hasn't called and told us anything."

"My baby was in the car?" Stiles turned and looked angrily at Leo who was standing behind him. "Why didn't you tell me my little girl was in the car, Leo?" he yelled.

"I didn't want to make you anymore upset than you already were. I wanted to wait until you made it to Memphis."

"How is my daughter?" he asked, looking from one person to another. "And where is she?"

"She's at Le Bonheur. The McCoy's, Detria's sister, and Cynthia are over there," Leo explained.

Stiles pulled his cell phone out of its case and dialed Brooke. No answer. Next, he called Hezekiah.

"Hello, Pastor McCoy. How is my baby?" Stiles was highly agitated.

"Pastor." Hezekiah's voice sounded weak and tired. "Are you back in Memphis?"

"Yes, I'm at The Med waiting to get word about Detria. They say she's in recovery. Tell me; how is Audrey?"

"I think you should get over here, Pastor," is all Hezekiah said.

Stiles hung up the phone abruptly. He looked at Leo. "Take me to my daughter. Poppa Mackey, I have to get to my daughter. Please call me as soon as you hear about Detria."

"What did Pastor McCoy say?" Brother Mackey asked. His face was lined with worry, and his eyes were red with bags forming underneath them like he hadn't slept in days.

"Only that I need to get over there."

"Lord, have mercy," Mother Mackey immediately started crying out, and then she tried calling Brooke again. There was still no answer. "I'm going with you," she insisted.

"Now, baby, Brooke is already there. Why don't you stay with me? Audrey is going to be fine."

"Look, he's right, Mother Mackey. I'll call you as soon as I get over there and find out what's going on. I promise." Stiles leaned over and kissed her tear stained cheek again.

"Please call me. Brooke won't answer her phone, and I need to know how my grandbaby is."

"Yes, ma'am. I will."

"You ready?" asked Leo.

"Yeah, I'm ready. Let's go."

Detria's doctor called for her family minutes after Stiles left.

"How is our little girl, Doctor?" Mr. Mackey asked.

The doctor looked at Mr. Mackey and then briefly looked at the other people in the room that he assumed to be Detria's family. "Your daughter sustained serious injuries. She's in critical condition. Her right arm was almost severed, but the good news is that we were able to save it from amputation. However, because of the extensive nerve damage, it's unlikely she'll ever be able to use it again. As for her other injuries, she sustained fractures to her pelvis and both of her legs. We had to place pins in both knees and another pin in her left ankle. Her right foot is fractured too." The doctor tilted his head slightly then straightened it. "As far as we can tell, she isn't paralyzed."

"Oh, Lord!" Mrs. Mackey stifled her own cries by covering her mouth with her hand. "Lord, please, Lord, take care of my child." Several of the church members gathered around her to comfort her. Mr. Mackey draped his left arm around his wife's shoulders.

"She is heavily sedated so when you do see her, try not to be alarmed if she doesn't respond. We want to make her as comfortable as possible because being fully awake, the pain would be unbearable."

"She *is* going to be able to walk when she comes out of this, isn't she?" Mrs. Mackey stepped forward, slightly closer to the doctor like she had to make sure she heard what he was about to say.

The doctor continued. "She's going to require extensive therapy, and even then she'll more than likely be wheelchair bound for months, maybe longer. I can't say."

Hearing the doctor's report, Mrs. Mackey staggered and almost fell down. Mr. Mackey led her over to the waiting room sofa. He carefully sat her down and wrapped his arm around her shoulder to console her. Several of the church members walked over to comfort both of them.

Mrs. Mackey looked up at the doctor, gasped again, then held her heart before leaning back over in her husband's arms and wailing.

Barely visible, tears flowed along the crevices of Mr. Mackey's light brown skin before dripping on his midnight blue oxford shirt.

41

"Some of us think holding on makes us strong; but sometimes it is letting go." Xavier Hesse

"Are you going to be here in time for us to go get something to eat?" Xavier looked down at his growling stomach. "There's nothing in the refrigerator worth eating," he complained.

"Honey, there's plenty of food in the fridge and some frozen fruit in the freezer. Oh, and there's almond milk in there too. Why don't you make one of those delicious smoothies you like? Umm," Fancy hummed into the phone, hoping to calm her unhappy son down a little until she and Hezekiah could make it home.

"A smoothie? It's not going to fill me up. You do know that don't you, Mom?"

"Yes, sweetheart. I know that. What I'll do is I'll call you when we're leaving the hospital. If you want us to stop and pick you up something on the way home, then we can do that."

"See, that's another thing. Why won't you let me drive? I have my learner's permit and in a few months, I can get my driver's license. If I was at home, Grandpa and Grandma would be letting me drive them around all over the place."

Fancy was growing frustrated by Xavier's complaints.

"Well, you're not in Chicago, Xavier. You're in Memphis with your parents. As far as we're concerned, you *are* at home. And you won't be driving anywhere unless one of us is in the car with you. And really, Xavier, now is not the time for this conversation."

"Still, I'm just saying. It's boring here."

She whispered into the phone as she stepped out of the waiting room and into the hospital hallway. "I told you the pastor's wife and his little girl were in a serious accident. So, please try to be a little more patient with me and your father." She waited on a response but there was none. "Xavier, do you hear me?"

"Yes. Bye, Mom," he answered with a mouthful of attitude.

"Good Bye, Son. I love you."

The phone went silent. Fancy remained in the hallway until she saw two doctors walk past her and into the private intensive care room where Audrey was.

Right away, she walked in behind them, eager to hear what they had to say. The poor child was lying in the bed, unconscious. Tubes and machines surrounded her like a shroud. The rise and fall of her chest was prominent as the breathing machine pumped life into her little body.

Stiles stood next to the bed holding her hand. It was the most difficult thing he'd ever had to do in his life. Seeing his little girl lying unconscious in a hospital bed, her face and body swollen beyond recognition, was heart wrenching. This was his little girl, and he couldn't help her.

"Please Father, heal my child. In your Word you said not to be afraid. You said if I just believe. Well, I'm believing, Father God, believing for healing for my Audrey," he cried while stroking the little girl's natural curly locks of coal black hair.

Hezekiah sat on the chair across from her bed, head bowed, and hands clasped as he silently petitioned for God's healing grace.

Both doctors came in the room and positioned themselves at Audrey's bed, one on each side.

"How is she?" Stiles asked, as his eyes flitted from one doctor to the next, revealing his worry and fear.

"Are you her father?" the African doctor asked in broken English.

"Yes, I'm her father. Tell me what's going on with my baby? When is she going to wake up?"

"Your daughter sustained a massive head injury and there's swelling on the brain. She has collapsed lungs, both of her arms are fractured, her left hip and her pelvis are fractured too. She has some internal bleeding, which we think is coming from a ruptured spleen."

The Caucasian doctor standing on the right of Audrey's bed spoke next. "She is on this ventilator, which is breathing for her. I'm sorry to have to tell you that your little girl has irreversible cessation of all functions of the entire brain, including the brainstem."

"Talk to me in layman's terms, Doctor. Tell me when my little girl is going to wake up. Tell me that she's going to be okay."

Brooke stood next to Stiles, her eyes overflowing with tears. She grabbed hold of her brother-in-law's trembling hand.

"I don't know if you're a praying man, but if you are, then now is the time to start praying," the doctor said.

The African doctor interjected. He spoke slowly, void of emotions, and had no bedside manners whatsoever. Listening to him, Brooke could only assume that he could not have had kids because then he would understand how difficult it was for a parent to hear devastating news about their child.

"Your little girl has no brain function. We are going to test her brain function again, but I don't expect any change. The ventilator is only prolonging the dying process by supplying oxygen, but it's not going to improve her condition."

Hezekiah got up and walked up to Stiles, planting himself next to Brooke. Fancy came up and stood next to her husband.

Looking from the father to the woman standing next to him, the Caucasian doctor reluctantly gave Stiles the news he knew they did not want to hear. "I'm sorry to tell you this, but she's clinically brain dead." This was one of those times when he hated his profession. He was about the business of saving lives, but when he had to tell family members and loved ones that their loved one was not going to survive, it hurt him to the core every time.

"You'll have to make a decision when to take her off the ventilator. But to be honest, she can expire before you even make that decision."

The doctor's voice unveiled a sense of knowing. It was if he could feel and understand what must have been going on in Stiles' already grief stricken mind. He looked at the other loved ones of the little girl, and it made him think about his two little kids at home. What would he do if one of them were lying in this hospital bed dying? Would his faith sustain him? Would his prayers to God give him the strength he would need to endure? He wasn't sure and he didn't want to find out, not ever.

Leo and Cynthia were stationed close to the door. He wrapped his arm around her shoulder, but other than that, he didn't move. It was like a magnet was holding him in place. The sadness he felt for his friend was overwhelming. He thought about his own kid and the thought of something like this happening was almost too much for him to take in. He held back his tears and told himself that he had to remain strong for Stiles.

Cynthia wiped the tears from her face with the back of her hand as she cried silently on Leo's shoulder.

The amount of grief, hurt and pain in the room was way too much for either of the doctors to take. They extended their sorrow before slowly exiting the room, leaving Stiles battered, bereft and broken.

42

"When the heart is burdened with grief, nothing
looks bright." Simran Khurana

Detria's wheelchair was stationed at the end of the church pew.
She had been out of the hospital less than twenty-four hours. Both
legs were encased in casts, and strapped together with black
neoprene belts. Her right arm was tucked against her chest in a sling.
She wept uncontrollably. She blamed herself for her little girl's death.
If only she had been more watchful, more careful, then maybe she
could have somehow gotten out of the path of the tractor-trailer. If
only she hadn't gone to the store. If only she hadn't been fussing at
Audrey. If only, if only, if only.

It didn't matter that the doctor's told her she would never have
use of her right arm again. It didn't matter that she could be
wheelchair bound for months. It didn't matter that her marriage had
fallen apart. Nothing mattered anymore, not even her baby boy who
was still in the hospital fighting for his life. This was her payback. This
was her lot in life, and she was going to have to live with her actions
and decisions for the rest of her life. It served her right. She felt like
this was God's way of paying her back for all the pain and hurt she'd
brought on her husband, her family, and her little girl.

Stiles sat next to Detria on the front row directly in front of
Audrey's tiny pink and white casket. He was unable to console her;
his own grief would not allow him to. Pain attached itself around his
heart like a leach, sucking the very life out of him. His eyes were
swollen from the tears that had continued to pour since Audrey took
her last breath one week ago.

Pastor and Josie, Francesca and her husband, Tim, along with
the Mackey family and other close family members, occupied the first
two rows.

Francesca hadn't seen or talked to her brother in months. When
Tim told her that Stiles had called the church they attended and
asked someone to get in touch with her, she was initially angry. She
had changed her phone number and the farthest thing from her mind

was reconciling with her family. Like Tim had told her, it was her duty to forgive her family for the hurt they'd caused in her life, and Francesca felt she had done just that. She had made peace with the way things were and she was actually happy. Many people with HIV/AIDS were living longer and some were even enjoying healthy lives. Francesca was one of them. She took good care of herself by trying to stay healthy, exercising and choosing to make better food choices.

When she got the news about her niece, Francesca felt awful. She may not have had a relationship with her niece, but it still caused a deep pain for Francesca. As badly as she wanted her and Tim to have children, the thought of parents having kids and then losing them so tragically weighed heavily on Francesca's heart. This was not the time for her to forsake her family. She had to be at the funeral for her brother, and her one and only niece. She was surprised to learn that Detria had given birth to a second child, but that wasn't Francesca's concern right now. She was at Holy Rock for one reason, and one reason only, to pay her last respects to the little girl lying in the casket looking like she was sleeping.

The church was packed. Many people had to be seated in the overflow room and watch the funeral services from a closed circuit television. Weeping and moaning could be heard throughout the sanctuary as people walked to the casket to view the little girl's body one last time.

As the service proceeded, Hezekiah rendered the eulogy. "There is nothing more heartbreaking than the death of a child. Little Audrey Graham may only have been two years old, but she lived a beautiful, happy life. She brought a smile and joy to Pastor Stiles and First Lady Detria. She was spoiled rotten," Hezekiah smiled, "by her grandparents." He looked directly toward the Mackey family. "I know we don't understand, and we can't see what He sees, but God really is in control. Some of you may ask, Lord why did this have to happen to an innocent little child? Why did you call her home at such a tender age?" Hezekiah didn't understand himself, but it was his duty, his responsibility, and his calling as a man of God to give the family something to hold on to.

Hezekiah looked out at the mass of people, then at Stiles and Detria. "Pastor...First Lady. We love you. Holy Rock is here for you during this difficult journey you are forced to embark upon. This journey through grief is not going to be easy. It's going to take time. It's going to take much prayer..."

Hezekiah continued delivering a heartfelt eulogy as he fought back his own tears.

Skip was seated on one of the pews toward the back of the sanctuary, with Meaghan sitting next to him. She hadn't told Skip about the encounter she'd had with Detria prior to the accident because she felt there was no need to. She had told Detria exactly how she felt and she didn't regret it. She did, however, feel bad that the little girl had died, but it wasn't her fault. If it was anybody's fault, it was Detria's. Meaghan thought about it. *Karma ain't nothing nice, nothing nice at all.*

Like they did almost every night, together Rena and Robert tucked their children into bed. "I love you," she told each of them as did Robert, followed by a kiss goodnight.

Rena hid the hurt as best she could. Her reason being, Robert had accused her of dwelling on her past far too much. She resented his accusation. Didn't he realize that a child had lost her life? When her mother told her about Audrey's death, Rena thought about how blessed she was to have not one, not two, but four children. Though Robert's two kids weren't biologically hers, they were hers since she had legally adopted them. The twins she and Robert had together were an added source of joy, and a blessing. She recalled how frightened she was about giving birth knowing that she had an incurable STD, but God had been faithful. She had a safe delivery and gave birth to two healthy babies. So to hear that Stiles and Detria had lost their only daughter sent Rena into somewhat of a mini-depression. She cried on and off for days. She wanted to go to Memphis to the funeral, but Robert had been totally against it.

"Rena, when are you going to move forward? I mean, I feel terrible that your ex," he emphasized, "lost his little girl. My God, that's awful. I don't know what I would do if we lost one of our children, but baby, going to Memphis? The man is no longer a part of your life. I'm your life," he pointed at his chest. "I'm your man. I'm your husband. And you are my wife, the mother of our children. I wish you could just let go of your past."

Rena listened but it was difficult for her to push her frustration under the rug and pretend like she wasn't bothered about what Robert was saying.

"I know that, Robert, but this man has lost his little girl."

"Okay, but what can you do if you go to Memphis, Rena? What?" Robert raised his hands like he was catching the 'spirit'.

Rena's eyes loomed open like suddenly she'd been enlightened, when actually she was slowly becoming angrier and angrier. "I know, he has a wife, so what are you saying? Are you jealous?"

"Jealous? Why would I be jealous? Would it be because every time my wife hears something unpleasant about her EX, she wants to run off to Memphis? Do you think that's what it could be?"

"I can't believe you could be so condescending. You know darn well it's not like that."

"Okay, then tell me what it is then, because obviously I'm missing something. I mean, what are you going to accomplish by going to Memphis?"

"Pay my respect. That's what," she yelled at Robert, then like a raging tornado, she whipped around and took two steps before she turned back around. She was poised to say something else, but he beat her to it.

"In case you forgot, let me remind you. He has a wife, Rena, and it's not you anymore!" Robert stood in the hallway, biting down on his lip and shaking his head.

Rena lashed out at him, the palm of her right hand, inches short of landing on his cheek. Robert intersected the blow by grabbing hold of her wrist.

"So this is what it's come down to? Huh? You ready to fight me over the next dude?" Robert roughly released her arm as a deep lined wrinkle appeared on his forehead. This time he was the one to walk off. He was getting tired of competing with her past. Something was going to have to change, and change fast, or he didn't know how bright their future would continue to glow.

43

"Sometimes you have to start over to have a happy ending."
Sonya Parker

Hezekiah reveled in the favor God was showing over his life. Having another chance to make things right was something he'd wanted for a very long time. He had made far more than their share of illegal choices. They sat across from their son at the restaurant. Xavier wolfed down, chomp by chomp, a gourmet double bacon, double turkey patty burger like he hadn't eaten in ages.

"Slow down, Xavier," his mother told him. "That food is not going anywhere." She put a forkful of her garden salad in her mouth then eyed her husband who had his phone in hand and was texting.

"Hezekiah, this is supposed to be family time. Will you get off that phone?"

"Okay, I'm sorry, babe. Deacon Jones just texted me. He wanted to know if I've heard from Pastor Graham today. I was just texting him back telling him that I hadn't."

"Humph, you need to tell Deacon Jones that you're not Pastor Graham's babysitter."

Xavier stopped eating long enough to look up at his parents and then he started laughing. "Yeah, tell him, Mom. That's what I'm talking about."

"Boy, you better shut yo' mouth or you won't be able to do nothing but gum your food after I put my fist through it." Hezekiah glared at his son, who with the quickness, stopped laughing and then picked up a steak fry and popped it in his mouth.

One thing Hezekiah detested was a disrespectful child. His son, though he hated to admit it, reminded Hezekiah of how he was when he was growing up. He used to have a smart mouth that kept him in trouble most of his young life. And still, today, Hezekiah had to tame his tongue so he wouldn't say something he would regret later. It had been two weeks since he had officially taken the helm as interim senior pastor of Holy Rock. He wasn't about to do anything to mess that up. Keeping his tongue and his past in check was something he was determined to do. He couldn't blow this once in a lifetime opportunity. Finally, no more financial woes for him and Fancy. No more dodging creditors and no more being tempted to rob Peter to pay Paul. Those days were over and done with.

"We need to get home so you can finish working on your sermon for Sunday."

"I think I just about have it together. I've been doing a lot of studying and practicing at church." Hezekiah poked the grilled tilapia with his fork, dipped it into the side of hot sauce, and then popped the flavorful fish into his mouth.

"I'm so proud of you." Fancy leaned over and kissed her husband on his cheek.

"When can I go back home? Memphis sucks." Xavier frowned, poked out his lips, and leaned back in his chair. "I miss Chicago. I miss my friends, and I miss Grandma and Grandpa. Memphis is so boring. There's nothing to do."

Fancy and Hezekiah looked at Xavier like they had no idea he was displeased.

"Things are not going to change, Son, so you might as well get used to them. You're going to stay in Memphis with us, and we're working on getting your brother transferred to a youth facility as close to Memphis as possible."

"What? Why do I have to stay? I hate this city. Anyway, why should I have to move here just because you and Ma have to hide from your past? You're making what you did my fault. Changing your names, all that stuff is stupid." Xavier stuck out his lip and rolled his eyes.

Hezekiah shook his head, bit on his bottom lip, and almost jumped up from his seat.

Fancy pulled on his suit coat, holding him down.

"First of all, I don't have to explain a thing to you. I am your father. You are my son. You do as I say." Hezekiah's fury was becoming evident as his voice raised and his hand curled into a fist. "As far as me and your mother's past, don't you ever in life say another word about me or your mother, or so help me—"

Fancy broke up the mounting tension between the two. "Calm down, Hezekiah. Xavier, settle your behind down too. Your smart mouth is one of the reasons you need to be here with us because you will not talk to us the way you talk to your grandparents. We are not going to tolerate it. Until you're out of high school and on your own, you will abide by our rules." Fancy was usually low key, and soft spoken but when it came to anyone, including her children, showing disrespect toward Hezekiah, she became a fierce 'stand by your man' woman.

Xavier rolled his eyes, then took a swallow of his soda.

"Do you understand me, young man?"

"Yes, ma'am." His baritone voice was almost inaudible.

The remainder of their family time at the restaurant was spent primarily in silence until Hezekiah's phone started ringing.

Fancy upturned her polished lips. She was happy for her husband and beside herself since she was now the first lady of Holy Rock, albeit was temporary. What she wasn't pleased with was the barrage of phone calls coming from the deacons, the trustees, and members without regard to the time of day or night. Her new role was going to take some getting used to, but as she sat at the table finishing her meal, she smiled. *Hezekiah McCoy, Senior Pastor of Holy Rock Church and none other than First Lady Fancy McCoy.* She was ready for the task at hand. Holy Rock was about to see what a real first lady was all about.

"Give me about an hour," Hezekiah said to whoever was on the other end of the phone. He placed the phone on the table and then called the server over and asked for the check. "You about ready?" he asked Fancy.

"Yeah. I'm finished. Who was that on the phone?"

"Sister Gloria."

"What did she want?"

"One of our senior members had a heart attack and is in intensive care. I'm going to drop you and Xavier off at home, then I'm going to the hospital to pray for him."

Fancy smiled.

"Why are you smiling?" questioned Hezekiah.

"Because I'm so happy for you, for us, Hezekiah." She looked over at Xavier who had his ear buds in his ear, like he was totally unaware of his parents and what they were talking about. "God has really given us a second chance," she whispered. "And we can't blow it, Hezekiah. Not this time. We have to keep our noses clean."

"We will, sweetheart. Don't you worry about a thing."

44

"For some moments in life there are no words." David Seltzer

Detria sat in front of the picture window in the family room. Time seemed to have stopped for her, yet it had been three and a half months since the accident, since she last walked, since she last smiled, since she brought one child into the world only to lose the other. The grief and feeling of loss was overpowering. A year before she became pregnant with Audrey, Detria had a miscarriage. After she had the miscarriage, the emotional pain was intense, but her loss back then was nothing compared to the loss she felt over Audrey's death. Each day she felt like she lost a little bit more of life.

Silent tears indented her cheeks, running down like a lake, drops landing on her melon green blouse. Elijah was sleeping soundly in the room in his pack and play. He had been home for just a few days.

"Mrs. Graham, your lunch is ready," Priscilla, the live in caregiver, told her, entering the room with a tray of food. She sat the tray on the TV stand in front of Detria.

Detria remained focused on the light rain cascading down from the sky. Tiny slices kissed the picture window.

"I'm not hungry."

"You have to eat," Priscilla insisted in a heavy New England accent. "I made one of your favorites; freshly made cream of broccoli soup and garlic toast."

"Thank you, but I don't have an appetite."

"Mrs. Graham, you have to eat if you want to get stronger. You want to be able to walk again one day, and take care of little Elijah, don't you?" Priscilla looked over her shoulder in the pack and play, at the sleeping baby. "He is such a beautiful little boy."

The little boy was nothing short of a miracle. After struggling for his life since he entered the world, he had beaten the odds. His doctors released him with a clean bill of health, and told Detria he should grow up without having any significant medical problems.

Priscilla prayed every day for Detria to get better. She was the same woman who had helped take care of Detria's mother last year when she had a bad lupus flare up. She did such a good job that she was the first person the Mackey's thought about when Detria was discharged from the hospital. The first month following the accident, Detria lived with her parents. After that, she was determined to go home, and she did, but the doctor told her that it was not good for her to live alone. Plus, if she planned on having Elijah with her, she had no choice but to have a live-in caregiver.

Priscilla was patient and showed love and compassion toward Detria. She took time to encourage her and to love on Elijah. She tried her best to convince Detria that she could care for her little boy regardless of being unable to walk, and having the use of only one arm.

The truth was, Detria couldn't think about taking care of Elijah. If she couldn't be a good mother to Audrey, what made people think she could be a good mother to Elijah? And how could she be his mother when she was bound to a freaking wheelchair and burdened with feelings of guilt over her daughter's death? Perhaps, if she had been a more patient, a more loving mother, maybe Audrey would still be alive. The last words her daughter heard from her were angry words, chastising her for crying so much. Now she would give anything to hear her daughter's cry. She felt hopeless and lost. Other than going to her scheduled doctors' appointments, Detria refused to go outside the house.

Her legs remained lifeless despite the intense physical therapy she received five days a week, followed by two days of at-home occupational therapy. Her arm was nothing more than a noodle. There were times Detria felt like it was all useless to live.

The occupational therapist was supposed to train her how to use assistive equipment to increase her independence. How many ways did they actually think she could maneuver a power chair? She found it quite humiliating instead of helpful. It was tough learning how to use her left arm and she easily became frustrated and angry.

"I'm going to leave your food here. Please try to eat. I will be back shortly to check on you and the baby."

Detria hugged herself as a shiver of cold ran up and down her spine. She continued staring outside. When she saw the familiar car pulling into the driveway, her heartbeat quickened.

"Priscilla," she called out. "Priscilla, hurry."

"What is it?" Priscilla ran into the family room. "What's wrong?"

"I don't want to see him," Detria cried.

Before Priscilla replied, the doorbell chimed. She looked toward the foyer. "Who is it?"

"Elijah's father."

Priscilla knew exactly who Skip was. She had heard the rumors about Detria's infidelity. But Priscilla wasn't one to judge. She'd done enough dirt in her life to last two life times, so she did her best to remain neutral rather than condemning when it came to people and the choices they made in life.

The doorbell chimed again, followed by a hard knock.

"What do you want me to tell him?" Priscilla wiped her hands on her apron.

"I don't know. I tell you what, don't answer the door."

"Don't answer it? Are you sure?"

"Yes," Detria said, her face distorted with anger. "Take Elijah upstairs. I'm going to the Study. He'll probably leave in a minute, just be quiet and do not go near that door."

Skip stood outside the door in his black trench coat, knocking on the door and ringing the doorbell. He had been calling and texting Detria ever since her little girl died, but Detria refused to answer him. He wanted to see his son, and not only that, he had an over the counter DNA test kit with him. It was time he found out once and for all if Elijah was his or not.

The one opportunity that he did have to talk to Detria was when she was still in the hospital. He went to see her and told her he wanted to have a paternity test done on the boy; she went ballistic. Skip had to admit to himself that it hadn't been exactly a good time to hit her with something like that, seeing that Elijah wasn't doing too well at the time and her daughter was on life support.

The day it all went down, Skip had gone to NICU to see Elijah, but was told by the nurse in charge that only the parents of the baby were allowed to see him. That infuriated him. He went straight to

Detria's hospital room and insisted that she have a paternity test done.

"I'm not going to do it. I don't want you in my son's life. I want to be left alone, and I want you to forget that you ever met me."

"Are you crazy? Do you actually think I'm just going to walk out of this hospital when I know I have a son? If you're so sure that he isn't mine, then you shouldn't have a problem giving me a paternity test."

"I told you, no. As far as the court is concerned, he is not your child," she screamed. "Now leave me alone, Skip."

"What are you talking about?" This broad was out of her freaking mind. What did she mean by as far as the court was concerned?

"Stiles and I are still married."

"What does that have to do with me and the fact that I'm that boy's father?"

"It means that legally, Stiles is his father. His name is on Elijah's birth certificate, and that's how it's going to stay."

Skip laughed at her. "Do you honestly think that man is going to let his name stay on that birth certificate after learning that it's not his baby? Look, I'm sorry for everything that's happened to you. I really am, but I'm telling you, if the kid is mine, I will not let you deprive me of being a father to him."

"I need you to leave, Skip. I can't talk about this right now." Detria turned her head away from him. The sound of her crying bounced off the walls. She began weeping so loudly that a nurse came into the hospital room. Seeing that Detria was visibly upset, the nurse insisted that Skip leave.

"I'm leaving, but you can't run from this, Detria. I won't let you. One way or another, I'm going to find out for sure if he's my son, and I'm going to be in his life, like it or not."

"Get ouuut!" Detria screamed again.

Meaghan was right; he was going to get Elijah tested by any means necessary, and there was going to be nothing Detria could do about it.

45

"Her absence is like the sky, spread over everything." C.S. Lewis

Stiles laid sprawled out on his cheap used sofa. The townhome looked like transients had been living in it. Half-empty cups once filled with soda, and left over saucers and plates of spoiled food had taken the place of a once spotless abode. Combined with his malodorous body odor from not having bathed or groomed himself in days, the smell in the apartment was like rancid meat.

The flat screen on the wall flashed scene after scene of Audrey, Stiles and Detria. The video had clips from when they brought Audrey home from the hospital. She was the most beautiful baby Stiles had ever seen. Another clip was at her first birthday party, yet another one showed her being christened at Holy Rock.

Stiles stared at the ceiling like he was in a trance. The pangs of grief had him bound. He had been inside his townhouse ever since he saw his daughter being lowered in the ground. He refused to see anyone, including Pastor. His phone went unanswered and he avoided text messages from Hezekiah and Leo. Even Francesca tried to reach out to her brother, but he turned her away like she had done toward him many times before.

Nothing could soothe him. Nothing could make him feel better. If no one could bring his little girl back, there was no need to talk to them or see them.

He lashed out at God and for the first time since he answered his call into ministry, Stiles doubted his faith and questioned God.

Day after day, night after night, he wept. Scattered around the townhouse were broken pieces of glass, vases and a turned over chair. He hated his life. He didn't want to keep living if it meant living with the knowledge of what had happened to his baby girl.

He thought about Detria. She never wanted Audrey in the first place. She was always putting her off on Mother Brown or Brooke.

The day of the accident, what could have happened? The police said she was sitting at the light, a light that had changed to green, so what was she doing? What had her attention that she didn't see the tractor-trailer? Was she talking to her lover, or was she screaming and hollering at Audrey for something stupid, like she usually did?

Stiles rubbed his grimy, matted beard in a show of frustration and anger. This was her fault. Detria was nothing but bad news and she had allowed the worst thing that could happen to him, and to their family. Their daughter was dead and it happened on her watch. He would never forgive her.

He mustered up enough strength to get up and search for his cell phone, which he hadn't recalled seeing in days. He searched on the floor, in his pockets, and around the house, but he couldn't find it. Going back over to the sofa, he looked between the pillows. His fingers came in contact with the Samsung Galaxy Note. Pulling it out of the sofa, he looked at it; it was dead, meaning he had to go find his charger. It didn't take long for that because he usually kept an extra charger plugged in the wall in his bedroom.

After the phone charged up, Stiles scrolled through his Contacts until he got to the name of Mitchell "Mitch" Tachowsky, his divorce lawyer. He left a message on the lawyer's voicemail.

Stiles had lost track of time. He didn't know what time of day it was, nor did he know what day of the week. He gazed up at the video that was now showing him, Detria and Audrey at the zoo. Audrey was sitting on his shoulders, laughing and pointing at the polar bears. Tears formed quickly and streamed down his face.

He turned away and went back into his bedroom, got the remote off the night table and sat on the edge of his bed. He turned on the television. It was Sunday night, close to ten o'clock. No wonder no one answered at the lawyer's office.

"Humph, Sunday. How ironic is that? God," he looked up, "you never ever cease to amaze me. Of all days for me to get up – it has to be Sunday. Humph. Well, well, well, what are you trying to do to me now?" His words dripped with anger and sarcasm.

He turned on the flat screen in his bedroom and blindly channel surfed, not looking for any program in particular.

Stiles heard his cell phone ringing. It was still in the living room where he'd left it. He ignored it and remained seated on the bed. The phone stopped then started ringing again. He ignored it again, but it kept ringing.

Finally after the sixth or seventh time, he slowly got up and dragged himself to get it.

"Leave me alone!" he screamed as he walked to answer the ringing phone. "I should have let that phone stay dead."

"Hello," he yelled into the phone as soon as he answered it.

"Stiles?"

Stiles listened to the familiar voice, a voice he once longed to hear but now meant nothing to him.

"Whadda you want?" he asked Rena in a biting tone.

"Uh, I've been trying to reach you but your phone kept going to voicemail."

"So, it was you calling me back to back, huh? Can't you catch the hint, Rena? If someone keeps ignoring your calls, that's usually a sign that person doesn't want to talk." Stiles was short and his words were cruel.

"It wasn't me. This is my first time calling," she paused, "today, that is. How are you?" she asked, ignoring his bitter tone.

"How am I? Hah."

"Yes. I'm concerned about you. I know it's been a few months since Audrey, since Audrey passed." She spoke slowly and cautiously. "But like I said, I haven't been able to reach you. I wanted to tell you that I am so sorry. God knows my heart goes out to you."

Stiles paced the floor. "Is that right? Well that's just fine, but I don't need your sympathy, Rena."

"Stiles, please. I didn't call to upset you. I just wanted to tell you that you're in my prayers. Honest you are. And if there's anything I...anything Robert and I can do for you, please let me know."

"Look, you have your family. You have your children. If you call yourself showing me that your life is picture perfect, then you've succeeded, so when are you going to stop rubbing it in my face, Rena? When?"

"I'm not rubbing anything in your face. How could you think something like that?" Her voice sounded wounded and hurt by his remarks.

"My daughter is dead. She...is...dead. Don't you get it? Can you bring her back, Rena? Can you do that?"

"You know that I can't. If I could, Lord knows I would."

"In that case, you know what, there *is* something you can do for me."

"Of course, anything."

"Leave me the hell alone." Stiles pushed the button and ended the call. Going back to the leather sofa, he stretched out on it again, picked up the TV remote from off of the cluttered table in front of the sofa, and started watching the video again.

46

"It doesn't really matter whether you grip the arms of the dentist's chair or let your hands lie in your lap. The drill drills on." C.S. Lewis

"You're going to have to reevaluate your finances," Stiles lawyer explained. You're no longer getting the salary from Holy Rock. The good news is that your contract states you will continue to receive an income equivalent to 30% of the salary you were paid at the time of your departure, being that your father is the founder of the church."

Stiles was quiet. He didn't care if they didn't pay him a dime. Money was of no interest to him now. Money couldn't buy happiness. Money couldn't heal his marriage. Money couldn't bring Audrey back.

"Are you listening to me?" his lawyer asked.

"Yeah, sure. But I don't care about any of that. Tell me how long before my divorce is final?"

"If your wife doesn't protest, we should be able to settle everything in four to six months."

"Why so long? I don't want anything from her. She can have it all. The house, the car, all of it. Maybe that'll bring her happiness. That's all she ever wanted from me anyway; the lifestyle I could give her. Mitch," he said, "I want this over and done with."

"I understand, and believe me, I'm going to make this as painless as possible. Your wife should be receiving a substantial sum of money from the accident, so she will be well taken care of."

Stiles frowned. His fist curled and his jawline flickered. "All at the expense of my daughter's life."

"It wasn't your wife's fault. That tractor-trailer plowed into her."

"So you're on her side?"

"This has nothing to do with sides. It's the truth of what happened. The only reason I brought that up was because in the divorce papers we are stating that your wife can only remain in the house if she is able to financially maintain the mortgage and taxes."

"Like I said, I don't want anything, just my freedom."

"Of course. You know she still isn't able to walk."

"And, you told me that for what reason?"

"For no reason, just letting you know."

"Who told you that? Leo?"

"Yes. Speaking of Leo, he says you still won't answer his calls and he's been over here numerous times, but you refuse to answer the door. Stiles, my brother, this isn't healthy. It's been almost four months since—"

Stiles pounced up from the sofa. "Don't tell me how long it's been, Mitch. Don't you think I know how long my daughter's been dead?"

"I didn't mean it like—"

"Tell me, what did you mean then? My daughter has been dead for 109 days, 11 hours, 25 minutes, and," he looked at the artistic clock hanging on the wall, "fourteen seconds."

"All I'm saying is, I wish you would get out. Fall is approaching. The weather outside has been perfect. Why don't you go for a walk? When is the last time you visited your father?"

Stiles remained quiet and pensive, as if he was digesting Mitch's words.

"I bet he would love to see you. And church...I know how much you love the church. Have you thought about going to one of the services?"

"All I've thought about," Stiles finally said, "is the loss of my little girl. I can't think about my father, the church, money, nothing. I miss her, Mitch. I miss my little girl."

Stiles broke down and wept. His heavy sobs seemed like they made the walls of the townhome vibrate.

Mitch embraced his client. "Man, I'm sorry. I'm so sorry," is all Mitch could say.

The knock on the door gave Mitch a much-needed reprieve and he rushed to answer it. Surprisingly, Stiles didn't object.

Mitch opened the door to Leo and Hezekiah. "Come on in," Mitch said, with the sound of worry emanating from his voice tone.

"He needs you."

The two men walked into the townhome and followed the sounds of Stiles' sobbing. They both rushed to him and embraced him. Right away, Hezekiah started praying.

"Stiles, man, let it out," Leo told his friend. "It's all right, bro. Let it out."

"Father God," Hezekiah prayed. "Have mercy on my brother. You know the anguish he feels. You know how deep the hurt runs. You said you would be close to the brokenhearted, Father. You said you would rescue those whose spirits are crushed. Rescue my brother, Lord. Comfort him."

Hezekiah continued praying. Stiles' sobs began to subside and Leo led him over to the chair to sit down.

"Stiles," Mitch said when Stiles finally stopped weeping. "I have everything I need to get things moving forward. I'm going to leave now. I have another appointment, but I'll be in touch."

Stiles nodded.

"Take care, my friend." Mitch picked up his briefcase from off the table, nodded at Leo and Hezekiah, then left.

Brooke pulled up in Detria's driveway. She pushed the remote and drove her car inside. Before she could let the garage door down, a candy apple red Dodge Charger pulled in behind her.

She got out of her car and walked around to the passenger's side, opening the door for Detria, but keeping her eyes on the car.

Skip got out of his car. "I want to see my son," he said in a non-confronting voice.

"Is that Skip?" Detria asked her sister.

"Yes, and Detria, why don't you just let him see Elijah. He is his father."

"I don't want him to see my baby," she countered. "Let the garage door down, and get me and Elijah out of the car."

It was too late for that because Skip came up to the car. He opened the back door and peered in at the round-faced little boy.

"Why are you here? Can't you leave well enough alone?" Detria asked in a pleading voice. If she was angry, it didn't show, rather she sounded more like a frightened and wounded animal.

"I'm not here to start anything, Detria. I just want to see my boy." Skip unbuckled him from the car seat and picked him up. Holding him up like Mufusa held up his son in the Lion King, Skip studied the boy and pride spread across his face. Brooke stared in silence.

"Can I come in?" he asked. "I want to spend some time with him."

"I...why don't you come back tomorrow."

"Why? I'm here now? Come on, get out of the car. I won't stay long. Brooke?" He looked at Brooke like he hoped she would speak up for him. She did.

"Detria?" she looked at her sister. "Is it okay?"

Detria slowly nodded.

"Skip, give me a minute to get her chair out of the trunk and get her and Elijah inside. Okay?"

"I'll help you. What kind of chair is it?

"Her wheelchair," Brooke answered, eyeing him like he had asked a stupid question.

"You still can't walk?"

Detria didn't say one word in response.

Brooke proceeded to walk to the back of the car. She popped the trunk and started getting the lightweight chair out of the car.

"Let me help you," Skip said, like he was coming out of a diabetic shock.

"Give me my son," Detria said bitterly.

Skip walked around the front of the car and tried to put Elijah in his mother's waiting arms. He paused when he realized that Detria had no use of her right arm.

"Put him on this side," she ordered without looking at him.

Skip didn't protest. He did as he was told, then he helped Brooke remove the wheelchair, steering it over to Detria's door.

"Thanks. I've got it from here." Brooke gently removed Elijah from his mother's arms and passed him back to Skip, who smiled as soon as he took hold of his son again.

He took a couple of steps to get out of Brooke's way, giving her room to help Detria get in the wheelchair.

Skip was surprised to see how weak looking Detria was. She was never a large woman, but now she looked like skin and bones and he noticed that she couldn't move her legs at all. He watched as she used her upper body and Brooke to maneuver from the car to the wheelchair. Her arm just dangled. He wondered if this was permanent? If it was, then there was no way she could properly care for his son.

"So, is this why you wouldn't let me in or answer my calls and text messages?"

"What are you talking about?" Detria looked back over her shoulder as Brooke pushed the chair toward the door leading into the house.

"Is that wheelchair permanent? And your arm? You can't use it at all?"

"I don't believe my medical condition is any business of yours. Now, I've agreed to let you come in and spend some time with your son. Don't push me, Skip."

"I'm just asking. I had no idea. That's all." He thought about the DNA kit he had in his car. Today he was going to find a way to swab his son's mouth.

"I left my phone in the car. Let me go get it. I'll be right back," he said while Brooke pushed Detria all the way into the house. "It'll just take a quick second." He hastily walked to his car, holding and talking to Elijah along the way. Unlocking his car, he opened the glove compartment and removed the test kit. He quickly used one hand to open it and put the Identigene® components inside his pocket. He hurried into the house, feeling confident that today was his lucky day.

"You can take him in the family room. It's this way," Brooke told him as she walked ahead of Skip.

"Where is Detria?"

"Oh, she'll be back. She went to her room."

"How much longer is she going to be in a wheelchair?" He bounced a giggling Elijah up and down on his knee, but was anxious to hear Brooke's answer.

"We aren't sure. The doctors say it could be a few months, which it's already been, or it could be a year or more. Only God knows.

"And her arm?"

"She'll never be able to use her arm again. The nerves were completely destroyed in the accident."

Skip looked horrified.

"You didn't know?"

Skip shook his head. "No. She won't see me, and she ignores my calls. When I come over here, she won't let me in. I'm just glad I caught y'all today. All I want is to see my son, you know?"

"She's going through a lot. She's depressed and she's grieving. Not being able to use her arm, or walk, is added pressure. I'm praying that she will make it through this. But honestly, I'm worried about her."

Brooke didn't understand why she was pouring her feelings out to Skip, but at this point, it didn't matter. Everything she said was true, and maybe, just maybe Detria would allow Skip to step up and be a father to Elijah.

"Who? How is she taking care of Elijah?"

"She has her family and a full time live-in caregiver."

Elijah began to fuss.

"You're ready for your bottle? Huh, sweetie," Brooke crooned. "First, we need to get you changed." She reached for the baby.

"Do you mind? I'd like to change him and feed him."

Brooke raised her eyes in a pleasant surprise. "Uh, are you sure you know how to change a diaper?" She smiled slightly.

"I used to change my little brothers and sisters when I was growing up."

"Okay, then, I guess it'll be fine. You go on in the family room. His pampers and wipes are in there in his pack and play. While you change him, I'm going to peek in on Detria, then I'll fix his bottle and bring it to you."

"Cool," Skip answered. This was the perfect chance and he was going to take it. He kissed Elijah on the cheek and carried him into the family room. He looked around to make sure no one was around. He pulled out the DNA kit, opened it, and swiftly swabbed the little boy's cheek with each of the three swabs, put them inside the envelope, sealed it, and put it back inside his pocket. He did the same for himself. After he finished, he smiled as he changed Elijah's pamper, and waited on Brooke to bring his bottle.

In two days, he would know, for certain, if this precious little boy was indeed his son.

"Holding on is believing that there's only a past; letting go is knowing that there's a future." Daphne Kingma

"It's time to come back to the church. It's time to come back to the Lord, Son," Pastor told Stiles.

"I don't think I'm ready. Holy Rock holds too many painful memories, if that makes sense. And I can't preach anymore."

"Give it time." Pastor reached out toward his son and took hold of his hands. "You know she was my little princess. I loved that little girl. She reminded me so much of your mother. Spunky, stubborn but sweet." Pastor smiled. "It hurts real bad to lose her. But I know that God makes no mistakes. We don't see it now, but even in this tragedy, there is something good that is going to come out of it. I believe that because I believe the Lord." Pastor's eyes swelled with tears.

Stiles began to cry softly. He didn't know if he would ever stop. Didn't know if there would come a time when he could remember his little girl without feeling the weight of grief.

Pastor leaned in and rested his hands on his son's shoulders and cried with him.

Leaving Pastor's house, and on the drive to his townhome, Stiles made a sudden decision, and instead of going home, he went to see Detria.

"Why are you here?" Detria asked. "If you've come to remind me that it's my fault our little girl is dead, go on and say it, and then leave me alone."

Stiles looked over at the woman standing in the doorway of the family room holding Elijah. She had introduced herself as Priscilla, Detria's caregiver. It was difficult for Stiles to look at the handsome little boy without feeling resentment and anger toward Detria. Nonetheless, he tried to focus on the reason he was there.

"I'm not here to argue, and I'm not here to put the blame on you. And as much as I want to hate you, I can't."

Detria turned away from Stiles in her wheelchair.

"I came to tell you that the divorce is in the works."

"I see." She turned back around and faced Stiles.

"This house, your car, the money in our joint bank account, everything, it's yours. I don't want it. I only want my freedom. I want to move on with my life."

"You always want to come off like the good guy, don't you?"

"Are you serious right now? Good guy? So that's what this is about? I'm penalized because I wanted my marriage to work, because I loved my family, because I expected my wife to be faithful, because I'm not slapping you around and spitting out mean and vicious words to you for letting my little girl get killed. I'm a good guy because all I want from you is for you to be out of my life?"

"Well, you have me out of your life, Stiles! I don't have any ties to you anymore. You think that this house," she waved her one good hand around and looked at her surroundings, "can make up for the fact that my child is dead? I will have to live with that for the rest of my life. For every day I spend in this wheelchair, I'm reminded of her death. Every time I try to use my arm and can't it reminds me of that God awful day, so don't you come up in here and act like you're the only one who's hurting."

"See, that's your problem, Detria. You've always been selfish. You think everything is about you. God knows I'm so ready to be done with this divorce, and everything connected with you."

"Look at me! I'm in a wheelchair. I don't know when or if I will ever walk again. My arm is nothing more than a noodle, and I will never be able to use it again. My baby is gone. So, this *is* about me."

Stiles smirked and shook his head. "You are a true piece of work. I thought I could come over here and somehow just end this peacefully between us. I thought you would go your way, and I could go mine, but you, you always have to..." Stiles threw up his hands. "I'm out." He turned around, dismissing Detria. "I'll send someone over here this week to get the rest of my clothes and any other personal items I have here. Have a good life!"

"You can go to hell, Stiles Graham!" Detria cussed and screamed but Stiles continued walking to the front door, refusing to respond. He yanked the front door open and almost ran chest to chest into Skip.

Stiles looked at Skip, shook his head, looked back over his shoulder at Detria, then stormed past Skip. He got in his car and sped off.

"Why are you here? You have no right to show up here anytime you feel like it," she blasted Skip.

Priscilla appeared, coming from the direction of the family area. "Mrs. Graham," Priscilla said, "are you all right?"

"Yes, I'm fine, Priscilla. Skip was just about to leave," she said, shooting an evil eye at him.

"Are you sure?"

"Yes, Priscilla. I'm sure."

Elijah started crying from the other room.

"Please, go on and check on Elijah."

"Okay, I'm going to go make his bottle."

"Will you get him ready for his bath after you feed him?"

"Yes, of course." Priscilla turned and walked away, leaving Skip and Detria alone in the foyer.

"I want you to leave."

"I'm not leaving until we talk."

"Talk? What is there to talk about? I don't have time for a two-timing, low-life dog like you.""

Skip stooped down in front of Detria. "Me? A dog? You gotta be kidding me. If I'm a dog, what does that make you?"

Detria pouted and began swearing. Get...out...of...my....house! Go back to that little tramp Meaghan. Just leave me alone!"

"So, that's what this is about? Another broad?" Skip shook his head. "You forget you had preacher boy, huh. You expected me to be true blue? Look, let's not even go there because long story short, she has nothing to do with me and you. Now, I'm here because I want to see my son."

"He is *not* your son. Your name is nowhere on his birth certificate."

Skip reached in his pant pocket and pulled out his wallet. He parted the money pouch and removed a piece of paper. Unfolding it, he held it out in front of Detria.

She studied the paper then looked up at Skip with eyes that could kill. "How did you get this? Who did you get to make this up?"

"Make it up?" Skip laughed. "This is far from being made up. Now, I want to spend time with my son. He is going to know who his father is, his real father. Now we can do this the hard way, or we can do it the easy way. The hard way? I take you to court and get preacher boy's name removed from the birth certificate, and then I ask for visitation with my son. The easy way..." Skip said, resting each hand on the wheelchair's armrest, and leaning in so close to her she could feel the warmth of his breath and smell the scent of his body like a vampire smells blood. It enticed her and momentarily she forgot she was in a wheelchair and unable to walk. She wanted to grab ahold of Skip's neck, pull him into her, and listen as his heavy breathing told her that she was the only woman who could ever satisfy him.

"The easy way is for you to go to court with me and get preacher boy's name off that birth certificate and replace it with mine."

Her defenses began to subside. "I hate you!"

"Really?" He seemed to enjoy watching her struggle to keep her composure. He moved in on her quicker than she could blink an eye. He sucked lightly on her bottom lip while using one hand to caress the familiar contours of her body.

Abruptly, and shaking her head like she'd come out of a trance, Detria pulled back as much as she could in her wheelchair. She met the intense stare of his eyes.

"Look," she stuttered nervously, "if you want to see Elijah, we'll work something out," she said with as much conviction as possible, hoping that it was enough to keep him from kissing her again. "But that's it. You will not come here anytime you feel like it. Is that understood?"

"Fair enough," Skip replied. "Now, where was I before you so rudely interrupted?" he whispered in her ear before kissing her on her earlobe and along her neck.

She closed her eyes and prayed that he would stop. If he didn't, she wouldn't be able to fight him off. She didn't want to. But why would he want her? She couldn't walk and she felt like the one-armed bandit. What could she do for him the way she was? Fear and shame pounded at her heart. How badly she wanted to be held by him. But things had changed. God had seen to that.

Skip stood upright and took one step back. Looking down at Detria, he smiled and extended both hands outward. "So you hate me, huh?"

"Oh, so this is some game you're playing? I should have known better. It's always about divide and conquer with you."

"It's not like that. All I wanted to see was if you hate me as much as you say you do. You forgot that I know you, Detria. I think I know you better than you know yourself."

"You think so?" she asked, trying to portray the hardcore tough girl so he wouldn't sense the overwhelming need she had to be close to him.

"I don't think so, I know so. You want the world to think that you're tough and invincible when the Detria I know is sweet, kind...," His words were soft and enticing, "...sensitive, passionate." He kissed her again.

Priscilla walked in, surprising both of them. Detria exhaled, placing her left hand over her heart like she was trying to still its beat.

"Ummm, Mrs. Graham, I'm getting ready to give Elijah his bath and then he's going down for his nap. Do you want to hold him before I bathe him?"

"Yes, bring him here, please." Detria turned in her chair and stretched out her left arm.

Priscilla walked over and lovingly placed the baby in the arm of his mother. "I'll be back shortly."

"Thanks, Priscilla."

"You're welcome," she replied before she turned and left out of the foyer.

Skip walked behind her wheelchair. Peering over her head, he looked down at his son. Sheer joy was evident on his face.

With a voice full of pride, Skip grinned. "Hey, look at him. Man, he's the spitting image of his daddy. It even looks like he's going to have my same color eyes." Skip kissed Detria on the top of her head while he used one of his hands to massage her upper body. His lips then trailed along her temple, her ear, and down to her neck. He stopped and lightly patted Elijah on the top of his head, before standing upright again.

"This boy here is going to be a lover just like his daddy." Skip pounded himself on the chest and laughed. "I'm telling you these little females better watch out. Lord help the world!"

Detria leaned her head back and boldly met Skip's eyes as her emotions melted away any resolve she may have had. For the first time in months, she laughed, and then shamelessly remarked, "Boy, you still silly."

48

"No matter how bad a heart is broken; the world doesn't stop for your grief." Susane Pieffer

How could it be? When had the hours changed into days; days into weeks; weeks into months? When had the seasons changed?

Here he was again, posted on the couch, surrounded by the deafening sound of a life of turmoil, heartache, and grief. His divorce from Detria had taken close to six months, just as his lawyer told him it would. Today marked two weeks that it was final, but instead of feeling like he had been set free, he felt like he'd been given a death sentence. Thursday night, and he was all alone in his townhome. Alone to fight the demons of self-pity and the surmounting realization that he had failed in his marriage and his ministry.

He was thirty-six years old, divorced twice, and both ex-wives were cheaters. He questioned his ability to choose the right kind of woman. Had answering his divine call to the ministry turned him into a pillow cushion with no backbone and no ability to recognize game? He questioned his manhood and his life's decisions. He questioned his sense of reasoning. What had happened to the days in high school and college when he could have any girl he wanted? He had gone from being a player to being played.

Stiles thought of Detria. She was a modern day Delilah; the beginning of his downfall. She appeared in his life when his mother was still alive. She was kind to his parents and to him. She was smart, intelligent, and she helped him forget about Rena. All the time she was out to destroy him. Right under his nose, she was sleeping with another man. The more he thought about it, maybe there had been others before Skip. Maybe, Skip just happened to be the one he caught her with.

Like Delilah did Samson, Detria captured Stiles' heart, and in the end, she had cost him dearly. He felt like a total and complete failure.

If God was trying to show him something, he wished that he would hurry up and do it, and make it real clear because he couldn't grasp what he was supposed to do next.

His nostrils flared as he pounded his fist full force on the coffee table. Anger, humiliation, frustration, embarrassment, and shame consumed him again. He could not control his tears. He cried over the demise of the life he had messed up, a life that he hoped would be pleasing to God. He fell back on the sofa, with his hands tucked under his head, staring at the ceiling.

He dozed off but was awakened by the sound of a strange voice on the television or had he been dreaming? He couldn't determine which just yet, but that wasn't important. He glanced around the room, shook his head, and then sat upright. *When you pass through the waters, I will be with you; and through the rivers, they shall not overwhelm you; when you walk through fire you shall not be burned, and the flame shall not consume you.*

He looked around again, like he was expecting to see God himself in the room with him; there was no one. The television was on but there was no sound coming from it. He didn't recall doing it, but the television was muted. The still small voice replayed in his mind and spirit. *The flames shall not consume you. I am the Lord, thy God. Is there anything too hard for me? Get up and live.*

He recognized it was God speaking to him in his spirit. Stiles got up then fell down to his knees and sobbed. He cried over the death of his dreams and the death of his daughter. The more he cried, the more the weight of his troubles seemed to lighten. *Do not be frightened, and do not be dismayed, for I am with you wherever you go.*

"I hear you, Lord. It's time to move forward, but I can only do it with you, Father God."

49

"We must be willing to get rid of the life we've planned,
so as to have the life that is waiting for us." – Joseph Campbell

It had been four months since Stiles packed his bags, loaded down his car, and drove nine hours nonstop until he arrived back in Houston, Texas. He was determined to see what he could do to reconnect the broken pieces of his life.

Tuesday evening he sat in Wallace's church listening to him teach about 'forgetting those things that are behind and focusing on the things ahead.' When he was at Holy Rock, he had preached from the same passage of scripture many times.

The more Wallace talked about letting go and moving forward to the things God has in store, the more Stiles thoughts regressed to his past, but he had to remind himself that he was not in Houston to dwell on the things of the past. He was here to take the next step in renewing his life and reestablishing his rightful relationship with God.

After Bible study was over, Stiles had a quick dinner with Wallace's wife and their five kids before he retreated to the guest apartment over Wallace's garage.

Stiles had been living with Wallace since his return. While he deeply appreciated Wallace's hospitality, it was time for him to get his own space and see what life really had to offer in Houston.

Tomorrow morning he was going to sign the lease on his new apartment. The apartment he chose was to his liking. Twelve hundred square feet, two bedrooms, two baths, nice size living room, a dedicated patio, and modernized kitchen with tons of amenities on site like a full exercise room, sauna, two pools, and housekeeping services.

Initially, he grappled with the idea of relocating from Memphis to Houston, until he reminded himself that there was nothing to keep him in Memphis. No wife, no church, no child. His father was living his own life too. Pastor's health had improved remarkably thanks to God's healing grace and his loving, attentive wife, Josie. Pastor was doing so well that for the past month and a half he had been able to return to attending church on a regular basis. Stiles was happy for his father.

Later that evening, while Stiles was laid back on his sofa watching football, Pastor called.

"Son, I thought you would want to know that we had the official vote after worship service today."

"Oh, yeah. How'd it go?" Stiles asked.

"The majority won. They voted to appoint Hezekiah as the senior pastor effective the first Sunday of next month."

"Good. To God be the glory. I know he's going to be a great leader. He's proven that time and time again since he was appointed associate pastor then interim senior pastor."

"Yes. I agree. I believe Holy Rock made the right decision."

Stiles could hear the satisfaction in Pastor's voice. Part of Stiles felt sad but he didn't say anything to that effect to Pastor. Although he accepted that his time was up at Holy Rock, the realization that someone else, namely Hezekiah, had assumed the position that he once reveled in, was a hard pill to swallow. Nevertheless, he swallowed it, and told Pastor he would call and congratulate his brother in Christ.

One day, if God directed him, he would pastor again. Until that time came, like Paul, Stiles made the decision that he would be content. Houston was his new home. He recalled tonight's scripture. *I do not consider myself yet to have taken hold of it. But one thing I do; forgetting what is behind and straining toward what is ahead.*

50

"Power does not corrupt men; fools, however, if they get into a position of power, corrupt power." George Bernard Shaw.

Hezekiah was enjoying his role as Holy Rock's senior pastor. It felt good to be in a position of leadership and authority, and he was determined to make the best of it.

The scandal and gossip about Pastor Graham and First Lady Detria had finally played itself out. What happened between the couple was rarely ever mentioned anymore, which was fine with Hezekiah. He had grown sick of hearing about Stiles and his world of mess.

Holy Rock, under his leadership, was moving forward. Almost every Sunday, and sometimes during midweek services, they were taking in new members. Hezekiah was carving new ground for himself and setting a new standard of operation for the mega church.

He had made a vast number of changes to Holy Rock, which he believed would improve the growth of the church and at the same time allow him to add his own set of pastoral footprints to the ministry. He had ruffled a few feathers along the way, first by replacing Stiles' longtime assistant, Sister Gloria with a much younger, and Caucasian assistant, named Juliana Webb.

Juliana was not a member of Holy Rock when he first met her. It was while attending a Pastor's Prayer Breakfast sponsored by one of the other churches that he was introduced to her. She was one of the volunteers who helped plan the annual citywide Pastor's Prayer Breakfast. In talking to her, he learned that she had been an executive assistant at a major company, but because of economic problems, the company was forced to close its doors, leaving Juliana unemployed. Hezekiah decided to bring her on board, believing that she would be loyal to him. He wanted a fresh group of people around him who would be just as dedicated and committed to him as those Stiles Graham surrounded himself with.

He replaced the armor bearers with men he felt would better serve him. Hezekiah didn't stop there. His biggest revamping came when he dismissed and then replaced eight of the twelve deacons who had served with Pastor and Stiles. Eyebrows raised and shockwaves spilled through the church when members heard that Deacon Jones was one of them, along with four of the seven trustees. This was all done as part of what Pastor McCoy called the Church Revitalization and Reorganization Ministry, which in layman's terms meant nothing more than getting rid of the old and replacing it with the new – his crew.

Hezekiah, unlike his predecessors Stiles and Pastor, was a hands-on type of pastor who insisted on studying the financial records himself, seeing that he held an associate's degree in accounting from a community college outside of Chicago. It was almost as if he was treating Holy Rock like a small church where the pastor assumed the role of treasurer, secretary, building engineer, the whole nine yards. Only Hezekiah mostly concentrated on the financial aspects of Holy Rock.

Fancy addressed her concern to Hezekiah about him being too involved with the church finances. She reminded him that it was his illegal financial dealing at previous churches that led to them doing prison time. She emphasized the importance of allowing the finance administrator to carry out his job, and for him to concentrate on being the shepherd of Holy Rock.

Hezekiah dismissed his wife's warnings. He had his own agenda, and it included making sure he had total access to the church's financial records. He received, in addition to his salary, two high limit credit cards, one primarily for his use and the other for Fancy. He made sure that he signed off on all financial transactions. Unlike large congregations such as Holy Rock, Hezekiah could withdraw money from the church's bank account without the approval of the trustees or deacons.

Despite her concern about some of the changes Hezekiah made, Fancy was having just as good a time as Hezekiah. She fitted the role of a first lady too, in Hezekiah's eyes. She was not only jazzy in her dress, in the way she carried herself, but she was smart and ambitious. She had basically revamped several of the ministries at Holy Rock, starting with the Marriage Ministry and the Youth and Young Adult Ministry.

When Detria was the first lady, she worked more with the children's ministry, but Fancy loved working with the older kids, something that surprisingly Xavier seemed to enjoy. He had met new friends, and even called himself having a girlfriend. Yes, things were working out for the McCoy's.

Khalil's time at the detention center was coming to an end in the next several weeks. Fancy looked forward to the day she would have both of her sons with her in Memphis.

"Hezekiah." Fancy walked over to where her husband was perched behind his mahogany desk.

"What is it, baby?"

"When are we going to properly christen your office?" She stood behind him and wound her arms around his neck, leaning over and kissing him on each side of his face.

He looked at the signature watch on his wrist. "I have a sermon to preach in an hour."

"So?" she said seductively. "A christening doesn't take long. I promise."

"Fancy, you're bad." He reached up and tenderly caressed a lock of her hair that rested against the nape of his neck. "Real bad."

"Is that right?" Fancy tilted her head and looked at him longingly. "So what are you going to do about it?"

"You're going to have to pay dearly for that." He turned around slowly in his office chair, pulling her down on to his lap.

"Give, and it will be given to you: good measure, pressed down, shaken together, and running over will it be put into your bosom. For with the same measure that you use, it will be measured back to you. That's what God's Word tells us. Holy Rock, let's be a giving church. My vision is for us to be 100% tithers," he told his congregation during Sunday morning service.

"God loves a cheerful giver. Are you giving? And if you are, are you giving your all? If we want to see this church grow beyond measure, then we have to learn how to be givers. The church doesn't run on love; it has obligations and bills to pay...."

The burly, short, casually dressed man named George sat in the middle section of the sanctuary next to his wife, listening intently at

Hezekiah preach about money, money, and more money. It reminded him of the song "For the Love of Money" by the O'jays. Considering himself somewhat of a music connoisseur, George easily recalled the words to the old R&B song. "Talkin' bout cash money - dollar bills y'all - come on, now..."

George and his wife had relocated from Chicago to be closer to their daughter and grandchildren after he retired his position in felony law enforcement. He was not a churchgoing man and did not consider himself religious, but his wife was just the opposite. During their thirty years of marriage, there was rarely a Sunday she missed going to church. George couldn't understand why his wife was so into church or Christianity for that matter, but God and the church was not a priority for him. It never had been.

Moving to Memphis didn't change his wife's routine. The first Sunday she visited Holy Rock, to his surprise, she joined the church. To keep his home life in check, he went to church with her, but certainly not every Sunday. He attended just enough to appease her and keep her off his back.

Seeing what he saw in the streets during his years in law enforcement reinforced his belief that if there was a God, then he certainly couldn't care about the human race or he wouldn't let so much evil go on.

Sitting in church, trying to keep from dozing off, he watched the charismatic man in the pulpit, amazed at how thousands of people packed the sanctuary Sunday after Sunday to hear this guy.

George didn't mention it to his wife, but the pastor and his wife looked familiar. He'd seen them somewhere other than Holy Rock. His cop intuition rarely failed him. It was once his job to be highly observant. He decided to make it his personal mission to delve deeper into the McCoy's past. Perhaps, doing a little investigating of the power couple would help him be able to sit through the Sunday ritual he hated.

George watched Hezekiah closely as he hooped and hollered from the pulpit. He didn't forget a face easily, and he had an uneasy feeling about this so called 'man of God.' He already distrusted men of the cloth, seeing them only as wolves dressed in sheep's clothing. Listening to this morning's sermon about money only added to his philosophy that all preachers were no more than bonafide hustlers, trying to get over on naïve people. If it was the last thing he did, he was going to find out just how much of a hustler this Hezekiah McCoy was and if there was something he was hiding.

51

"You can only fully understand what you've done to others, when someone does the same to you." Nishan Panwar

Detria couldn't believe the time had passed so quickly. Elijah was a thriving seventeen month old, and in Detria's eyes, the sweetest little boy ever. He made being a mother easy. She didn't want to compare him to Audrey, but there were times she found herself doing exactly that. Audrey used to have temper tantrums, rarely slept through the night, and constantly worked Detria's nerves to no end. Elijah was just the opposite. He had a calmness about him, rarely cried, and had been sleeping through the night since the day Detria brought him home from the hospital. He was quite the happy child.

Skip adored his son. He came to see Elijah almost every day. The more he came over to spend time with his son, the more at ease Detria became around him. She was almost back to acting like her old self since she'd let Skip back into her life.

She was still doing therapy five days a week. Lately there had been remarkable improvements in her mobility. She was getting stronger daily, probably because she pushed her body to its max, determined to walk again. Much of the tingling feeling in her legs was gone and she could stand for minutes at a time with an assistive device. It was much harder since she had no use of her right arm, but she was not going to give up. Soon she was able to take tiny steps, then bigger ones, until she could walk several feet. One day she would be able to walk without the support of the crutch, but for now, she was starting to feel happy again.

Many Sundays she went to church with Donna, one of her occupational therapists. Much to her surprise, she enjoyed the quiet, warm, and gentle-spirited people at Donna's church. The woman pastor was soft spoken, yet her messages were practical to everyday living. Detria liked that.

Her bouts of grief were becoming less and she gave the credit to having Skip and Elijah in her life. Sometimes she thought about her ex-husband, and wondered if he still blamed her for their daughter's death.

When Brooke told her that Stiles had moved out of town a few months ago, after resigning his position at Holy Rock, Detria wondered if he'd run off to find solace in Rena. That was unlikely since Rena was married with kids, and probably no longer interested in him. Then again, Detria would never put anything past Stiles when it came to Rena.

She also found it hard to believe that Stiles had really moved out of Memphis. The Stiles she knew would never leave Holy Rock. The fact that he had stepped down as Senior Pastor didn't mean that he had left Holy Rock altogether. Not Stiles; Holy Rock was his life, which as far as Detria was concerned, was the main reason their marriage couldn't survive, though Stiles would never admit that truth. He seemed to find it easier to put the blame all on her.

Skip walked into Detria's considerably large bedroom. She was seated on the sofa in the sitting room area of the bedroom. Her wheelchair was parked next to the sofa.

"Hey, where's my mini-me?"

"Priscilla just put him down for a nap."

"I wish you had let him stay up a little longer so I could see him."

"Believe me, I tried, but you know how he loves his sleep. He was up playing longer than usual."

"That's because he's growing."

"Yeah...he is."

Skip's eyebrows raised and he smiled a devilish smile. "Well, well, what do you suppose we can do until he wakes up?"

Detria leaned her head back, resting it on the back of the sofa. "Uhh, I have no idea," she responded in a seductive tone.

Skip walked over and sat down next to her. In one swift move, he gathered her into his arms and started kissing her. He didn't stop, despite her subtle protests. Unable to move her legs on her own, Skip took the liberty and guided her body back on the sofa. Using one hand to lift her left leg, he put it up on the sofa, giving himself easy access to where he wanted to go.

For a moment, Detria felt the bout of low self-esteem attack her as she imagined how it used to be between them. Before the car accident their lovemaking had been wild, brazen and uninhibited.

"Skip..."

"Ummm," was his answer.

"I love you," she cried as she felt the electricity of his touch. "I love you so—"

She gasped, as he silenced her words with his mouth on top of hers.

52

"Little by little one walks far." Peruvian Proverb

The sun was shining but the temperature still hovered just above freezing. A light snow had fallen the night before, blanketing the ground and trees in a spectacular display of beauty.

Brooke drove cautiously through the city, understanding that since the accident, Detria would sometimes have panic attacks when she rode in a car. They were rare, but there were no warning signs when one would come.

"What are you going to do with all that money?" Brooke asked her sister as they left Detria's attorney's office.

After going back and forth with the insurance company for the past year and a half, Detria's attorney made a high seven figure out of court settlement with the trucking company responsible for Detria's injuries and Audrey's death, quickly thrusting her into the multi-millionaire's club. She was set for life, but no amount of money could restore the use of her arm, help her walk again, or bring her little girl back.

Her doctors told her that they were confident that the day of being wheelchair bound would soon pass; they just didn't know how much longer that would be. So, she continued to work hard with the physical and occupational therapists.

"Well, I know we are going to have the best Christmas ever," Detria answered as she looked out the passenger window at the busyness that was attributed to the season. The streets were laced with cars, filled with people preparing for the holiday.

"Before I do anything, I'm going to meet with a financial advisor. I need to know how to handle this much money, where to deposit it, and what to invest it in. I can't just go to the bank and deposit it into my checking and savings account. The FDIC only guarantees up to $250,000, you know."

"I never thought about anything like that. No wonder when people win the lottery, you don't hear from most of them right away. I guess they're busy trying to figure out what to do."

"My lawyer did suggest that I look into depositing it into what's known as a Certificate of Deposit Account Registry."

"A what?" asked Brooke.

"A CDAR. From what I understand, my money would be put into CDs issued by members of their network. That way the principal and interest are eligible for FDIC insurance. I would still get one regular consolidated account statement."

"Never heard of it." Brooke looked baffled, shaking her head.

"Me neither, until now, that is. Anyway, once I get all of that settled, I'm going to pay off my mortgage, Mom and Dad's mortgage, and any other bills they have. I'm going to do the same for you and John. I'm going to make sure we're all totally debt-free."

"Oh, my gosh! Really?" Brooke screamed with joy. "Oh, Detria," she cried. "I can't believe you're going to do something like this for me. It's going to give me, John, and the boys the kind of life I've always dreamed of. Thank you, Sis." Brooke leaned over and quickly pecked her sister on the cheek.

"You deserve it, and so do Mom and Dad." Detria smiled, but didn't say much after that. She focused back on the cars zooming past.

Brooke turned on the street leading to Detria's neighborhood. She stopped at the Stop sign and looked over at her sister. Placing her hand on top of hers, she said, "I know no amount of money can change what happened. I know this has to be hard for you."

Detria turned and looked at Brooke. Tears were streaming down her face, landing silently on her teal winter coat.

"I'm okay. It's just hard to be happy when I've lost so much in the process."

Brooke pulled off from the Stop sign and continued driving to Detria's house. "Yeah, I know, but, hey, let's not think on that. Let's just go home and see Elijah."

"Sounds like a plan," Detria responded.

They arrived at Detria's house. Priscilla greeted them at the door, and helped Detria inside.

"Would you like me to prepare something for the two of you to eat?" Priscilla asked.

Detria looked over at her sister as they went into the family room. "You want something to eat?"

"Yeah, that'll be cool." Brooke looked at Priscilla. "Do you have something already prepared, Priscilla?" I don't want you going out of your way for me."

"It's no problem. I can fix my famous club sandwich with fresh romaine lettuce, tomatoes, and bacon, with chips on the side, and a cup of my special spiced hot herb tea."

"Oh, my Lord," Detria remarked. "Priscilla's club sandwiches are to die for, Brooke."

"Okay, sounds good to me," Brooke replied.

"Okay, two turkey club sandwiches with chips coming up." Priscilla turned and left the sisters in the family room to talk.

Detria enjoyed Brooke's company, that is, until Brooke started talking about her relationship with Skip. That always hit a sore spot with Detria. She didn't understand why Brooke had to be all up in her business, when she never questioned or interfered with her and John's marriage.

"How much time does he spend over here?"

"Duhh, not that it's any of your business, but he comes almost every day. His son lives here, remember?"

"I'm just saying, Detria."

"Just saying what?"

"That he's the reason for your divorce. I know he should be able to see his son. That's understandable. But why can't he pick him up and take him to his house? I mean, after all, he is the reason for a lot that has gone wrong in your life, and I just wish you'd stop messing around with him."

"Who say's I'm messing around with him? I told you, he comes to see Elijah."

Detria wasn't about to tell her that she and Skip were intimately involved again, and had been for months. It wasn't Brooke's or anybody's business about her personal life. She loved Skip and he loved her. They had even talked about getting married a few times, but she wanted to wait until she had fully recovered and was able to walk totally on her own. If she was going to be a bride again, she wanted to walk down the aisle, not roll down it.

"Have you heard anything from Stiles?"

"No. Why would I? The man practically hates my guts, and it's not like I'm all goo-goo over him either. I mean, I know I was the one who cheated. God knows, you've reminded me of that a zillion times." Detria huffed and shook her head like she was disgusted with the conversation they were having, and she was.

"But I'm past all of that now. I wish Stiles well, and I've moved on. God has forgiven me. I've paid for my mistakes. Brooke, in case you forgot, my child is dead, and I'm...well...look at me. Don't you think that it's hard to deal with the fact that I'm in the position I'm in because God is punishing me?"

"God is not punishing you, and you know it. You were involved in a car accident that was no fault of your own, so I'm not going to let you go around saying that God caused your accident, and that God let my niece die all because you were sleeping with Skip. No way. God doesn't operate like that."

"I can't help it. That's how I feel at times." Detria bowed her head.

"If you feel that bad then why are you still with Skip? You're saying one thing, but you're doing something else."

"Look, you have somebody, Brooke! You have a man. Do you think I want to go through life alone? Do you think it's fun being tied to this chair and never having the use of my arm? You think that's a good feeling or something? Well, it's not."

"Dang, it still doesn't mean you have to settle for Skip. How do you know God doesn't have someone better out there for you? What you need to do is pray. Ask God to take away the feelings of guilt you have toward yourself. Ask him to take away this need to have a man in your life until *He* brings the right one along. When He does, then that man will love you and accept you for who you are, and how you are."

"How do you know that man isn't Skip?"

Brooke inhaled deeply, then got up from the couch. "You know what, I'm going to leave on that note. Sometimes you act like you don't have the sense of a goldfish. You can't see that the man is using you."

"Using me how, Brooke? Tell me," Detria fumed.

"You get a disability check. You have this huge house," Brooke stated pointing and looking around. "And now you're a multi-millionaire." Brooke folded her arms. "What does he have?"

"For your information, Skip has a home of his own and a job. Anyway, it's none of your business what he has and doesn't have. If you're trying to say that he's only with me because of what I have, then you don't know me at all. Why can't you believe that he loves me? Huh? Why is that so hard for you to digest? You think that you're the only one who can be happy and have a good life with a good man?"

Detria pushed the On button on her chair and navigated the joystick on it, turning herself away from Brooke. She took off toward the door leading to the side driveway.

"You're right; I think it's time for you to go. I'm tired."

Brooke eyed her sister, rolled her eyes, then picked up her purse. "I'm out of here. I'll talk to you later."

Priscilla appeared with the sandwiches.

"I'm sorry, Priscilla," Brooke told her. "Something came up. I have to go."

"Oh, okay," Priscilla replied, as she looked over at Detria, and placed the sandwiches on the table in front of her.

"Will you take my food up to my room?"

"Of course." Priscilla retrieved the tray of food and left.

Detria waited until she was sure that Brooke was gone. She went to her room and parked her chair on the side of the bed. Priscilla had brought the food like Detria asked and sat it on the side table next to her bed. Detria took several bites out of the sandwich, ate a few chips, and took several sips of the hot tea.

Next, she grabbed her cell phone and threw it on the bed. With expert precision, just like the occupational therapist taught her, she transferred herself from her wheelchair to her king-sized bed. She sat up in the bed, got her cell phone, and called Skip.

"I have some good news. Can you come over?"

Epilogue I
Two years since the accident

"A hard beginning maketh a good ending." John Heywood

"When are you going to wake up and stop being stuck on stupid?"

"You know what? You are my sister, Brooke, so don't get it twisted; you do not control me."

Brooke was so angry and disappointed in Detria, she couldn't see straight. The foolish girl was like a wild child. She had done what she said and made her immediate family members debt-free since receiving her settlement. She had upgraded all the furniture in her already perfect home, and she told Brooke that she gave a sizeable donation to the church where she had been attending.

If things had ended there, Brooke would have been good, but seeing how ignorant Detria was acting, made her want to choke some sense into her.

"Somebody needs to control you," Brooke countered. "I can't believe how you're spending money on Skip. What's wrong with you? Are you that hard up for a man that you have to buy his love and attention?"

"I beg your pardon? Are you jealous? I mean, hey, what more do you want from me? I got you out of debt, bought you and John new vehicles, paid for my nephews to attend a private school, and you still aren't satisfied? You're biting on me because I'm happy for once in my life?"

"Happy? Girl, please. You're only fooling yourself. You're nothing but an insecure woman who thinks that buying fancy cars, name brand clothes and shoes for that fool you call your man is going to keep him. But I'm telling you, and this is out of love; you are only setting yourself up to get hurt."

"You'd like that wouldn't you, Brooke? You hate the fact that me and Stiles got divorced. You always thought he was so special, but you don't know Stiles like I do. You don't know how he was behind closed doors. You, Momma and Daddy, all of you want to come down hard on me because I cheated." Detria threw her good arm up in the air. "Okay, so I screwed up, but it wasn't all my fault. If he wasn't so busy up at that church, or running to that university doing any and everything but be with me, then maybe Skip wouldn't have been able to step into Stiles' place so easily. And, yes, I had a baby by another man, but again, I didn't plan for that to happen!"

"You know what? I get it. You think you don't deserve any better than Skip? You're still blaming yourself for Audrey's death. You hate the fact that you've lost the use of your arm and that you walk with a limp. So you think he's all you can get. Detria," Brooke pleaded, "don't keep doing this to yourself. Let him have visitation rights with his son, and leave it at that. Move on with your life. Please."

Detria stared at Brooke. A flood of thoughts played through her mind. Part of her felt what Brooke was saying. There were times when she did feel less than, but Skip seemed to come at just the right time and always made her feel that she was his queen. And what was wrong with buying the man she loved gifts? What woman didn't do things for her man, and now that she had money and plenty of it, she was more than happy to cater to him.

She paid off the mortgage on his house, bought him his dream car and truck, and gave him a huge sum of money to start his own business. They were going to get married soon, so what difference did it make anyway.

"Not that it's any of your business, but me and Skip are going to get married."

"Ha, married? You really believe that? Think about it, Detria. Skip has had all the time in the world to marry you, that is, if he really wanted to. Especially since you keep saying that he is so madly in love with you. Now that you have him living like a king, you rarely see him, and he hardly ever spends time with Elijah anymore. I bet that little boy doesn't even recognize his own daddy, for Christ's sake!"

"That's a lie. He knows his daddy." Detria was becoming more and more upset. She was sick and tired of being judged. Why couldn't Brooke and her parents understand the relationship between her and Skip?

"You spend all your time cooped up in this big old house, hoping and praying that he'll drop by."

"How do you know what I do or what I think? You don't live here. You don't run my life."

"Believe me; I know you don't have a life outside of that man. You don't even take time with Elijah."

"I go to church almost every Sunday. I've made friends there. And me and Donna have become friends too, so you don't know what you're talking about." Detria gave her sister an evil look.

"And what about Elijah? He sure as heck isn't in here with you. You know why? It's because you're no better than Skip. You never have Elijah unless it's when Skip is coming over. You let Priscilla take care of him twenty-four seven. It's not like you aren't able to care for him. Just because you have one arm, you think you aren't capable of being a mother to that precious little boy?"

"It's time for you to go. I will not listen to any more of this nonsense. I'm fed up with your sanctimonious garbage. Even if what you said is true, then it's still my business and not yours. I'm a grown woman. I make my own decisions. I'm living my own life. If you, Mom and Dad don't like it then you don't have to come around."

Brooke's eyes bucked. "You mean you're ready to cut off your family for a man?" Brooke picked up her designer bag from off the island, placed it over her shoulder, and turned to leave. "You really do have a serious problem. I'm going to keep praying for you. I just hope you wake up before it's too late."

"Whatever, Brooke. Just leave."

"Gladly," Brooke countered and stormed out of the house.

Epilogue II

"When one door closes, another opens, but we often look so long and so regretfully upon the closed door that we do not see the one which has opened for us." Unknown

Stiles, through Wallace, heard that the small congregation of Full of Grace Ministries was searching for a new pastor after their former pastor died from a massive heart attack. With Wallace's prompting and pushing, Stiles submitted his pastoral résumé. He understood that even if he was offered the pastoral position that he would be making pennies compared to his salary at Holy Rock, but that was okay with him. Money didn't buy happiness, and he wasn't in the ministry for the money anyway. He wanted to serve God with all of his heart, mind, and soul. The fact that he had gone through some of the darkest times of his life, hadn't changed that.

A few weeks after submitting his résumé, Stiles was contacted by the church's Pastoral Search Committee and invited to bring forth the Word at Full of Grace. Stiles accepted the invitation. Standing in the pulpit, looking out on the congregation, he felt the presence of the Holy Spirit as he rendered the Word to the people of God. At that moment, he understood his true calling. In spite of everything that had transpired in his life, he still had the burning desire within to preach God's word. It was who he was and what he was born to do.

After preaching that first time at Full of Grace Ministries, Stiles was called to come preach at the church five more times over the next six months. Two weeks after the last time he preached, Full of Grace Ministries unanimously voted Stiles in as their new pastor.

Today had been Stiles' installation service. He was now officially the pastor of Full of Grace Ministries. At the end of the service everyone left out of the sanctuary and went to the fellowship hall to further enjoy the sit down dinner in honor of their new pastor.

Stiles stayed behind, explaining to his new pastoral staff that he would join them shortly. Once he was alone, he surveyed the empty 200-hundred-seat sanctuary. He never envisioned his life being like this. He thought he would be like Pastor, and stay at Holy Rock until he no longer could stand in the pulpit and preach the Word. He experienced a gamut of emotions as he thought about pastoring again. It had been a long time in the making, and he hoped that he was ready to stand in a position of leadership again.

He stood stationary before the altar and began to pray. "Life has a funny way of turning out the total opposite of our plans," Stiles told God. "I don't know why my life has turned out the way that it has, but I'm asking you to help me to accept the things I cannot change. Give me wisdom. Help me to let go of yesterday and move into the future you have for me. Enable me to go forward with the knowledge that your plans for me are for my good, and not to bring harm to me."

"Uh ummm."

Stiles stopped praying when he heard the soft sound of someone clearing their throat. He looked back over his shoulder, curious to see who had entered the sanctuary. He swallowed hard when he saw the beautiful young woman standing just inside the entrance. She was one of the deceased pastor's daughters.

"I'm sorry. I didn't realize you were praying." The lady turned around to leave.

"Wait," Stiles told her. "You don't have to go."

"But I interrupted your prayer. I didn't mean to." She spoke softly.

"Really, it's not a problem. I was done. Plus, me and God go a long way back. He understands." Stiles chuckled lightly.

The woman smiled. "I was asked to come tell you that the food is ready, and everyone is in the fellowship hall waiting on you, Pastor Graham."

Kareena was twenty-seven years old, single, no children, and loved the Lord. Her soft coffee brown eyes seemed to hypnotize Stiles. Her smooth ebony skin set against her petitely sculptured body caused him to swallow hard. He had not entertained the thought of another woman in his life since before his divorce. With both of his marriages having failed, he felt inadequate and unsure of himself. He even wrestled with the fact that maybe God didn't want him to have a wife. Maybe he was meant to be alone and not have a family. He recited first Corinthians verses eight and nine in his head. *Now to the unmarried and the widows I say: It is good for them to stay unmarried, as I do. But if they cannot control themselves, they should marry, for it is better to marry than to burn with passion.*

He didn't think he had any passion left. He had all but lost his desire to have someone in his life again. Too many losses, too much heartache. He decided that the only thing he would totally pour his heart into was the ministry. When the offer came from Full of Grace Ministries, he felt this was just the place to do that. What he hadn't expected was his feelings to be awakened again.

"Thank you, Kareena. I'll be right there."

"If you'd like, I'll wait and walk back with you," she offered. Her voice sounded like sweet music to his ears. His body seemed to come alive, like it had been hibernating for the past two plus years.

As he walked beside her, his mind recalled another bible verse: Proverbs, eighteen verse twenty-two. *He who finds a wife finds a good thing....*

"If I cut you off, chances are you handed me the scissors." Unknown

Skip was living life to the fullest. Things had definitely turned around for the better. He had plenty of money in the bank. Thanks to Detria's generosity and his business savvy, he was financially secure, meaning he no longer needed to rely on Detria's monetary handouts, although he would gladly take it when she offered.

Detria had given him enough money to open his own franchise. His lifelong dream of owning his own restaurant was now a reality. He had two Subway franchises and business was booming at both establishments. He had plans in motion to open two more locations.

As for spending a lot of time with Detria and Elijah, it was quite limited because he was pouring everything into his business, among other things.

Detria walked into the Subway location where Skip usually was on Tuesdays and Thursdays. The other location was farther away from where she lived. She had Priscilla to drive her over because she hadn't driven a car since the accident, and she was nervous about driving with one arm. She hadn't seen Brooke in weeks, and though she missed her, she was not going to be the one to call. She didn't want to listen to her sister talk bad about Skip. It was all she seemed to do every time they talked on the phone or saw one another, and Detria was tired of hearing it. If Brooke wanted to talk to her, she needed to call, apologize and promise Detria that she would stop berating her baby's daddy.

Detria had been walking on her own for several weeks. She still was unable to walk at a normal pace, but she could walk and that was all that mattered to her. She had a new sense of freedom. She couldn't begin to describe how it felt not being tied down to a wheelchair anymore.

She enjoyed taking short shopping trips and going out to eat. Today she thought she would surprise Skip by coming to have lunch with him. She had brought Elijah along with her, but left him outside in the car with Priscilla until she made sure Skip was inside the restaurant.

A customer leaving out of the restaurant held the door open for her and Detria slowly walked inside. She stopped dead in her tracks when she saw Skip coming from the back of the restaurant. Her smile turned into a frown when she saw Meaghan walking next to him.

Meaghan stopped and stood behind the cash register.

Skip whispered something in her ear.

Meaghan giggled, then looked at Detria and slyly rolled her eyes.

Skip happened to look up. "Hi. Welcome to Subway." He looked surprised to see Detria. "Hey. What are you doing here?"

Detria turned as swiftly as her weak legs could carry her. She hobbled out of the restaurant, but not before seeing another smile of satisfaction spread across Meaghan's face.

"Detria, hold up," Skip said as he followed her outside.

"Let's go, Priscilla," Detria told her as she tried to get inside the car.

Skip easily caught up to her. Standing next to the passenger's door, he didn't stop Detria from getting inside the car. He looked in the back seat and saw his son. He patted Elijah on his stomach and ruffled the thick head of hair on his head.

"What are you doing here?" he asked Detria as she pulled the door closed.

"I didn't know I needed permission to come out," she bitterly snapped. "I see why you don't have time for your son...or me."

"Look, there you go, jumping to conclusions. You see Meaghan and the first thing you do is start thinking all crazy. The girl needed a job, Detria. That's it. You know how this economy is." He tilted his head to the side. "I'm just trying to do my part to boost the economy, and give the unemployed people in this city a job. Meaghan included."

"I'm ready, Priscilla. Take me home, now, please."

Priscilla put the car in gear, leaned down, and looked past Detria, and over at Skip. "You heard her, Mr. Madison. We're leaving."

"I'll be over later tonight. This isn't over." He tried to kiss Detria but she turned away from him.

"Bye, Sport," he said to his son. "Daddy will see you tonight."

Skip sat in the all-season room looking at Detria. Her eyes were bloodshot from crying. The heat outside was nothing compared to the heat he was feeling inside from her cold, heartbreaking stare.

"What made you come to the restaurant like that? I mean, you could have called. If you and Elijah wanted something to eat, all you had to do was pick up the phone, call me, and let me know. You know I would have brought it to you,"

"You were kissing her. How could you do me like this, Skip? How could you go behind my back, and especially with Meaghan?"

"I told you. She works at the restaurant, Detria. Don't start with all the insecurities. I don't need this."

"You don't need this? You're the one who was caught lip lapping all over her, and you tell me that you don't need this? After all I've done for you. After all I've given you."

"Hold up. Don't start that crap. I hate it when people give you stuff then act like you owe them something. You gave me what you gave me, no strings attached. I didn't ask for any of it. Now you tripping, trying to throw it up in my face." His eyes tightened, and he stood to his feet.

"I did more than give you stuff, Skip. I gave you a son. I gave you my life. My marriage fell apart because of you. My child is dead because of you."

"Because of *me*? How are you going to blame me for that? I'm sorry about your kid. I really am. But don't try to put that off on me. You know what? I never pegged you for the insecure, jealous type, but you are, and I can't deal with it."

"What do you mean you can't deal with it? I've given you everything. Helped you start that business, bought you cars, gave you money, plenty of it, and this is how you repay me? You said we were going to get married, but I seriously doubt that you were serious, after what I walked in on today."

"Look, let's be real here. We have a child together. But as far as anything else, I can't do it. You've changed, Detria, and it's time that I be honest with you."

"Yeah, why don't you do that? Be honest for a change. Let me hear what you have to say."

"You want to hear the truth? Is that what you really want?"

"Yes, that's what I really want. Tell me the truth."

"Okay, I will. Meaghan is pregnant."

"Did you say *pregnant*?" Detria grabbed hold of her head. Suddenly, it felt like she was going to pass out. She steadied herself by holding on to the armrest of the sofa. Detria's lips drooped in utter disbelief and her face distorted in anger.

"You're telling *me* that that heifer is having *your* baby?" Detria was stunned. You could see the arteries throbbing in her neck like little electronic pulses. Her hand flew up to her chest, settling over her heart as tears flowed and she began to spew out one venomous word after another.

"That's right. She's having *my* baby. Elijah is going to have a little sister or brother. But there's one thing you're wrong about."

"And...what is that, Skip? I'm all ears. Tell me what it is that I'm so wrong about," she cried.

"She's no heifer. She's my wife."

The End

Words from the Author

"He who commits adultery lacks sense; he who does it destroys himself." Proverbs 6:32 ESV

The act of betrayal can be costly. When we deceive others, it can never turn out right. In *My Wife My Baby...And Him,* we get a firsthand look at how adultery, deceit, and lies can have a trickle-down effect and destroy lives. The saying 'we reap what we sow' is apparent and it is so true. Stiles, Detria, and Skip although they are fictional characters, represent an overwhelming and increasing number of spouses who cheat. I researched the statistics concerning women who cheat and here they are: Fifty-four percent of women admit to committing infidelity in any relationship they've had. Fourteen percent of married women have strayed at least once during their married lives. Sixty-eight percent of women say they would have an affair if they knew they would never get caught, and three percent of children are the product of infidelity. (statisticbrain.com)

In today's society, everything is 'watered down' and more and more and more ungodly things are acceptable, but that still does not make it right. We have a standard of excellence that we as individuals, as people, whether male or female, should always strive to meet. We should be people of integrity, with moral character instead of giving in to the desires of our flesh.

Detria had a hard time being happy in her marriage. She was not prepared or ready to be a mother to Audrey, nor was she prepared to take on the roles and responsibilities that come with being a pastor's wife.

Stiles, like his father, poured his all into being the shepherd at Holy Rock, rather than being more committed and dedicated to the wants, needs, and desires of his family.

When one discovers that a spouse is cheating, it can be absolutely painful and debilitating. It forever changes the scope of the relationship, and the persons involved.

The death of a child is even more painful and gut wrenching because children are supposed to outlive their parents. Detria and Stiles felt the agonizing pain of grief over the loss of their child. Detria blamed herself and Stiles blamed Detria, which is never a good thing to do. The only way to make it through adultery and the death of a child is seeking God, praying to Him for healing, for comfort, for the strength to move forward. You will never really "get over" it, but slowly, and in your own time, you can learn to live with the loss. It is a wound that never heals, but with God by your side, in time you can learn how to keep living.

Lastly, remember that there is no mistake and no wrong that you have done that God will not forgive. He also calls for us to forgive so we can be forgiven. Does it mean we have to accept that person back into our lives and into our space? Personally, I don't think so. As long as you have made the conscious decision to truly forgive, and mean it with all your heart, then I feel that is all that is required.

Reading Group Discussion Guide

1. What differences/similarities do you see, if any, between Rena, Detria and the late First Lady Audrey Graham?

2. How do you perceive Stiles? Should he have sensed or known that his wife was cheating? Why or why not?

3. Was Detria justified in having an affair since Stiles was never around?

4. Could Stiles and Detria's marriage have been saved? Why or Why not?

5. Did Skip truly love Detria at any time during their adulterous affair?

6. Was Stiles' anger justified? Why or Why not?

7. What are your thoughts about Hezekiah and Fancy McCoy?

8. Do you believe Hezekiah is going to revert to his old ways? Why or Why not?

9. What kind of woman in your opinion is Fancy McCoy?

10. What do you think is next for Holy Rock?

11. What are your feelings about the way Stiles dismissed Rena when she called to see how he was doing?

12. Do you think it took a tragedy to bring Francesca around? Do you believe she can now forgive her family and have a relationship with them? Why or Why not?

13. Why do you think Rena visited Holy Rock when she was in the city? Shouldn't she be over Stiles?

14. Do you think Kareena and Stiles will develop a relationship? Do you want to see him develop a relationship with her?

15. Was Stiles wise to move from Memphis or is he merely running away from his problems?

16. Do you think Stiles should move back to Memphis? Should he try to return to Holy Rock?

17. Does having lots of money change people? Did it change Detria? Did it change Skip? How?

18. If you came into a huge amount of money would you spend it on your 'boyfriend' or 'girlfriend'? Would you spend it on your lover? Why or Why not?

19. What are your thoughts about the relationship between Skip and Meaghan?

20. Would you like to see the *My Son's Wife* series continued? Why or Why not?

A Personal Invitation from the Author

If you have not made a decision to accept Jesus Christ as your personal Lord and Savior, God himself extends this invitation to you.

If you have not trusted Him and believed Him to be the giver of eternal life, you can do so right now. We do not know the second, the minute, the hour, the moment, or day that God will come to claim us. Will you be ready?

The Word of God says:

"If you confess with your mouth, 'Jesus is Lord,' and believe in your heart that God raised him from the dead, you will be saved. For it is with your heart that you believe and are justified, and it is with your mouth that you confess and are SAVED" (Romans 10:9-10 NIV, emphasis added).

+++++++++++++++++++++++++++

To arrange signings, book events, or speaking engagements
with the author, contact
books@shelialipsey.com

Connect Via Social Media
http://twitter.com/shelialipsey
Shelia E. Lipsey Readers on Facebook
Urban Christian Authors Group on Facebook
http://www.shelialipsey.com

Thank you for supporting my literary career!

Remember to
Live Your Dreams Now!

Shelia E. Lipsey, God's Amazing Girl

2015 Shelia E. Lipsey Titles
The McCoy's of Holy Rock
The Real Housewives of Adverse City
The Secret Life of Payne (Book II Fairley High Series (YA)

CPSIA information can be obtained at www.ICGtesting.com
Printed in the USA
LVOW11s1139050914

402625LV00001B/43/P